Hangups
From
Way
Back

Historical Myths and Canons

Hangups From Way Back

Historical Myths and Canons
Volume I

Frederick Gentles
Melvin Steinfield

San Diego Mesa College

Canfield Press
San Francisco
A Department of Harper & Row, Publishers, Inc.

O world of men, what is your happiness?
A painted show. Comes sorrow and the touch —
a wet sponge — blots the painting out.
And this moves pity, sadder still than death.

—AESCHYLUS

HANGUPS FROM WAY BACK: Historical Myths and Canons, Vol. I.
Copyright © 1970 by Frederick Gentles and Melvin Steinfield

LIBRARY OF CONGRESS CATALOG CARD NUMBER: 78-119012

Design by Michael Rogondino
Illustrations by Robert Bausch
Copyediting by Jacqueline Handley

Contents

Contents

Contents

Contents

Preface

The blame for student criticism of the lack of relevance in their education—for their feeling that what they are studying somehow does not relate to the world they live in—must be shared by teachers and the books they use. Although teachers of world and Western civilization defend their courses—justifiably—as being necessary to an understanding of today's world, it is clear many have failed to communicate history's relevance. Obviously, more effective teaching tools are needed.

This book attempts to demonstrate this relevance. And what is more relevant today than the way man handles myth, an idea that seems eternal but is actually only transient? "A myth," as Ashley Montagu observes, "is something which is in fact not true, but in which we believe and act upon as if it were true." Myths later become canons—that is, rules, regulations, and laws, the correct and accepted ways of doing things. We build our cultures on myths; indeed, myths are necessary for the stability of a culture. All of us live by myths and canons, taking them for reality. And for certain myths that man has held dear, he has become involved, frustrated, paranoid, and even vicious.

Here we are concerned with some ideas that have caused endless controversy and bloodshed throughout history. The intoxicating, man-made idea is the myth, the canon, the hangup. By seeing how myths have determined man's behavior in the past and how some of them are still with us, perhaps we can better resist their influence. It is, of course, not enough to simply *say* that history is relevant; it must be shown. The selections in each chapter, therefore, focus on those basic patterns of intellectual, social, political, military, and economic history—the myths—that especially pertain to today's problems.

It is impossible to acknowledge every individual who assisted in the development of this book, but a few names do stand out for the magnitude of their contribution. Among the reviewers, Melvin Lesser of Los Angeles City College read the manuscript twice and offered many valuable suggestions. The entire Canfield Press staff— especially Joseph Dana, Brian Williams, and Wendy Cunkle— offered expert assistance in many ways. Thanks are also due our wives, Marian and Dorothy, for their patience. Of course, the authors assume responsibility for all interpretations in their essays and any errors that might appear in the book.

Frederick Gentles
Melvin Steinfield

1 Some Concepts of Man and Society

If you love must you also hate? Some people say yes, it is instinctual;
others say no, we learn to love and hate. In other words, we may be
programmed for peace and programmed for violence, and there has been a
lot of both on this small planet far out from the center of our Milky Way
Galaxy. It is with the hate and violence in the world today—and the
possibility of greater violence tomorrow, now that man possesses the ultimate
weapons—that the following essay is concerned. The author believes the
student beginning a study of civilization should know something about
the twentieth-century viewpoints of man's behavior so that he can analyze
and interpret the men and events of history.

Love and Hate on Planet III

Frederick Gentles

On the moon's Sea of Tranquility is a plaque with the names of
the American Apollo 11 astronauts and President of the United
States Richard Nixon, plus the legend: WE CAME IN PEACE FOR
ALL MANKIND. This ideal of peace has been a goal of mankind since
the earliest days of civilization. From time to time in history, man
seems to have realized the dream, but the world has been a violent
one too—at the time of the 1969 moon landing a cartoonist pictured
a shattered earth posted with a battered placard with the caption:
HERE MAN FIRST SET FOOT ON THE PLANET EARTH, #%00 B.C.
WE CAME IN PEACE FOR ALL MANKIND. It was signed by man,
Adam, and by woman, *Eve*.[1]

Why is it we have not achieved the permanent peace and order
long desired? Is it man's nature that he loves but also hates and fears
his fellow men? Is he naturally so aggressive and self-interested that
he will always try to destroy others—and very likely himself?

In the "nature versus nurture" debate some scientists say these violent traits are innate—an inborn part of man's "nature"—and there
isn't much we can do except try to redirect these instincts so they will
not harm others. Other scientists say man's nature is actually "nur-
tured"—he has learned to be what he is because of conditioning
processes in his society. Some people, they say, are conditioned to be
aggressive and some to be passive, some to love and some to hate.

Despite all the studies on the nature of man, there is obviously, considering the intensity of violence in the world, a scandalous gap
between our ability to scamper about on the moon and our ability to
solve great domestic and foreign problems. As far as learning how

to control ourselves and solve age-old problems, we are still in the Middle Ages. One factor is that men are set apart in rather isolated groups all over the world and grow up with many different ideas about the values and meaning of life. Thus, we are all provincials, even those living in the big cities.

Members of an old religious order claim that if they can direct a child's mind for seven years, his religious thinking will be determined for the rest of his life. Of course, the training of a child in *any* particular culture will usually result in his behavior reflecting the customs and values of that culture. A Greek thinks as a Greek, a Roman as a Roman, and a clansman as a clansman. Consider for a moment what has determined your thinking—family and friends? neighborhood and nation? newspapers, television, books, magazines? It is difficult to rise above the parochialism of one's own village, state, or country and think in larger terms; even one of the Apollo 11 astronauts, when in the vicinity of the moon, said he felt homesick for the earth. However, with the perspective of space and time, together with knowledge and understanding, one can hope to rise above local and narrow paths of thought, in spite of the gravitational pull of the old neighborhood.

Two cases illustrate how the trauma of sudden change can affect thinking and routine. Although the examples involve what might be called simple people, there is no reason to believe the rest of us are any less immune to the shock of cultural change.

After the British forbade headhunting in the Eddystone Islands in the last century, the "primitives" demonstrated less of an interest in life, and their population dwindled. Before, each individual and village had a certain amount of "spirit power," and they added to this by taking heads from neighboring villages. With the new "civilized" law, there was no longer head power or so much spirit power, and a major institution of the culture was destroyed. After all, what was the fun in life if one couldn't go headhunting?

In another instance, the natives of a village in India found the essence of their culture destroyed when American technicians piped running water into their huts. Since the well had been the social center of the village, the people became unhappy—they no longer saw their old friends and life was dull at home all day. They decided, therefore, that the village must be restored to its old ways and that the pipe system must go. It went.

As a creature of habit, man may be trained to believe in all sorts of ideas, even absurd ones. These ideas become a part of his life, and existence becomes meaningless without them. Indeed, he may be willing to die for what he believes in, whether it be headhunting, village wells, or apple pie.

Although historians generally believe that knowledge of self and understanding of life is revealed through the study of man and his institutions, some scientists now urge that it may be through the study of the biological structure of the cell and the nature of animal behavior. This is a controversial area among scientists, and students of history should at least be aware of it, if only to remind themselves that human affairs involve *both* biological and environmental factors. Accordingly, a brief description follows of the so-called "nature versus nurture" controversy.

Biochemists have intensively studied the make-up of the single cell, and results indicate that the nature of a Clyde Barrow, a Mahatma Gandhi, or a Charlie Brown is tied, at least in part, to his genes. The nucleus of the fertilized cell in the mother carries information from both parents which leads to the development of such particulars as skin, eye, and hair color, mental capacity, nervous characteristics, height, susceptibility to various diseases, and memory capabilities in the new individual. These inherited characteristics are sometimes very important factors in the behavior of individuals and groups.

As an example of the importance of body chemistry in the behavior of an individual, the story is told of Sir Walter Raleigh, traveling on Roanoke Island in 1585 in the New World, coming to a fork in the road and taking the right turn, which lead off to the legendary Tabac Indians. Here he was offered the peace pipe, which he enjoyed so much that he took it with him back to England. Soon all of England and then the whole world was smoking the delicious weed of the Tabac Indians; moreover, there were many wars, and much history was made after this time. But, so one popular version of this tale goes, had Sir Walter taken the turn to the *left,* he would have come upon another tribe, the Mari Wanna Indians. They too would have offered him the peace pipe; he would have taken their weed back to England to spread the habit throughout the world—and, in that case, there would have been no history worth mentioning for nearly 400 years. Instead, according to the marijuana converts, there would have been beautiful people living in beautiful harmony. Although the story is fanciful, the point is that the body chemistry can be changed, and with the change can come changes in behavior. Chemicals can tame a man and make him docile, or they can make him vicious and violent—and the stimulant and the tranquilizer are fashions in our time.

Homo homini lupus—"man is a wolf to man"—is a phrase used

by some scientists who see man behaving in ways like animals. In his *Civilization and Its Discontents,* psychoanalyst Sigmund Freud used the phrase to emphasize man's animal nature, then asked:

> Who, in the face of all his experience of life and history, will have the courage to dispute this assertion? As a rule this cruel aggressiveness waits for some provocation or puts itself at the service of some other purpose, whose goal might also have been reached by milder measures. In circumstances that are favorable to it, when the mental counter-forces which ordinarily inhibit it are out of action, it also manifests itself spontaneously and reveals man as a savage beast to whom consideration towards his own kind is something alien. Anyone who calls to mind the atrocities committed during the racial migrations or the invasions of the Huns, or by the people known as Mongols under Jenghiz Khan and Tamerlane, or at the capture of Jerusalem by the pious Crusaders, or even, indeed, the horrors of the recent World War—anyone who calls these things to mind will have to bow humbly before the truth of the view.*[2]

Freud, who scorned to distinguish between a culture and a civilization, wrote this in a book published in Vienna in 1930. There have been a few wars since then, and there have been the Hitlers and the Stalins and the massacre of millions from Indonesia to Biafra.

In another book, *The Future of an Illusion,* Freud says that civilization has to be protected against the individual and that every individual is virtually an enemy of civilization. "It is remarkable [he writes] that, little as men are able to exist in isolation, they should nevertheless feel as a heavy burden the sacrifices which civilization expects of them in order to make a communal life possible."[3] In other words, he says, man can't live contentedly either with or without his fellow man; man is simply discontent, and arguments are of no avail against his passions.

Civilization, Freud continues, is built upon coercion and upon renunciation of instinct. All men contain destructive and antisocial attitudes; these trends in a great number of people determine the collective nature of their society. Furthermore, educating man toward a life of reason and kindness is unlikely because the ability of the masses to absorb education is limited. Freud sees hostility, protest, and revolt

*Reprinted from *Civilization and Its Discontents* by Sigmund Freud, translated from the German and edited by James Strachey. By permission of W. W. Norton & Company, Inc. Copyright © 1961 by James Strachey. Also by permission of Sigmund Freud Copyrights, Ltd., The Institute of Psycho-Analysis and The Hogarth Press, Ltd., Vol. 21 of the Standard Edition of the Complete Psychological Works of Sigmund Freud.

ahead, especially where a society accepts great inequalities between privileged and underprivileged.

Ethologists, who study animal behavior in the natural habitat, think man has important lessons to learn from the animal kingdom. The extremes of brutal behavior do not belong to animals but to man; it is man who is the beast. While there is fighting among animals, most of it is ritual, and there are appeasement ceremonies by both victor and vanquished. Animals habitually kill only for food; they do not slaughter their own kind, or any other kind, in wholesale numbers.

Konrad Lorenz, the director of the Max Planck Institute for Behavioral Physiology in Bavaria and an eminent naturalist and zoologist, believes that "Expert teaching of biology is the one and only foundation on which really sound opinions about mankind and its relation to the universe can be built."[4] In his best-selling book *On Aggression*, he says that the same aggressive instincts that help preserve life may also destroy it if carried to extremes. As with Freud, he appeals for some redirection of our aggressive instincts; man has become so self-centered and so possessive that these traits could destroy him. Lorenz still has hopes, however, that man's knowledge and his humor will save him.

In *The Territorial Imperative*,[5] a follower of Lorenz, Robert Ardrey, makes the point that the drive for the acquisition of territory is common to men and animals. This drive often brings individuals and societies into conflict, depending upon which aspect of our dual nature is uppermost. Ardrey defines this duality as the code of *amity,* in which there is a capacity for love, kindness, friendship, generosity, sympathy, and so forth; and the code of *enmity,* in which there is a pronounced capacity to hate, to be cruel, to destroy. Ardrey thinks this amity–enmity is basic to man's nature because of his animal-inheritance. And man, he says, is a willing subject to this dual code. We love our friends, and we hate our enemies. Some of us say, no, we don't hate our enemies, we just hate the things they stand for. At any rate, we are willing to kill them.

Rats, as men, are exceptions in the animal world to killing their own species in great numbers. While a rat will seldom kill another rat in his own pack, one pack will mercilessly attack and kill members of another pack. Evidently there is a process by which rats as well as men distinguish between murder and war.

In a war, people of one nation will kill people of another even though they are of the same religion, the same race, and even having the same language and culture. Only an imaginary line separates them. An idea separates them. People, tribes, and nations are always drawing lines—and rat packs, apparently, draw them too.

But men are not rats, says Professor David Krech, who calls him-self a rat-brain psychologist: "It is not true that a brain is a brain is a brain. The rat is a rat and he hath a rat's brain; the child is a child and he hath a child's brain—and each, according to my hypothesis, re-quires its own educational nutrient."[6] He believes that the study of language and how it is acquired may provide understanding of the basis of our mental life. Being human, he says, means that people have the power of cognition or knowing.

Which brings us at last to the other side of the nature-nurture con-troversy. The idea that man has a brain with acquisitive or percep-tive powers not characteristic of other animals leads other scientists to object strenuously to the Lorenz school's emphasis on nature. That school, they believe, is dangerous—man might simply accept his ag-gressive and destructive ways, pass them off as natural, and go on committing outrageous deeds upon his fellow man. Instead, man is what he has sensed in life. Man experiences, man learns. This is the empiricism of Locke and Hume, who believed that all knowledge is founded upon experience. This is nurture, and Alexander Pope was right, they say, in his *Essay on Man*, when he wrote, "The proper study of mankind is man." If man is programmed for violence, it is not programming done by instincts but programming done very largely by fellow man. Witness the Eddystone Islander with his headhunting and the civilized man with his warfare.

In *Patterns of Culture*,[7] Ruth Benedict described three cultures. In one the orientation of life was toward peace and serenity, in the two others toward conflict and aggressiveness. The Zuñi of New Mexico live in a society where the emphasis is on harmony and the quiet, peaceful life. The Dobu in eastern New Guinea, however, live in one where conflict with fellow man is the essence of being—one may steal, kill children, maim one's neighbor, and commit other deeds that our Western society would consider crimes. The whole atmosphere of the Dobu culture is one of hostility and fear.

In the Kwakiutl Indian culture of the Pacific Northwest, the drive in life was for one to accumulate possessions so that he might gain prestige by giving to others so that they too might possess. This was the acquisitive society par excellence. The Kwakiutl orientation recalls that of the American "robber barons" of the nineteenth century, who accumulated massive wealth and then set up foundations to distribute it for charitable and cultural purposes. The Carnegie, Rockefeller, and Morgan foundations still help support science, medicine, colleges and universities, museums, and so on.

One of Miss Benedict's purposes in writing the book was to suggest that cultures have different orientations and that those individuals who demonstrate or who object to the traditions of their particular culture are not necessarily and fundamentally evil in not conforming to the set standards of their society. At the moment, long hair, sideburns, beards, and sandals represent a challenge to the traditional ways in our society.

The way of life that emphasizes harmony and peace, like the Zuñi's, is called *Apollonian*, after Apollo, the Greek god of beauty and harmony. Apollo 11 astronauts landed in the moon's Sea of Tranquility, "in peace for all mankind"; Apollo 12 landed in the Ocean of Storms —a perfect, if unconscious, symbolism for man's other side, conflict, called *Dionysian* after the Greek god of wine. Although Dionysius (Bacchus in Rome) could be kind and gentle as he went about his world teaching the cultivation of the vine, this perfect peace alternated with revelrey, orgy, cruelty, and suffering, and after harvest time, Dionysius descended to the underworld, where he was the only god who was tortured. He has been called the tragic god, and the Dionysian-type societies named after him re-enact this same rhythm of life: peace, love, conflict, cruelty, and often violent death. But Dionysius' resurrection in the spring each year also represented hope for mankind, and there was a great festival (Bacchanalia) celebrating the new life.

According to Claude Levi-Strauss, the French anthropologist:

> No society is perfect. Each has within it, by nature, an impurity incompatible with the norms to which it lays claim; this impurity finds outlet in elements of injustice, cruelty, and insensitivity. . . . It will eventually become plain that no human society is fundamentally good; but neither is any of them fundamentally bad; all offer their members certain advantages, though we must bear in mind a residue of iniquity, apparently more or less constant in its importance.[8]

What he has to say about the imperfections and inconsistencies of societies applies to individuals as well, and with both individuals and societies, declared purposes and objectives are often inconsistent with actual day-to-day living. The United States is certainly one of the freest countries in the world; even so, to what extent has its people really lived up to the ideals of the Declaration of Independence and the Bill of Rights? With liberty and justice for all or with liberty and justice for some? Of course, there are greater inconsistencies between claims and practices about justice in the Soviet Union, the Republic of South Africa, and many other countries one could name. What Levi-Strauss seems to suggest is that we are a world-community of sinners.

Some people and some cultures have more readily accepted change in their patterns than others. Progress may be thought of as two kinds: *circular progress*, where there is little change in the political, social, and economic institutions from one generation to another, and *linear progress*, where people have been willing to make changes in their institutions in order to improve and refine their ways of living. The mind of the primitive (his is not a primitive mind, however) seeks order and in order finds safety. He hesitates to change; he fears the unknown, though change, if meaningful, will be assimilated into the traditional culture. Usually, however, he is the most conservative of the conservatives.

The mind of civilized man, beginning with the Sumerians, seeks change, a way of thought that has culminated in several Herculean and portentous events of the twentieth century: the Bomb, the Pill, the moon landing, and, of course, TV. Politically, socially, and economically, however, linear progress has left something to be desired. There is a marked cultural lag between scientific progress and progress that involves man's ability to get along with his fellow man and to supply everyone with the necessary goods of life.

Linear progress may be described as a line inclined upward from right to left, conservative to liberal. One student suggested that the line might better be described with a spiral running through it, since change comes gradually, and we maintain a circular progress with our traditions and customs while change is going on. Another student suggested that the spiral should turn to the left for the liberals and to the right for the conservatives.

At any rate, the symbolism of circle, line, or spiral can stand for the progress of a society or the progress of an individual. Some individuals experience linear progress up through high school and then settle down to circular progress for the rest of their lives at an eight-to-five job fifty weeks a year, with TV from six to bedtime. Others may go on through college and then settle down to a routine. Routine, however, is not just a behavioral pattern of Western Civilization; in one fashion or another, it is universal. Meanwhile, the battle of the bumper stickers goes on among those who are pretty well satisfied with the status quo and those who are not. One example of the recurring conflict: AMERICA: LOVE IT OR LEAVE IT answered by AMERICA: CHANGE IT OR LOSE IT.

Rapid and marked change is an unsettling experience for the psyche. It leads to bewilderment and sometimes to violence, say Ivo and Rosalind Feierabend and Betty Nesvold in their studies on the aggressive habits of nations.[9] Their analyses of the internal stability of

84 countries between 1948 and 1965—riots, revolutions, assassinations, strikes, and demonstrations were considered with other data—showed the following scores: [10]

Finland	0
Luxembourg	0
Japan	32
USSR	81
United States	97
Union of South Africa	158
Indonesia	190

They found that violence tended to increase when social achievement failed to keep pace with social expectations. That is, on the chart of a society of rising expectations, the actual achievement line turned at a point and started to descend in what is called the "J-curve." The greater this gap between expectations and achievement, the more likely it is that violence will occur.

The J-curve is applied by another author, James C. Davies, to account for the French Revolution, the American Civil War, the Nazi Revolution, and the Black uprisings in America. In all these cases, there was a long period in which the lines of expectation and achievement rose together on the charts, but when achievements failed to keep pace and the gap widened, violence broke out. [11]

What hope is there for survival of the species or of civilization in the light of man's behavior? Oswald Spengler, in the *Decline of the West*, said there was none—that it was already too late for Western Civilization because the decay was so far advanced. He viewed societies as being organic in nature, each with a vigorous springtime of growth and development, a summertime of maturity, an autumn of decline, and a winter of decay and death. Western society, Spengler thought, was in its wintertime, and only a few gloomy decades remained before the non-white races of the world would take over and build on the ruins of the West. To Spengler, as to his contemporary, Freud, World War I was proof of this decay.

In 1968 a London newspaper ran a series of articles on the so-called "Savage American," describing the history of violence in America prior to the assassinations of Martin Luther King and Robert Kennedy. Another newspaper followed with a series on "The Politics of Hate in America." Communists, Birchers, KKK, labor groups, business men, the poor, the middle class—all hate and fear some other individuals and groups they consider evil and dangerous. They have been conditioned by newspapers, television, neighborhoods, friends, and so on, to think and behave in ways common to the group. They firmly believe in their righteousness. Perhaps it should be put: *we* firmly believe in *our* righteousness. Given other conditions we could think in ways quite contrary to our present views and be equally positive. No wonder Shakespeare wrote, "What fools these mortals be!" No wonder Pilate asked, "What is truth?"

Viewed from space the earth is such a beautiful blue and white planet! By 2001 we may have discovered what Mars is all about. Will we have discovered ourselves? This book is one endeavor, at least, to see ourselves in the perspective of time and recurrent problems.

Notes

1 Cartoon by Paul Conrad, *Los Angeles Times,* July 17, 1969.

2 Sigmund Freud, *Civilization and Its Discontents* (New York: W. W. Norton, 1962), pp. 58–59.

3 Sigmund Freud, *The Future of an Illusion* (Garden City, N.Y.: Doubleday-Anchor, 1964), p. 3.

4 Konrad Lorenz, *On Aggression* (New York: Harcourt, Brace & World, 1966), p. 298.

5 Robert Ardrey, *The Territorial Imperative* (New York: Atheneum, 1966).

6 David Krech, "Psychoneurobiochemeducation," *California Monthly,* June-July 1969, p. 18.

7 Ruth Benedict, *Patterns of Culture* (New York: Mentor, 1951). This book is one of the classics in cultural anthropology.

8 Claude Levi-Strauss, *Tristes Tropiques* (New York: Atheneum, 1965), p. 385.

9 Ivo K. Feierabend, Rosalind L. Feierabend, Betty A. Nesvold, "Social Change and Political Violence: Cross-National Patterns," in *Violence in America, Historical and Comparative Perspectives,* Hugh Davis Graham and Ted Robert Gurr, eds. (New York: Signet, 1969), p. 606.

10 *Ibid.,* p. 626.

11 James C. Davies, "The J-Curve of Rising and Declining Satisfactions as a Cause of Some Great Revolutions and a Contained Rebellion," in Graham and Gurr, *ibid.,* p. 671 ff.

London-born Ashley Montagu, today one of America's leading anthropologists, here refutes the theses of Lorenz, Ardrey, and Golding that man's behavior is closely connected to animal behavior. Man is not naturally depraved, says Montagu; he is only trained to behave in a depraved manner. The idea of innate depravity is very dangerous because it may give man an excuse to pass off his aggressive behavior as natural and, therefore, to do nothing about it. What proof does Montagu offer that man is not naturally aggressive? What, according to him, is the fatal defect in the work of Ardrey and Lorenz?

The New Litany of "Innate Depravity," Or Original Sin Revisited

M. F. Ashley Montagu

It is said that when the Bishop of Worcester returned from the Oxford meeting of the British Association in 1860, he informed his wife, at tea, that the horrid Professor Huxley had declared that man was descended from the apes. Whereupon the dear lady is said to have exclaimed, "Descended from the apes! Let us hope it is not true, but if it is, let us pray that it will not become generally known."

It would seem that the last forty years of anthropological research and discovery in the field and in the laboratory, taken together with the findings of the behavioral sciences, place us in much the same position as the Bishop's lady, for while the findings of these disciplines are wholly opposed to the deeply entrenched view that man is an innately aggressive creature, most people tend to dismiss these findings out of hand or ridicule them as a rather eccentric idealistic heterodoxy, which do not deserve to become generally known. In preference to examining the scientific findings they choose to cast their lot with such "authorities" as William Golding who, in his novel *Lord of the Flies*, offers a colorful account of the allegedly innate nastiness of human nature, and Robert Ardrey who, in *African Genesis* and more recently in *The Territorial Imperative*, similarly seeks to show that man is an innately aggressive creature.

The first part of *African Genesis* is devoted to a demonstration, which the author brings off quite convincingly and with éclat, of the validity of Professor Raymond Dart's claims for an osteodontokeratic culture among the australopithecines. It is in the second part that Mr. Ardrey makes one of the most remarkable extrapolations from the first part I have ever encountered in any work. Mr. Ardrey argues that since the australopithecines made use of tools, and employed some of them as implements with which to bash in the skulls of baboons, the australopithecines were therefore "killers," and that *therefore* human beings are "killers" by nature! Mr. Ardrey's book constitutes, perhaps, the most illuminating example of the manner in which a man's prejudices may get in the way of his reason and distort his view of the evidence. Mr. Ardrey refers to some of his early personal experiences of violence which convinced him of the murderousness of human nature. Hence, when through the distorting glass of his prejudgments he looks at a tool it becomes not simply a scraper but a weapon, a knife becomes a dagger, and even a large canine tooth becomes "the natural dagger that is the hallmark of all hunting mammals," while in "the armed hunting primate" it becomes "a redundant instrument." "With the advent of the lethal weapon natural selection turned from the armament of the jaw to the armament of the hand." . . .

The evidence does not support Mr. Ardrey's theories. Whatever "the basic primate instincts" may be, they are not what Mr. Ardrey implies. Indeed, when he forgets himself, he writes of "the non-aggressive, vegetarian primate," which is precisely what all primates tend to be. But Mr. Ardrey would have us believe the contrary: the basic primate instincts according to him are aggressive. And, of course, with the assumption of hunting as a way of life, these, according to him, would become intensified. But in previous pages, and at greater length elsewhere, I have given the evidence for the contrary view. This evidence renders Mr. Ardrey's interpretations quite unacceptable. Everything points to the non-violence of the greater part of early man's life, to the contribution made by the increasing development of cooperative activities, the very social process of hunting itself, the invention of speech, the development of food-getting and food-preparing tools, and the like. These facts are never once mentioned by Mr. Ardrey, except perhaps obliquely as a doctrine which scheming scientists have foisted upon an unsuspecting world. The truth is that Mr. Ardrey is arguing a thesis. It is the thesis of "innate depravity." It is an unsound thesis, and it is a dangerous one, because it perpetuates unsound views which justify, and even tend to sanction, the violence which man is capable of learning, but which Mr. Ardrey erroneously believes to be inherited from man's australopithecine ancestors.

When man hunts he is the predator and the hunted animal is the prey. But prehistoric man did not hunt for pleasure, in order to satisfy his "predatory instincts." He hunted for food, to satisfy his hunger, and the hunger of those who were dependent upon him. He did not hunt because he was a "killer," any more than contemporary men are "killers" who kill animals in abattoirs so that others may eat them. Prehistoric man was no more a "killer" than we are "killers" when we sit down at table to consume a chicken or a steak which, by proxy, someone else has "killed" for us. It would be interesting to know who are the "murderers," the men who are paid to slaughter the animals we eat, or we who pay the cashier at the supermarket? Or perhaps it is really the owner of the store in which we buy meat who is the "murderer," the "killer"? Prehistoric man hunted because he desired to live—*that* hardly makes him a killer, any more than our continuing in the habit of eating meat makes us killers.

When Mr. Ardrey admiringly presents us with *West Side Story* as a "vivid portrait of natural man," in which "we watch our animal legacy unfold its awful power," in the form of juvenile delinquents in their "timeless struggle over territory, as lunatic in the New York streets as it is logical in our animal heritage," we can only say, "in police parlance," that it is worthy of William Golding's *Lord of the Flies,* in which a similar view of the depravity of human nature is unfolded. In Golding's novel two groups of children, abandoned on an island, take to hunting each other to the death. This novel has a wide readership on American college campuses, and it has recently been made into a film. Its appeal to young people is not strange, for in the world of violence in which they live Golding's novel supplies them with an easy "explanation." I understand that the novel is used in some sociology courses as a good illustration of "innate depravity," of the alleged natural nastiness of man. It could hardly be expected to be otherwise.

Mr. Ardrey has further elaborated his views in a book entitled *The Territorial Imperative,* published in August 1966. In this work Mr. Ardrey endeavors to show that man's aggressiveness is based on his allegedly innate territorial nature. Man, he argues, has an innate compulsion to gain and defend exclusive territory, preserve or property. The territorial nature of man, he says, is genetic and ineradicable.

Mr. Ardrey devotes the greater part of his book to a discussion of territoriality in many different kinds of animals. He attempts to show that territoriality in animals is innately determined. The informed student of these matters would be interested in knowing why the evidence has not been considered which leads to the opposite conclusion. Mr. Ardrey writes that "The disposition to possess a territory is innate. . . . But its position and borders will be learned." Certainly it is biologically and socially valuable for many animals to possess their own special territory, and certainly there are strong drives in most animals to defend their territory against trespassers, but such drives are not necessarily innate. They may be learned in just the same way in which animals learn the position and borders of their territory. Territory is defined as an area defended by its occupant against competing members of the same species. But there are many animals that do not exhibit such behavior. The California ground squirrel, adult male long-tailed field mice, she-wolves, the red fox, the Iowan prairie spotted skunk, the northern plains red fox, and in the superfamily to which man belongs, the Hominoidea, the orang-utan, the chimpanzee, and the gorilla, as well as many other animals. As Bourlière has observed in his admirable book, *The Natural History of Animals*, "It would seem that territorial behavior is far from being as important in mammals as in birds." Somehow, Ardrey manages to neglect to consider the significance of these many exceptional cases. And while he does mention the chimpanzee, he omits any reference to the orang-utan and the gorilla. On the naturally amiable chimpanzee's non-territoriality he comments, "The chimpanzee has demonstrated, I presume, that we must reckon on some degree of innate amity in the primate potential; but as I have indicated, it is a very small candle on a very dark night." . . .

What is the explanation of the appeal such books have for so many people? Golding's novel is a rattling good story. Ardrey's books are excitingly written and hold the reader spellbound. But these qualities are not the secret of their appeal. What, then, is?

Such books are both congenial to the temper of the times and comforting to the reader who is seeking some sort of absolution for his sins. It is gratifying to find father confessors who will relieve one of the burdensome load of guilt we bear by shifting the responsibility for it to our "natural inheritance," our "innate aggressiveness."

If it is our "nature" to be what we are, if we are the lineal descendants of our "murderous" ancestors, we can hardly be blamed or blame ourselves for the sin of being little more than made-over apes. Our orneriness is explained, and so is the peccant behavior of children, juvenile delinquency, crime, rape, murder, arson, and war, not to mention every other form of violence. It is all simply explained: it is due to man's innate aggressiveness.

There is nothing new in all this. We have heard it before. During the latter half of the 19th century, and during the early part of the 20th century, this viewpoint formed the foundation for the doctrine of "Social Darwinism." It was implied in such ideas as "The Survival of the Fittest" and "The Struggle for Existence," and in such phrases as "The weakest go to the wall," "Competition is the life-blood of a nation," and the like.

Such ideas were not merely taken to explain, but were actually used to justify, violence and war. As General von Bernhardi put it in 1912, "War is a biological necessity . . . it is as necessary as the struggle of the elements in Nature . . . it gives a biologically just decision, since its decisions rest on the very nature of things." One wonders what von Bernhardi would have said after the "biologically just" defeat of Germany in two World Wars? No doubt, the general would have had little difficulty in finding an "explanation."

The new liturgy of "innate aggression," as an explanation of man's proclivities to violent behavior, does not seek to justify that behavior, but by thus "explaining" it to point the direction in which we must proceed if we are to exercise some measure of control over it. Toward this end, Dr. Konrad Lorenz, one of the founders of the modern science of ethology—the study of behavior under natural conditions of life—has dedicated himself in his latest book, *On Aggression,* published in April 1966.

In *On Aggression* Lorenz has set out his views at length. In many respects they parallel those of Ardrey.

Ardey's and Lorenz's views suffer from the same fatal defect, namely, extrapolation from other animals to man.

Why do reasonable beings behave so unreasonably, asks Lorenz. And he answers, "Undeniably, there must be superlatively strong factors which are able to overcome the commands of individual reason so completely and which are so obviously impervious to experience and learning." "All these amazing paradoxes, however, find an unconstrained explanation, falling into place like the pieces of a jigsaw puzzle, if one assumes that human behavior, far from being determined by reason and cultural tradition alone, is still subject to all the laws prevailing in all phylogenetically adapted instinctive behavior. Of these laws we possess a fair amount of knowledge from studying the instincts of animals."

It is in these sentences that the flaws in Lorenz's argument are exhibited. First he assumes that man's frequent irrational behavior is phylogenetically based. Second, this enables him to conclude that the "laws" derived from the "study of the instincts of animals" are applicable to man.

There is, in fact, not the slightest evidence or ground for assuming that the alleged "phylogenetically adapted instinctive" behavior of other animals is in any way relevant to the discussion of the motive-forces of human behavior. The fact is, that with the exception of the instinctoid reactions in infants to sudden withdrawals of support and to sudden loud noises, the human being is entirely instinctless.

Those who speak of "innate aggression" in man appear to be lacking in any understanding of the uniqueness of man's evolutionary history. Unacquainted with the facts or else undeterred by them they insist on fitting whatever facts they are acquainted with into their theories. In so doing they commit the most awful excesses. But, as is well known, nothing succeeds like excess. Lorenz's assumptions and interpretations are typical.

"There is evidence" he writes, "that the first inventors of pebble tools—the African Australopithecines—promptly used their new weapon to kill not only game, but fellow members of their species as well." In fact there is not the slightest evidence for such a statement.

Lorenz continues, "Peking Man, the Prometheus who learned to preserve fire, used it to roast his brothers: beside the first traces of the regular use of fire lie the mutilated and roasted bones of Sinanthropus pekinesis himself."

Lorenz's interpretation of the "evidence" is one he shares with many others, but it is gravely doubted whether it is sound. The cracked bones of Peking man may represent the remains of individuals who died during a famine and who may well have been eaten by their surviving associates. This sort of thing has been known to occur among most peoples of whom we have any knowledge. There is, however, no record of any people, prehistoric, nonliterate, or anywhere in the annals of human history, who made a habit of killing their fellow men in order to dine off them. It is absurd to suggest that Peking man used fire "to roast his brothers." Does Lorenz seriously believe that Peking man made a practice of "roast brother"? As another possibility it does not appear to have occurred to Lorenz that, like some contemporary peoples, burning the corpse may have been Peking man's way of disposing of the dead. . . .

Lorenz knows a great deal about the behavior of animals, but with respect to man he apparently knows very little else that is not in the realm of nineteenth-century desk anthropology. Like Ardrey, he extrapolates his dubious interpretations of animal behavior to still more dubious conclusions concerning man. . . .

Given the limits set by his genetic constitution, whatever man is he learns to be.

Throughout the two million years of man's evolution the highest premium has been placed on cooperation, not merely *intra*group cooperation, but also upon *inter*group cooperation, or else there would be no human beings today. Intra- or intergroup hostilities, in small populations, would have endangered the very existence of such populations, for any serious reduction in numbers would have made the maintenance of such populations impossible. There is not the slightest evidence nor is there the least reason to suppose that such conflicts ever occurred in human populations before the development of agricultural-pastoral communities, not much more than 12,000 years ago.

The myth of early man's aggressiveness belongs in the same class as the myth of "the beast," that is, the belief that most if not all "wild" animals are ferocious killers. In the same class belongs the myth of "the jungle," "the wild," "the warfare of Nature," and, of course, the myth of "innate depravity" or "original sin." These myths represent the projection of our *acquired* deplorabilities upon the screen of "Nature." What we are unwilling to acknowledge as essentially of our own making, the consequence of our own disordering in the man-made environment, we saddle upon "Nature," upon "phylogenetically programmed" or "innate" factors. It is very comforting, and if, somehow, one can connect it all with findings on greylag goslings, studied for their "releaser mechanisms," and relate the findings on fish, birds, and other animals to man, it makes everything all the easier to understand and to accept.

What, in fact, such writers do, in addition to perpetrating their wholly erroneous interpretation of human nature, is to divert attention from the real sources of man's aggression and destructiveness, namely, the many false and contradictory values by which, in an overcrowded, highly competitive, threatening world, he so disoperatively attempts to live. It is not man's nature, but his nurture, in such a world, that requires our attention.

Like Ashley Montagu, Geoffrey Gorer was born in London in 1905, but he
remained in Britain, where he is a leading anthropologist. In this article,
he says that man may be a killer, but it is not because of his instincts.
Why, then, does man take pleasure in killing? Why does he hate?
Gorer compares rat packs to the nation-state and speaks of the advantages
of the nation-state over the territory of the clan and the tribe. What are
the advantages? What are the disadvantages of the large nation?

Man Has No "Killer" Instinct

Geoffrey Gorer

One of the most persistent and widespread beliefs about "human
nature" held by men of goodwill in most of the advanced societies in
the world is that human beings are "naturally" peaceful and gentle,
considerate of their fellow human beings and unwilling to hurt or kill
them save under the (assumedly) exceptional conditions of war.

This belief in the essential gentleness of "human nature" can only
be maintained by a wilful blindness that refuses to recognize the evidence which history, social anthropology, the daily newspapers and
television so constantly provide of man's willingness to hurt and kill
his fellows, and to take pride and pleasure in so doing.

In recent months we have read detailed accounts and seen gruesome
pictures of Ibos and Hausas gleefully slaughtering one another in
Nigeria, of massacres of Indonesians and Chinese in Java and other
islands of the archipelago, of Chinese youngsters with red armlets self-
righteously humiliating their elders, not to mention both sides in Vietnam. If we try to console ourselves by claiming that most of these
slaughters and humiliations were the acts of people who were not civilized and not Christian, this consolation should be short-lived. The
Boers and white Rhodesians claim Christian justification for the ill-
treatment of their fellow citizens with darker skins; the pictures of the
school at Grenada, Miss., are surely not forgotten; and no recorded
"uncivilized" nation has equaled the systematic humiliation and
slaughter practiced by Christian Germany and her allies a bare generation ago.

All known societies make a distinction between murder—the killing of a member of one's own group—and the killing of outsiders. We
can understand murder for jealousy or gain or safety, however much

are (so to speak) subhuman, and killing them is not murder. This primitive type of rat-thinking is never far below the surface, even among the civilized and sensitive.

Where human beings differ from rats is in their very varying definitions of who shall be included within the pack. Usually, the pack is the society or tribe, people who speak the same language (typically unique to the tribe) and between whom real or suppositious bonds of kinship can be traced; but there are variants in both directions.

The smallest packs known to me are those described by Dr. and Mrs. Ronald M. Berndt, who studied four contiguous language groups in the Eastern Highlands of New Guinea. Here the people one should not kill are certain specified kinfolk and a few relations of one's wife or wives. Everyone else, irrespective of ancestry or language, was fit prey for the "deadly game" of death, for only by killing can a man earn power and prestige. The dead were eaten and, in the case of women, raped either before or after death.

The only reason why these packs had not exterminated one another before the Australians pacified the area a bare decade ago is that they practiced a policy of preservation of human game. They seldom killed more than they could eat, and left the temporarily weak in peace to breed. The gleeful, guiltless accounts that Dr. and Mrs. Berndt gathered from the participants in these orgies of slaughter, cannibalism and rape read like a nightmare vision of human savagery.

New Guinea also contains one of the relatively few tribes described by anthropologists in whom the joy of killing seems to be completely absent. These are the Arapesh, studied by Dr. Margaret Mead and Dr. Reo Fortune. They will be discussed in more detail subsequently.

For most of humanity, the tribe is the unit within which killing is considered murder, and outside which killing may be a proof of manhood and bravery, a pleasure and a duty. Such killing may be done by individuals—head-hunters, scalp-collectors, as part of a vendetta or raid—or by groups; in the latter case the killing is called "warfare." The differences in quality and scope between tribal warfare and modern war between nation-states are so great that it might be useful if different words were used for the two activities.

The nation-state was invented after the Neolithic revolution, less than 10,000 years ago; and this is a very short period in man's evolutionary history. One of the advantages of the nation-state is that it greatly extended the area within which killing would be murder; a number of tribes were brought under the same law and equally protected from mutual slaughter. This amalgamation is not now an easy one, as the sad condition of contemporary Nigeria or Indonesia demonstrates; and it probably was no less difficult in the past. There are no reliable contemporary records of the establishment of the first nation-states, mostly along the great rivers of Asia and North Africa; by the time adequate historical records commence, a dominant group had succeeded in preserving peace among the component tribes. The pack was successfully extended to include and protect most of the inhabitants of a given geographical area, even though slaves and captives were usually excluded.

The nation-state is really the last successful human invention for extending the size of the pack, within which killing is murder. In the past 4,000 years a number of religions have been founded which would include all believers inside the pack; but no religion has commanded worldwide allegiance; and regularly the outcasts, infidels, untouchables, heathen or heretics could all be humiliated or killed with added pleasure and self-righteousness, because they were members of the devil's pack.

The founders of the great world religions, Gautama Buddha, Jesus, Lao-Tzu, Mohammed, all seem to have striven for a worldwide brotherhood of man; but none of them could develop institutions which would include the enemy, the unbeliever, and give him the same protection from anger, hatred and the lust for killing which they decreed within their own congregations.

Within the last century and a half, various millennial ideologies—democracy, Socialism, the Communist internationals, the United Nations—have taken over the goal of the traditional religions: the establishment of a world-wide brotherhood of man, a single pack. They have been no more successful than their predecessors in protecting the enemy, the unbeliever, from the horrible results of righteous anger.

In recent centuries, most men of goodwill have at least paid lip-service to the ideal of a universal brotherhood with equal protection for all, whatever might be their actual behavior or that of their compatriots. But this century has seen a most sinister recrudescence of rat-pack ideology, in which human status is denied to all persons who do not share one's hypothetical ancestry or visible skin color: Fascism, Nazism, white supremacy, black power all justify hatred and contempt for those outside the pack; and recent history shows how easily, how very easily, this justified hatred and contempt develop into humiliation, torture and killing.

The evidence could be endlessly multiplied to demonstrate that man, as a species, has no inhibitions against killing his fellow men who do not belong to the same pack, however the pack may be defined, and often gets intense pleasure and a sense of pride from so doing. But to admit this is not the same as positing a "killer instinct" as part of man's hereditary endowment. There is no logical reason for hypothesizing such an instinct, and indeed some arguments, to be advanced shortly, against doing so.

Because men have no innate instinctual inhibitions against hurting and killing other members of their species, this offers some human beings a potential source of intense pleasure, as do incest, homosexuality and other sexual deviations. Man has no built-in inhibitions against these sources of pleasure either; did he possess them, laws would be unnecessary. Whether any of these pleasures will be sought, how frequently, and by whom, depends on the values of a specific society at a given time and the vicissitudes of individual lives.

Because man can and does gain intense pleasure from humiliating, hurting and killing his fellows, the speculative novels of the Marquis de Sade are extremely important documents, whatever their literary qualities. Save in a directly sexual situation (when he relished flagellation), de Sade was an affectionate, humane and very courageous man. In his 13-year-long solitary confinement he looked without flinching into the deepest recesses of his unconscious fantasies and reported, in fictional form, the pleasures to be derived from the unfettered exercise of power over one's fellow men and women.

De Sade linked these pleasures with the pleasures of sex; this was the only metaphor which contemporary science made available to him and it was congenial to his temperament. Even so, there are many episodes in the novels when power is used for its own sake— power to humiliate, hurt or kill—without any overt sexual gratification. De Sade wished to portray "the spasms of man's loathsome heart and fearful passions" because he was convinced that only by acknowledging the truth about human nature, as he saw it, could a safe and just society be built.

Classical psychoanalysis has in good part confirmed de Sade's pessimistic diagnosis of "man's loathsome heart." Freud always maintained the central position in his theory of the Oedipus complex; and the little Oedipus had murder in his heart, the killing of his father—a point which many contemporary psychoanalysts tend to gloss over. According to the findings of the late Melanie Klein and her followers, the inchoate hatred and rages of very young children produce wishes which, when translated into verbal metaphors,

parallel the fantasies of de Sade: cannibalism, poisoning, eviscera-
tion, castration, murder.

The history of civilized nations in the century and a half since de
Sade's death also confirms his pessimistic diagnosis of human behavior. Although he placed no bounds on his imagination, we have
been witnesses to far greater horrors than de Sade could dream of;
man can be an even more savage monster than he guessed. It is possible that, had de Sade's diagnosis of human potentialities been taken
consistently into account, the fanatics, torturers and murderers would
have had less impunity in the indulging of their fearful passions.

There are, however, a few rays of hope, a few societies where
men seem to find no pleasure in dominating over, hurting or killing
the members of other societies, where all they ask is to be at peace
and to be left in peace. These societies are, of course, small, weak,
technologically backward, and living in inaccessible country; only so
could they survive the power-seeking of their uninhibited neighbors.

Among these gentle societies are the Arapesh of New Guinea,
mentioned earlier; the Lepchas of Sikkim in the Himalayas (whom
I studied); and, most impressive of all, the pygmies of the Ituri rain-
forest in the Congo, studied by Colin Turnbull. These small societies
(there are several others) living in the most inaccessible deserts and
forests and mountains of four continents, have a number of traits in
common, besides the fact that they do not dominate over, hurt or kill
one another or their neighbors, though they possess the weapons to
do so. Many of them, including the pygmies and the Lepchas until a
couple of generations ago, rely almost exclusively on hunting for
their protein food.

What seem to me the most significant common traits in these
peaceful societies are that they all manifest enormous gusto for
concrete physical pleasures—eating, drinking, sex, laughter—and
that they all make very little distinction between the ideal characters
of men and women, particularly that they have no ideal of brave,
aggressive masculinity.

Men and women have different primary sexual characteristics—a
source of endless merriment as well as of more concrete satisfactions—and some different skills and aptitudes. No child, however,
grows up with the injunctions, "All real men do . . . " or "No
proper woman does . . . ," so that there is no confusion of sexual
identity: no cases of sexual inversion have been reported among
them. The model for the growing child is of concrete performance
and frank enjoyment, not of metaphysical symbolic achievements or
of ordeals to be surmounted. They do not have heroes or martyrs to

emulate or cowards or traitors to despise; their religious life lacks significant personalized gods and devils; a happy, hard-working and productive life is within the reach of all.

As far as the history of these small tribes can be reconstructed, they have always chosen to retreat into ever more inaccessible country rather than stand their ground and fight with invaders. There is no reason to suppose that their psychological or physiological potentialities are different from those of their more aggressive neighbors, but their values certainly are; for them peace and the absence of quarreling and jealousy are far more important than a reputation for bravery and virility. And while the tribes are not broken up, it is likely that these values will continue to prevail. When the tribes are broken, individuals, unsupported by the traditional ethics, might easily revert to rat-pack mentality. Save that they have so far survived, these small tribes have not been conspicuously successful in the struggle for existence and terrain against more ruthless neighbors. Nevertheless, they may offer a paradigm of ways to diminish the joy of killing in the uninhibited human race.

By contrast, the cannibals in the New Guinea Highlands have a highly aggressive ideal of masculinity; and so, in general, do all the peoples who prize the martial virtues and self-righteously kill their enemies or their "inferiors." The New Guinea Highlanders frankly enjoy sex, especially if it approximates to rape; but many other martial societies repudiate all sensual pleasure as unworthy of a Real Man. If our gods and heroes are killers—Lords of Hosts, warriors, successful revolutionaries—and if masculinity is demonstrated by the willingness to give and take "punishment," then the joy of killing is always likely to re-emerge.

It seems possible that the youth international, which has developed nearly the whole world over in the last generation, has inarticulately sensed the necessity to redefine the concepts of a "real man" and "a true woman" if we are not to destroy ourselves completely. The long hair, dandified dress and pleasantly epicene features (which so infuriate their elders) are a physical repudiation of the ideal of aggressive masculinity which has been traditional in all their societies in recent generations, and which is still maintained by the conventional and the neo-Fascists (white supremacists, Empire loyalists, Birchites and the like) in the same societies.

Even idiotic slogans such as "Make love, not war" (as if the two activities had ever been incompatible!) and the use of drugs make the same point. Mankind is safer when men seek pleasure than when they seek the power and the glory.

If the members of the youth international—the beats and the swingers, the *provos* and the *stilyagi*—maintain the same scale of values and the same sex ideals 20 years hence when they themselves are middle-aged and parents, then they may, just possibly, have produced a permanent change in the value systems and sex roles of their societies, which will turn the joy of killing into an unhappy episode of man's historic past, analogous to human sacrifice, which ascribed joy in killing to the gods also.

The attempts to devise a social unit more inclusive than the nation-state, a brotherhood of man, have all been unsuccessful to date. It is just possible that the youth international, with its emphasis on shared sensual pleasure and its repudiation of the ideal of truculent "manliness," may succeed where the grandiose schemes of idealists have always failed. For man has no "killer instinct"; he merely lacks inhibitions.

What is there about violence and violent sports that is so attractive
to so many people? We have our much talked about violence on television,
our long attraction for the gun, our history of the Wild West, and our
gangsters and gangster   movies. Stimulation and excitement is headlined
on both the front page and the sports page. Bob Oates, "Los Angeles Times"
staff writer, surveys the sports world and the nearby academic world
in search of answers.

Violent Sports: Furious Tribal Instincts Freed?

Bob Oates

The invitation had come from the coach of the San Diego Chargers; "Let's put it on the screen." And now, as he turned on the lights,
Sid Gillman was smiling. "Beautiful," he said.

In the movie, three linebackers had assaulted a quarterback, knock-
ing him down and out.

Gillman said, "I have never known a football player who didn't
want to hit you with everything he had. Hitting is the nature of the
animal and the game."

In the country today, this is a popular view. The more violent
sports, from hockey to auto racing, are attracting more attention each
year. Every football coach endorses, and teaches, violence.

"But I am convinced there is right and wrong violence," Gillman
said, pointing to a newspaper headline. "I'm in favor of the football
kind—not the Harvard campus kind."

This also is a popular view in America.

Answers Sought Elsewhere

A contradiction of the era is that whereas violence is deplored on
streets and campuses, it seems to be admired and encouraged in
stadiums.

Why? Are humans instinctively violent? In their sports prefer-
ences, are the American people expressing socially unacceptable im-
pulses in acceptable ways? Or is there another explanation for the
expanding interest in rougher sports?

The answer may be in two parts:

1—Most psychologists and sociologists believe that man's disposition to violence is not an instinct. Rather, it is learned. The thing

that distinguishes man, they say, is a capacity for generalized learning. And in recent years he has been conditioned to appreciate both the fury and the science of more active games.

2—Athletes and sports fans alike are attracted by the interplay of both elements: (a) the violence and (b) the science (skills, techniques and ability founded on training, discipline and experience).

Football Violent Sport

A sport which tends to be one-sided—emphasizing skills without much savagery, or vice versa—engages the attention of fewer Americans than a sport based on the combinations.

The essential interest comes from the art and science of each sport. The excitement comes from the violence: from athletes testing their skills in situations of "the right kind."

Both elements are illustrated in professional football.

Says all-pro Merlin Olsen of the Rams: "Frankly, what I like about football is that it gives me a chance to demonstrate my ability and courage at the same time. I've never cared for non-contact games of skill—but I don't get any kick, either, out of beating up a guy just for the hell of it. I need a reason to hit him."

"In football," he says, "you've got to intimidate a man physically and dominate him intellectually. You have to show him who's boss and who's smarter. That's the challenge, and I love it."

Along with most football players, Olsen accepts rather than revels in the violence. But he doesn't underestimate it.

"Aggressiveness," he says, "is what puts football in tune with the times, more so than baseball or other sports. This is an aggressive country. Our economic system is the most aggressive in the world. School kids are taught to compete aggressively for scholarships. Aggression is all over television and the newspapers. It's only natural that the most aggressive games are the best liked."

What it may come down to is that a rough sport is a picturesque example of the "American way."

Lance Alworth, for instance, and Rudi Nureyev are men of similar skills and size, although one is a pro football player for the Chargers and the other a ballet dancer. To American spectators, Rudi is interesting—whereas Lance is both interesting and exciting.

Alworth's thing is Nureyev's thing in a setting of violence. The slim Alworth as an all-pro pass receiver is grace in action—but his stage is a booby trap. It can and has blown up under him.

"Moves Elegantly"

Alworth moves elegantly through a mine field of roughnecks; he extends his great talent along the brink of a total wipeout.

And it is this that draws Alworth, and the spectators, to football.

In Los Angeles, ice hockey is the newest major league manifestation of this kind of art and malice—though an ineffective team has held down the crowds that illustrate the point more convincingly elsewhere.

Says Larry Regan, general manager of the Kings:

"The most violent hockey team usually wins. Hitting is half of this game, and a collision gets the crowd on its feet every time. But the other half—speed and skating—is just as vital.

"Hockey," says Regan, "is the only sport in which to play it skillfully, you have to learn another skill first—skating. Any American boy can swing a bat or carry a football or a hockey stick. The trick in hockey is not just to put a stick on a baseball or a golf ball or a puck —but to do this when you're speeding along on a sheet of ice, or cutting sharply, and all the time keeping yourself balanced on two little blades one-eighth of an inch thick. And at the same time, keeping your eye open for a guy who wants to bust you heels over tea kettle."

Boxing's Attraction

Boys and men alike are attracted to hockey by these double challenges to ability and inner fortitude—and much the same is true of boxing, although this sport is better known for violence than skill.

Boxing is widely considered to be the prima facie example of the most violent thing one man can do to another without a weapon. Under supervision in a licensed ring, however, this is a sport less violent than football, according to promoter Aileen Eaton of the Olympic.

"A 200-pound quarterback," says Mrs. Eaton, "is fair game for a 290-pound defensive lineman. We'd never allow that in boxing. Before a match is made, the whole object is to get athletes of even weight, even strength and even ability.

"This is the only sport," she says, "that is so concerned about those things—in terms of injury and punishment. In football, certainly, the object sometimes seems to be just the opposite."

Boxing also is the one sport in which the goal is to knock another human being senseless. This is the aspect which repels non-boxing fans. But in the majority, those who like boxing are probably no more bloodthirsty than the average of the rest of us.

"Violence is the least part of boxing," Mrs. Eaton insists. "The appeal is a pair of well-matched athletes on their own in a small ring—with no help coming from a defensive platoon or a home-run hitter batting fourth. Who's the better man? That's boxing."

Auto Racing Too

That's automobile racing, too—in the judgment of those who compete in one of America's fastest-rising sports.

The late Tony Bettenhausen once said that the appeal of an Indianapolis ride rests on its "extended challenge" to each man to prove himself.

"Any good motorist can navigate one turn," he said. "The challenge is 200 laps: you alone against determined men and machinery."

Machine racing remains under fire in this country both for its "unnecessary" risks (Bettenhausen was killed testing a race car at Indianapolis) and for its "unhealthy" stimulus to the race public. But those who have studied race crowds for many years doubt the charge that the typical race fan is "blood-thirsty."

Says former Ram linebacker Les Richter: "The race driver balances on the fringe of disaster, of total tragedy. You're there to see him dance on the fringe, not go over. The 'almost' accident is the thrill, not the tragic accident."

Richter, now the president of Riverside International Raceway, was regarded as the roughest linebacker of his time. He once provoked a Coliseum opponent to take off his helmet and swing it like a hammer on Richter's head. Richter speaks as a two-sport expert when he says:

"Facing . . . Violent End"

"Football fans are there to see John Unitas with his back to the wall—facing a violent end at the hands of Deacon Jones—and they want Unitas to stand there and take it. They want him to try for a touchdown pass instead of taking the easy way out and running off with the ball.

"It is the same in racing. The thrill is watching human beings weave through murderous traffic at 150 m.p.h. with their life in their two hands. But if a man is hurt, everybody feels it; everybody hurts."

Richter expands on this thought with a theory about sports crowds that may be definitive.

"Every sports fan, including me," he says, "is a Walter Mitty. He puts himself in the car or on the hockey rink and wishes he were brave enough to do what he is seeing. Bravery is the pull."

Psychologists agree in general that athletes and spectators are "psychologically similar." Thus it is likely that the rise of public interest in the more violent games (as compared with the more passive games: baseball, soccer, track and field, etc.) is due in part to the public's growing appetite for (or tolerance of) violence.

There are other reasons. Speaking of team sports as a whole, their overall appeal probably rests to a large extent on their entertainment value and two other things:

1—The fan identifies with the hometown team and when it wins, he is happier. He feels better. HE is a winner.

2—When his team loses, it wasn't the fan who lost the game. The spectator, who was only mentally engaged on the field, can now dissociate himself from the players and blame them. They are now "bums."

Accordingly, the fan is invincible. He can win, but he can't lose.

In this context, the violent side of sports is an extra dimension— a bonus thrill.

The lure, in some respects, is synthetic: hockey fans hope to see sticks in the air and blows landed, but sociologists can find no proof that they are ecstatic when skulls are fractured.

At baseball games the fans may holler, "Stick it in his ear." They may implore the pitcher to knock the batter down.

"But the fans don't really mean it," says Bill Rigney, the manager of the California Angels.

"They're just blowing off steam," Rigney believes. "Nobody wants to see a player beaned."

Curiously, the introduction of the protective batting helmet in recent years may have changed baseball in subtle ways—and not entirely for the better. Batting, to begin with, is something more than "the most difficult sports skill to master," as Ted Williams calls it. It is an act of bravery. A man standing at the plate with a bat, but without a helmet, commits his life to the accuracy of the bullet throwers of the major leagues.

But put him under a helmet and some of the fear leaves him, and some of the concentration, too.

Says Rigney: "I often think they get careless standing there under those magical hats. They don't have to think about getting hurt any more, and pretty soon they aren't even thinking about what they're doing. If the pitchers would brush them back more often, they'd be doing them a favor.

"But baseball today frowns on the brushback pitch," Rigney sighs. "It used to be that a manager could sit in a dugout and yell to his pitcher, 'Knock him down.' But no more. Today, the rules forbid it."

The irony is that as the rest of the world grows more violent, baseball, which has never been the most savage national pastime, gets safer. It has the helmet now and more scruples.

Losing Ground

It has been speculated that the sport is losing ground for this reason. In a national poll (the Harris Survey) last month, football was listed as the "favorite sport" of more Americans (31%) than any other. Baseball, second with 28%, had never been out of the lead before. Five years ago when baseball was first with 40%, football had 25%.

In the nominally non-contact game of basketball, acts of physical aggression have a different meaning.

Says Jerry West, the Laker star : "In the NBA, the first thing you have to show the old pros is that you can 'take it.' "

Answering a question about [former] UCLA All-American Lew Alcindor's professional future, West says:

"Much depends on how Lew handles the rough stuff. He will be shouldered, elbowed and stepped on. Big men will drive through him if they can. I think Lew can take it, but we'll have to wait and see."

Track and field is the perfect example of the one-sided non-violent sport demanding the most carefully refined skills.

Says USC track coach Vern Wolfe: "In our sport, if a runner so much as steps in front of another runner, he is disqualified. I guess the most exciting thing that ever happened to us was the day a shot putter wound up and punched another shot putter in the nose."

There is a correlation between lack of violence and lack of public interest in track—and also in such sports as swimming, diving, tennis and golf.

Coach Wolfe, speaking for the artists of the non-contact sports, says: "They work just as hard as football men. And they have just as many skills. They have everything but the crowds."

In some sports, it has been shown that sex appeal is box office— when combined with violence. Hockey and wrestling are examples.

Says Regan of the Kings: "Women love hockey, and many come un-escorted. They like to get close to big, strong men who do violent, masculine things. There isn't as much sex appeal in football, where the field is far away. It's hard for á girl to identify herself with a face-less man. In hockey you can almost touch the man. When he's hit, you can see the expression change on his face."

On wrestling nights at the Olympic, where simulated violence is continuous, there also is a large proportion of women, many un-escorted. It has been suggested that some are sexually attracted.

An oddity of wrestling is that its fans are among the most violent in sports and its participants among the least.

Soccer, in one sense, is like wrestling. There isn't much genuine vio-lence in soccer, yet it provokes violent outbursts in the crowd. In Peru, a moat around the field separates fans and athletes. In other countries there are chain-link fences.

And there may be another link—between the non-violence of soc-cer and its furious fans, who, herded into a packed stadium, achieve no emotional release from the game because nobody has been beaten up.

Social scientists are not united on this explanation. But most of them appear to be in agreement with Mike Ditka and other football players that the action of a forceful game serves as an outlet for ten-sions.

Ditka, now with the Dallas Cowboys, feels "more calm" in the autumn pressures of the football season than he does in the winter and spring. He doubts the popular notion in America that acts of violence "stimulate" aggressors to more aggressions.

"Build Anxieties"

"A lot of football players," says Ditka, "build up anxieties in the off-season because they have no outlet for them. I'm most relaxed when I'm playing football. If I'm not getting rid of my energy this way, I blow it off in some way that isn't proper in this society."

Many hockey and football fans might make a similar self-analysis.

Says a USC psychologist, Dr. Donald J. Lewis: "Most of us get a release out of a controlled, forceful spectacle like football."

Lewis concedes that public interest in violence is rising. So is re-search on the subject on the torn campuses of the nation, where the usual starting point is a question: Were the agitators (or the football players) born violent?

Psychology's answer: There is no evidence that violence is trans-mitted in the genes from one generation to the next.

Dr. Lewis says, "The only instincts—or at least the only unlearned reactions built into the nervous system—are, first, the drives for sex, food, water and oxygen; second, the need for activity and rest after activity; avoidance of pain. Some psychologists might add one or two things to the list and some would subtract one or two."

It is clear to most scientists that there is no inborn, powerful need for violence as such.

A belief widely persists, nonetheless, that there is a "fighting instinct" in man. Otherwise, why do athletes and spectators tend to choose violent games of skill over non-violent games of skill?

Social scientists hold in general that "man is mostly what he learns to be." In an aggressive environment he is aggressive. Introduced to games combining skill and aggression, he likes the combination.

Psychology approaches the subject from a viewpoint explained by USC's Dr. Lewis in a comment on the effects of televised violence: "Each man's reaction is determined by his social training. For a small percentage, violence leads to violence. For others, it is a cathartic. The majority simply adapts to it—and the more violence, the more widely tolerated."

Psychology finds, furthermore, that aggression is related to frustration. Dr. Lewis says:

"If any organism (including man) is blocked or thwarted in its efforts to reach any instinctive goal, it flails out immediately. This is a basic attempt to remove one frustration. But the form this takes is purely learned. A man can say 'gol-darn it' in a letter to the editor or he can put on a football uniform. These are both expressions of aggression."

Violence Taught

In sports terms, the interest in violence often is not so much "learned" as "taught" (or coached). This has been the contribution of such men as Vince Lombardi, former Green Bay Packer coach now with the Washington Redskins, and Punch Imlach, coach of the Toronto hockey team.

A pertinent comment is found in anthropology. Dr. Sally Carrighar, a British anthropologist, writes:

"Aggressiveness can be taught . . . It also intensifies when it is exercised and atrophies when it is not . . . When men began to settle in communities, they learned the irritations of being crowded . . . With words they could incite hatred against neighboring tribes.

"A leader—coveting power or property—could, with propaganda, instill in his subjects admiration for warlike attitudes."

In American sports, it will be recalled that for nine years in Green Bay, coach Lombardi "instilled in his subjects admiration for warlike attitudes."

Moreover, "coveting power and property," he admitted that he incited hatred against neighboring tribes.

Football is a good modern example of man's tribal pulls to both cooperation and aggression. A football team is a cooperative of 40 men. And the mainspring of the game is violence.

"Cooperation is teamwork," says San Diego's coach Gillman, "and only two things mean more: courage and skill."

Through the pen of Joseph Alsop, Konrad Lorenz explains some of his beliefs and replies, in part, to his critics. The excerpt is taken from a much longer article that appeared in "The New Yorker" magazine. It is apparent that the nature-versus-nurture debate will continue.

A Condition of Enormous Improbability

Joseph Alsop

. . . Animal behavior, in all its aspects, is the ethologists' study. Eventually, I feel sure, the work of the ethologists will have very great sociological and philosophical impact. Philosophically, the problem of the origins of behavior is on the level of the twin problems of the origins of the universe and the origins of life, for which scientific solutions are also just beginning to be put forward. Ethologists have already turned up much that is suggestive if applied to man's behavior as a social animal. Looking at man's present plight on earth, in truth, one can easily perceive all sorts of permutations and derivations of the four basic animal drives that the ethologists have identified—reproduction, hunger, fear, and aggression. In one way or another, the four basic drives lead on to a good many lamentably recognizable social phenomena, like territoriality (or acute possessiveness, even grabbiness about territory), intra-specific fighting (such as the war in Vietnam), and the contest for places in the pecking order that is the henyard version of status-seeking. The ethologists themselves have lately begun to be excited by the potential applications to human society of their numerous discoveries. Dr. Konrad Z. Lorenz, the Austrian zoologist, who played the largest part in the foundation of this new discipline in the inter-war years, recently published a strikingly interesting book entitled "On Aggression." There have been ethological congresses on the same disturbing subject. And popularizers have caused a certain stir with books like Robert Ardrey's *Territorial Imperative* and Desmond Morris's *The Naked Ape*.

Because I had been attracted by this aspect of ethology, I went to Germany not long ago to visit Dr. Lorenz, at the Max Planck Institute of Behavioral Physiology, of which he is now the ethological co-director. When I reached Seewiesen, in the lovely Bavarian plain, where Dr. Lorenz's Institute is situated among woods and meadows by a little lake, I soon discovered that in terms of its original purpose my journey to see the founder of ethology was a bit premature. There was a duty, Dr. Lorenz had evidently felt, to sound the fairly anguished note of warning to the human species that is the essence of *On Aggression*. But as a serious researcher, discussing the stage that his discipline has reached so far, he proved hard to move beyond the much firmer ground already established by studies of the behavior of lesser species, such as whydah birds and European polecats. My conversations with Konrad Lorenz nonetheless illuminated quite wonderfully, if sometimes ominously, many of the philosophic and scientific puzzles of the origins of behavior. . . .

When I asked Dr. Lorenz to talk further about the relationship between innate behavior and learned behavior, Mrs. Lorenz said, "Now you have started something." She was smiling in an amused way, for she knew what I did not—that this is a matter that has created grave controversies among ethologists and, to an even greater degree, between ethologists and psychologists. Sure enough, there was an echo of past battles in Dr. Lorenz's academically severe tone when he replied with a warning that he had been "using the word 'innate' in a shorthand sense." He went on to say, "Nothing is truly innate except the blueprint in the genome. A baby may have a genetic blueprint for the most beautiful nose in Western Europe, but if bad diet makes the baby rachitic the blueprint will not be realized. Yet the approximate realization of the genetic blueprint is still the normal result, so it seems to me quibbling to refuse to apply the word 'innate' to behavioral and other characteristics whose blueprints are demonstrably transmitted in the germ plasm. All the same, we ethologists were mistaken in the past when we made a sharp distinction between 'innate' and 'learned.' Viewed in one light, all life is a learning process. No animal species or lower organism could survive for very long without adaptedness, and evolutionary adaptation molds each species or organism so that it fits its own environmental niche and therefore survives. This molding to fit an environment really amounts to forming an image of that particular environment within the species or organism, and one can quite properly speak of information concerning the environment being acquired by adaptation. Hence, there are really two ways of learning— genetically and by individual experience—and these two ways of learning, though different in kind, nonetheless form a continuum, as W. N. Russell has pointed out. In a good many cases, genetically transmitted information is not subject, or is hardly subject, to revision or correction by individual experience. One example is the computing mechanism in a starling's nervous system which enables the bird to know the points of the compass by the sun's motion across the sky. A similar mechanism plays the primary role in the route-finding of homing pigeons. Another example is the human nervous system's computing mechanism which enables you to see that this is a pencil"—he brandished one—"whether I point it at you or hold it upright. Human optical illusions result almost invariably from false premises being fed into our innate mechanism of *Gestalt* perception. But these nervous mechanisms into which individual learning does not enter, or hardly enters, are only one part of the story. In every individual's system of fixed motor patterns and innate information there are pre-formed places where individual learning can be fitted in. The number of these pre-formed places for individual learning increases in proportion to the complexity of the organism. Hence, higher animals are capable of much individual learning, while insects have a rather limited capacity."

To illustrate, Dr. Lorenz began with bees. For route-finding, bees use irregularly shaped objects, like rocks. Thus, they can be very easily taught that artificially placed objects of irregular shape mark the road to the home hive, and they are then completely put off their course if the artificial markers are moved. But flowers are always, in greater or less degree, radially symmetrical. It is useless to offer bees a rich artificial nectar supply if the attached marker-object is irregular in shape. Their innate information is that food sources are invariably associated with symmetrical shapes, and they cannot be taught the opposite, however often the opposite is made to be true by human contrivance. On the other hand, pigeons have been taught a fair number of interesting, albeit simple, lessons by specialists in "operant conditioning"—psychologists studying learning who have shown, for instance, how fast rats can be made to learn their way through mazes by a combined system of mild punishments, like electric shocks, and food rewards. "But you cannot make a pigeon-prostitute by such rewards and punishments," Dr. Lorenz went on, and explained that this failure resulted from what he called "the wrong feedback." In other words, pigeons will never perform their courtship rituals without some sort of identifiably sexual stimulation. In the same fashion, the operant conditioners, while teaching rats to do many astonishingly clever things, have never managed to make rats go into their copulatory posture by rewards and punishments—again because of the wrong feedback. These are simple indications of the nature and the limitations of Dr. Lorenz's pre-formed places for learning. If the right pre-formed place is not hit, learning does not occur. Yet in many mammals some learning enters even into the reproductive act. Dr. Eibl-Eibesfeldt found that his male polecats learned the correct posture in their infantile social play but had much initial difficulty if reared in isolation.

"To understand individual learning," Dr. Lorenz added, "you must begin with the fact that we and all the rest of animal creation start our lives with a substantial store of innate information that can be amplified by the right kind of experience. The information is put there by adaptation for just that purpose. Much of the innate information takes a rather simple plus-or-minus form, telling us, 'This feels good, that feels bad—do this again, don't do that again.' I am not speaking here, either, merely of feeling pain from a cut or satisfaction after a good meal. It's more complicated than that. For example, P. N. Richter and John Garcia have done quite fabulous experiments with rats. One was to break down the needed protein component in the rats' diet into the constituent amino acids and offer these separately. Judging by their weight gains, the rats quickly learned to take just enough of each amino acid to get the equivalent of their optimum protein requirement. And, obviously, they synthesized their protein requirement so correctly—think of that!—because they felt better that way. Another experiment was to give the rats saccharin water, which they like. Nausea was then induced quite a bit later, by injections of apomorphine, or something similar. Since the saccharin water was the last thing that had entered their stomachs, the rats at once associated the nausea with the saccharin water, and they refused it thereafter. But when other kinds of discomfort were inflicted on the rats, no matter how frequent and severe, these were never associated with food or drink—the discomfort had to be the kind that bad food normally causes in order to induce this special kind of learning. Per contra, the rats could never be conditioned to go here, or avoid going there, or do the other things that operant conditioners think up, by infliction of discomforts normally caused by food. Electric shocks and the like rapidly conditioned the rats in these ways, but not nausea. You see what I mean, then, by pre-formed places for learning. It doesn't stop with 'This feels good or bad' either. In some species, for instance, the innate schoolmarm, as I call it, is also able to say, 'This sounds good.' Father James Mulligan, of St. Louis University, and one of the really able younger men, Masakazu Konishi, of Princeton University, began to wonder how song-birds learn to sing. So song sparrows were reared in isolation, in sound-proof rooms. Eventually, by a kind of trial-and-error process of lonely song, the sparrows produced rough but recognizable approximations of the standard song of their species. And when they were taken out of isolation and allowed to hear other birds —not song sparrows, though—they borrowed this additional note or that until their own songs were perfect down to the last trill. Song sparrows, therefore—but not all bird species, by any means—are demonstrably born with what you can only call a clear idea of how their song *ought* to sound, but without the song itself. Yet they have to hear in order to be able to judge. When deafened very young, Konishi's experimental sparrows never got nearer to the true song than a kind of amorphous twittering. When deafened after they got the song right, however, Konishi's sparrows continued to perform it correctly— it had become a fully learned motor pattern. And, like countless other bird species, the sparrows also proved to have certain innate calls that were, in reality, nothing but fixed motor patterns. Even when deafened very young, they always gave the song sparrow's characteristic warning call, *trank, trank, trank,* whenever they were frightened." . . .

In the light of all this, I asked Dr. Lorenz, as my parting question, whether he regarded the aggressiveness of men equipped with H-bombs, or the human overpopulation of the planet that increases year by year, or some other factor in the quite new human situation of this strange century, as the worst of the looming dangers that now darken the horizon of the human future.

"I wrote *On Aggression*," he replied, "because it seemed to me so urgent for all of us to understand that we belong to a dangerously aggressive species, now that more and more of us are gaining possession of weapons that can partly, or even quite largely, put an end to life on earth. But now that you phrase the question in this more general way, I am not sure that I really know the answer. To begin with, the relation of the human species to its environment is now quite different—at any rate, in the industrial societies—from the relation of any other animal species to its environment at any time in the history of the earth, and quite different, too, from man's relation to his environment at any time in human history up to the Industrial Revolution. Of course, there have always been many, many species whose adaptedness included a fairly dramatic power to change their environment to suit themselves. The big African termites' nests are marvels of instinctive architecture, and such a nest constitutes a change in the environment going far beyond the temporary nests of leaves and branches that gorillas often make for themselves at nightfall. Man, however, has not attained the power to make much more than merely local changes in the environment, as by digging irrigation systems or building walled cities or other old-fashioned activities of that sort; man today is hard at work, albeit not consciously at work, changing the entire world environment in much more radical ways, by altering the chemical composition of the air all creatures breathe, by polluting lakes and rivers, by using insecticides that cause profound ecological changes in huge areas of the earth, by killing off—for sport or by crowding them out—more and more species of the larger animals, and so on and on. In this situation, who can say where the greatest danger lies? To man himself, moreover, there are other obvious dangers perhaps as grave as aggressiveness plus H-bombs. My father used to say, 'Every humanitarian advance is dangerous to the human species,' and in a sense there was much truth in my father's pessimism. Among many human populations, the progress of medicine has now suspended the normal processes of genetic selection. Thus far, we have been able to live quite well on the genetic capital accumulated in the past, but it is obvious that more and more harmful human mutations are being preserved by medical science, and if this continues indefinitely the gene pool will be heavily contaminated. In the same fashion, medicine, plus modern transport that delivers food where there is famine, plus several other factors, have clearly combined to produce the increase of population that you asked about. All biological experience suggests that this cannot go on indefinitely without leading to very dire results. Altogether, life itself—not just human life but all life—is a condition of enormous improbability. And now that the balance of life on earth is being progressively upset, none can foresee the final consequences. Yet one must not lose hope. For if man would just use science to find out and to face the facts about himself, and if man would also use science to guide his activities a little, so that the environment that supports life is not blindly and fatally damaged, then hope for the future would be justified."

Questions

1 Is man a riddle?

2 What hopes can you find for man with his record of love and violence? Some anthropologists say that culture provides for more than binary choices.

3 "It is not true that a brain is a brain is a brain." Explain.

4 Why is Ashley Montagu so concerned about the books by Lorenz, Ardrey, and Golding? How does he refute their theses?

5 According to Geoffrey Gorer, why did the founders of the world's great religions fail to make their teachings universal?

6 How do you explain the sports fan who cannot lose? Why was Green Bay so successful, according to the article by Bob Oates?

7 Are cultural differences really a handicap to world cooperation?

8 How does Konrad Lorenz qualify the thesis of innate behavior?

2 The Brilliant Beginnings of Civilization

Men become absorbed in a fixed idea about head-hunting or burning crosses and are so sure that they have the truth that they consider others as lost souls. We are all subject to the hangup of a fixed idea, and as civilized people we have been hung up on certain ideas and issues from ages past. The first civilizations had varied but definite ideas about material goods and government. In seeing them deal with the problems of goods and services we see something of ourselves.

A Few Old Hangups From the Bronze Age

Frederick Gentles

Some five hundred years ago Machiavelli said that what has happened in the modern world happened first in ancient times. There is, he said, a genuine resemblance of things present to things past, and the reason for this is that man has ever had the same passions. Civilized man, indeed, has gone round and round with the same old issues from the Bronze Age to the present, and these issues—and passions— are as vital and as unsettled in the present world as they were in the old.

From the beginnings of civilization in ancient Mesopotamia and Egypt, man has been concerned not only about his larger relations with god and country but also with such immediacies as the power of government over his affairs. He has been troubled about local states' rights versus a larger centralized authority. He has worried about taxes, justice, wealth, security, power, and prestige. He has been caught up with the man-made institution of property. Should property be common to all, concentrated in the hands of a few, or privately held but widely distributed?

In hanging on to ideas about these problems, man has often become a true believer, letting the ideas dominate his thinking and life-style unto death; so many of the ideas he lives by are taken as truth when in fact they are myth. "A myth," Ashley Montagu reminds us, "is something which is in fact not true, but in which we believe and act upon as if it were true." A myth is a convenient belief. The problems are old; only the characters and the sets are changed from one age to another. There are, as Machiavelli said, present resemblances to things past.

As record-keeping man appears out of the haze of prehistory, we find him concerned primarily with practical matters such as barley and beer, turnips and onions, sheep and cattle, and the buying and selling of property, slaves, and fields. He has harnessed the Tigris and Euphrates in order to produce regularly and abundantly, and he has invented such practical gadgets as the plow, the wheel, wagons, boats, and copper and bronze implements for tools and weapons. This was, indeed, a remarkable new frontier and a great society that began to take form in the Sumeria of five thousand years ago. Over 90 percent of the tablets discovered in this ancient land pertain to business transactions of private individuals or to bureaucratic governmental agencies administering social or community property. Businessmen and bureaucrats appear at a very early time in history.

It has been suggested by some scholars that a basic inspiration for the development of writing was the need to keep track of property, and that this was accomplished in the land of two rivers (Mesopotamia) by scratching symbols and numbers of sheep, barley, or other property on clay tablets. The temple gods (with priests acting in their names), the kings, and the nobles had extensive property holdings, and there is abundant evidence of property transactions among the common people. The large holdings of temples, kings, and nobles were worked by serfs and slaves or were leased to tenant farmers who gave up a good percentage of their produce as rent. Thus, the old institution of tenant-farming that has plagued both Eastern and Western civilizations through long ages, began with the first civilized peoples. There have been government-imposed land reforms ever since, many of them resulting from peasant protest and revolt, but, typically, land always seems to flow back to the few who charge exorbitant rents and keep the masses poor. America, too, has its poor tenant-farmers and sharecroppers.

One gathers from reading about the Sumerians that the great temples were used as much for business undertakings as for religious purposes. The priests at Lagash, for instance, supervised not only tenant farmers but also bakers of bread, brewers of beer, clerks, smiths, spinners, weavers, and other artisans in a communal-type operation that eventually resulted in wealthy priests taking advantage of poor workers by paying them low wages, overcharging for burials, and treating the communal property as their own. The temple accounts of the goddess Bau in Lagash have been preserved almost intact and report that in her temple worked twenty-one bakers who were assisted by twenty-seven female slaves, twenty-five brewers with six slaves assisting, forty women preparing wool from the goddess's flocks, female spinners and weavers, a male smith, and other artisans working with tools provided by the temple. In addition, Bau had a personal estate worked by tenant-farmers and wage-earners.[1] In this brief but well-kept record, we find we are already in the age of socialism, free enterprise, specialization, bureaucracy, and—with Bau importing a stud bull from the mountains to cross with her lowland cattle—scientific farming. And all this long before 2000 B.C.

Goods and gods were not far apart. To a great many people, they are one and the same, then and now. The priests had their vested interests and maintained their power by perpetuating the myths, which, of course, became reality to people living out the symbolism of gods and goddesses, rites and sacrifices. Kings, frequently in competition with priests, perpetuated their power with the help of myths, police, and soldiers.

There was a form of socialism in the temple economy, but a socialism that operated a bit differently from modern concepts of the term. There was also a form of capitalism, both private and temple, that operated in ways unique to the Sumerians and their successors, the Old Babylonians. Samuel Noah Kramer, in the article following this essay, says that even the poor owned farms, gardens, houses, and cattle in a mixed economy that was socialistic, capitalistic, and state-controlled. There was even the idea of the pooling of resources to form a type of corporation separate from the state.

> The degree of the trader's freedom of disposition and individual financial responsibility and initiative can not yet be established with any clarity. Only from Ur of the early Old Babylonian period have we evidence that the importers of copper from beyond the Persian Gulf transacted their business by pooling their funds and by sharing the risks, the responsibility, and the profits. These texts repeatedly mention the *karu*, a merchant organization with a seat and a legal status of its own, outside the city proper.[2]

No name is given for the company. (Could it be Anaconda?) In any case, capitalism and socialism were taking form and people were reacting to them just as they do now to Wall Street and Red Square.

From the records and from the codes of law, it is obvious there was much class conflict in the ancient world of the Near East. Gordon Childe says that:

> The surplus produced by the new economy was, in fact, concentrated in the hands of a relatively small class. Such concentration was doubtless necessary for the accumulation of absolutely small individual contributions into reserves sufficient for the great tasks imposed on civilized society. But it split society into classes and produced further concentration in the new economy. For it limited the expansion of industry and consequently the absorption of the surplus rural population.[3]

Shades of Karl Marx and Sigmund Freud! It was Marx in the *Communist Manifesto* who claimed that the great conflicts of history were due to the creation of classes, and it was Freud who said that civilization's discontents were due to man's inability to satisfy all his selfish desires.

As a respected Sumerologist, Kramer is also particularly interested in behavioral patterns, and in 1958 he wrote an article entitled "Love, Hate, and Fear: Psychological Aspects of Sumerian Culture" in which he described the motivations and values of that society whose settlements date from about 4500 B.C. down to about 1750 B.C. Although marriage might be for love, he said, it was also a business affair in which the almighty shekel counted in making the nuptial arrangements. There was also divine love, love of country and city-state, love of family, friends, and last, but definitely not least—self. Although much of it was probably pure love, it is obvious that some of it was tainted with material motives. The Sumerians loved possessions; possessions added meaning to life.

Kramer believes that hatred played a dominant role in Sumerian behavior because the political, economic, and educational institutions were characterized by aggressive competition and conflict between individuals. Even the gods displayed hatred, and stories were told of the laying of curses upon the cities of Sumer by enraged deities. Foreigners were frequently hated, and there was even cause to fear and hate those in one's family or town, and, of course, those who were rulers. Many letters have been found filled with protest, cutting remarks, and general invective. The Sumerians placed great stress on ambition, success, prestige, and honor. There was competition, and there was love, hate, and fear in ancient Sumeria. These were the beginnings of the civilized games that civilized people play.

Though the Sumerian was a materialist, he was deeply involved spiritually with both his religion and his state, which were considered nearly one and the same at one time and rather separate at another. At one time there was a conflict between temple and palace, and at another time the king came to control the temple and there was a close association of god and country. A fierce loyalty led, at least in part, to fierce wars between the city-states. The worst catastrophe that could befall a city was to have the enemy destroy the holy places; the flag is such a sacred symbol among nations today. Lamentations deploring the destruction of the cities were composed by survivors of the persistent and bitter conflicts among our ancestors.

Warfare with its soldiers and armaments became an institution for protecting the city-state and enlarging its boundaries, for bloating its ego and gratifying its lust for wealth. One city or another succeeded in dominating the battlefields of Sumer, but, as in the nation-states of Western society, its domination lasted only until decline and decay set in. There was a power struggle between Ur and Nippur; the victor was named King of Kish. There was a border dispute between Umma and Lagash; the King of Kish arbitrated a settlement. The treaty of peace was violated; the Ummaites burned and looted Lagash. It reads like our daily paper. Says Kramer:

> Sad to say, the passion for competition and superiority carried with it the seed of self-destruction and helped trigger the bloody and disastrous wars between the city-states and to impede the unification of the country as a whole, thus exposing Sumer to the external attacks which finally overwhelmed it. All of which provides us with but another historic example of the poignant irony inherent in man and his fate.[4]

What are the attitudes of people toward local control of their political, economic, and social affairs when there is a challenge by a giant national organization? The people of the United States have acted and reacted to the issue of states' rights versus federalism from the time of the Constitutional Convention on. From 1787 to the Civil War on through to the New Deal and Nixon's New Federalism, this issue has always divided the country. Why? In ancient Egypt there were about forty-four states. How did the Egyptians face this issue?

Egypt never had the concept of city-state; it instead developed around provinces called *nomes*, each ruled by a governor, or *nomarch*. There were about twenty-two nomes each in Upper and Lower Egypt, and the history of that land is one of wars between those wanting unification and those wanting local independence. First Upper and Lower Egypt were unified separately as two rival kingdoms, and then about 3100 B.C. the two were brought together under one king, or *pharaoh*. There were at least three political loyalties of the people: to the nome, to Upper or Lower Nile cultures, and to Egypt's king. From time to time one or another took precedence in claiming the prime loyalties of subjects; however, for the better part of 2000 years, the idea of king-power prevailed, largely because the pharaoh was considered as a god and because he had priests, police, and military might to maintain his law and order. As late as King Tutankhamen (King Tut, about 1350 B.C.) there appear two symbols on his beautiful gold crown—the vulture, representing Upper Egypt of the south and the cobra, representing Lower Egypt of the northern Nile delta. Sectionalism persisted in Egypt as it persists in the U.S.A.

Despite its isolation from neighboring peoples and its achievement of stability over a very long period, Egypt, like America, was a polyglot nation of many foreigners and racial mixtures. In the south there was a mixture of black Nubians of the Sudan with brown-skinned peoples of the desert. Queen Nefertiti was a striking Eurasian, while Queen

Tiy, the daughter of two prominent Thebans of Upper Egypt, was a Nubian beauty. The delta was a land of foreigners from Asia and Mediterranean lands, and because of the differences in culture between north and south there was discrimination and conflict. The discrimination seems to have been based on differences in culture rather than on skin color, possibly because there was little difference in color between the black-skinned people with wooly hair and the swarthy people from the desert and Asia. Even today, the people of North Africa and of the Holy Land of Judaism, Christianity, and Islam are predominantly dark-skinned. Could it be that Abraham, Moses, the prophets, Christ, Paul, and Mohammed were all very dark people? Professor Pierre Montet of the College de France has an excellent description of races in Egypt as he interprets them from inscriptions, paintings, and statues.[5]

For all their physical and cultural differences, however, the Egyptians considered themselves a nation apart and felt very proud, even superior. Besides isolation, two other compelling reasons for unity in the disunity of Egypt are the success of the king in persuading the people to think of him as the godhead and the conquest and occupation of Egypt by foreigners. Though Hans Kohn in his excellent book *The Idea of Nationalism* does not speak of the idea in Egypt as he does in Israel and Greece, many Egyptologists insist there was the idea of nationalism in Egypt.

There was a feeling of being an Egyptian over and above that of being loyal to the pharaoh. Just before 1700 B.C., the Hyksos from Asia overran Egypt and imposed such a harsh rule over the land for almost 200 years that they were ardently hated by all who could call themselves Egyptians. It was at this point that a great national feeling developed; it approached in intensity modern-day romantic nationalism, where people experience a strong national bond despite sectional or provincial ties. They were proud to be Egyptians, and they hated the barbaric and inferior foreigners. Myths, canons, and hangups had already developed around the institution of nationalism.

After the Hyksos were driven out, the Egyptians created a military-imperialistic state to seek empire in Asia and Africa. The Empire Period led to an overextension of resources, to a military hierarchy to go with the entrenched civil and ecclesiastical hierarchies (not entirely unlike the three dominant institutions in Latin American history of church, nobility, and military), and to the decline and decay of a brilliant culture. The gods, and the pharaoh as god, were questioned by larger numbers than ever before. Self-interest became the rule, with increasing violence and the breakdown of law, order, and justice.

Professor John A. Wilson says that:

> The great effort of building up and maintaining a new organism such as an empire of remote frontiers, required national unity, and, in the first surge of vengeful patriotism after the Hyksos, that unity was formed out of the devoted fervor of all Egyptians. However, the burden of maintenance was of indefinite time, and the fruits of empire were not shared equally by all. Of course, the wealth pouring into Egypt affected everybody in some degree, but it also created and widened a gap between the governing class and those who were governed. Those who took the lead in the national adventure became increasingly powerful and wealthy. As time went on, they did not need to march with the armies but were tied down at home with their increasing investments and local concerns. . . . There was a class cleavage, and it was no longer possible—theoretically and exceptionally—to move upward in the social scale. That high value set upon the individual Egyptian, down to the ordinary peasant, in the early Middle Kingdom was a thing of the distant past.[6]

And so Egypt, as other civilized nations, fell into decline and decay and was overrun and conquered by Persians, Greeks, Romans, Arabs, Turks, French, and British.

This seems to be the story of our civilized lives from the beginning of our civilized time: We rise to great heights of wealth and beauty only to descend to depths of corruption, worshipping the material gadgets of our own creation. Not truth, not beauty, not even the gods deter the personal ambition that so often brings about personal destruction.

Why?

Notes

1 Gordon Childe, *What Happened in History* (Baltimore, Md.: Penguin, 1961), pp. 94–95.

2 A. Leo Oppenheim, *Ancient Mesopotamia, Portrait of a Dead Civilization* (Chicago: University of Chicago Press, 1964), p. 91.

3 Childe, *op cit.*, p. 99.

4 Samuel Noah Kramer, *The Sumerians, Their History, Culture and Character* (Chicago: University of Chicago Press, 1963), p. 268.

5 Pierre Montet, *Eternal Egypt* (New York: New American Library, 1964).

6 John A. Wilson, *The Burden of Egypt, An Interpretation of Ancient Egyptian Culture* (Chicago: University of Chicago Press, 1965), p. 186.

We see reflections of ourselves in the peoples of the ancient lands of
Sumer and Egypt. They too were once hung up with problems of socialism,
capitalism, social justice, goods and gods. They were involved with the
problem of states' rights versus centralized government. History, it is said,
repeats itself. "The fact is a testimony to human stupidity," said
Edith Hamilton, the eminent classical scholar. And yet, she said, history is
really a chart to guide us. In this selection, Kramer shows that the people
of Lagash 4500 years ago had many of the same problems about
material things that people have today.

The First Case of Tax Reduction

Samuel Noah Kramer

The first recorded social reform took place in the Sumerian city-
state of Lagash in the twenty-fourth century B.C. It was directed
against the abuses of "former days" practiced by an obnoxious and
ubiquitous bureaucracy, such as the levying of high and multifarious
taxes and the appropriation of property belonging to the temple. In
fact, the Lagashites felt so victimized and oppressed that they threw
off the old Ur-Nanshe dynasty and selected a ruler from another family
altogether. It was this new *ishakku*, Urukagina by name, who restored
law and order in the city and "established the freedom" of its citizens.
All this is told in a document composed and written by the Urukagina
archivists to commemorate the dedication of a new canal. To better
understand and appreciate the contents of this unique inscription,
here is a background sketch of some of the more significant social,
economic, and political practices in a Sumerian city-state.

The state of Lagash, in the early third millennium B.C., consisted
of a small group of prosperous towns, each clustering about a temple.
Nominally the city of Lagash, like the other Sumerian city-states, was
under the overlordship of the king of the entire land of Sumer. Actually its secular ruler was the *ishakku*, who ruled the city as the
representative of the tutelary deity to whom, in accordance with the
Sumerian world view, the city had been allotted after the creation.
Just how the earlier *ishakku's* came to power is uncertain; it may well
be that they were selected by the freemen of the city, among whom
the temple administrators (*sanga's*) played a leading political role. In
any case, the office became hereditary in time. The more ambitious
and successful of the *ishakku's* naturally tended to augment their

From *History Begins at Sumer* by Samuel Noah Kramer (Garden City, N.Y.:
Doubleday Anchor, 1959), pp. 45–50. Reprinted by permission of Dr. Samuel
N. Kramer.

power and wealth at the expense of the temple, and this led at times to a struggle for power between temple and palace.

By and large, the inhabitants of Lagash were farmers and cattle breeders, boatmen and fishermen, merchants and craftsmen. Its economy was mixed—partly socialistic and state-controlled, and partly capitalistic and free. In theory, the soil belonged to the city god, and therefore, presumably, to his temple, which held it in trust for all the citizens. In actual practice, while the temple corporation owned a good deal of land, which it rented out to some of the people as share-croppers, much of the soil was the private property of the individual citizen. Even the poor owned farms and gardens, houses and cattle. Moreover, because of Lagash's hot, rainless climate, the supervision of the irrigation projects and waterworks, which were essential to the life and welfare of the entire community, necessarily had to be communally administered. But in many other respects the economy was relatively free and unhampered. Riches and poverty, success and failure, were, at least to some extent, the result of private enterprise and individual drive. The more industrious of the artisans and craftsmen sold their handmade products in the free town market. Traveling merchants carried on a thriving trade with the surrounding states by land and sea, and it is not unlikely that some of these merchants were private individuals rather than temple representatives. The citizens of Lagash were conscious of their civil rights and wary of any government action tending to abridge their economic and personal freedom, which they cherished as a heritage essential to their way of life. It was this "freedom" that the Lagash citizens had lost, according to our ancient reform document, in the days before Urukagina's reign. It was restored by Urukagina when he came to power.

Of the events that led to the lawless and oppressive state of affairs, there is not a hint in the document. But we may surmise that it was the direct result of the political and economic forces unloosed by the drive for power that characterized the ruling dynasty founded by Ur-Nansho about 2500 B.C. Inflated with grandiose ambitions for themselves and and their state, some of these rulers resorted to "imperialistic" wars and bloody conquests. In a few cases they met with considerable success, and for a brief period one of them actually extended the sway of Lagash over Sumer as a whole, and even over several of the neighboring states. The earlier victories proved ephemeral, however, and in less than a century Lagash was reduced to its earlier boundaries and former status. By the time Urukagina came to power, Lagash had been so weakened that it was a ready prey for its unrelenting enemy to the north, the city-state of Umma.

It was during these cruel wars and their tragic aftermath that the citizens of Lagash found themselves deprived of their political and economic freedom. In order to raise armies and supply them with arms and equipment, the rulers found it necessary to infringe on the personal rights of the individual citizen, to tax his wealth and property to the limit, and to appropriate property belonging to the temple. Under the impact of war, these rulers met with little opposition. Once domestic controls were in the hands of the palace coterie, its members were most unwilling to relinquish them, even in peacetime, for the controls proved highly profitable. Indeed, our ancient bureaucrats devised a variety of sources of revenue and income, taxes and imposts, that might well be the envy of their modern counterparts.

But let the historian who lived in Lagash almost 4,500 years ago, and was therefore a contemporary of the events he reports, tell it more or less in his own words: The inspector of the boatmen seized the boats. The cattle inspector seized the large cattle, seized the small cattle. The fisheries inspector seized the fisheries. When a citizen of Lagash brought a wool-bearing sheep to the palace for shearing, he had to pay five shekels if the wool was white. If a man divorced his wife, the *ishakku* got five shekels, and his vizier got one shekel. If a perfumer made an oil preparation, the *ishakku* got five shekels, the vizier got one shekel, and the palace steward got another shekel. As for the temple and its property, the *ishakku* took it over as his own. To quote our ancient narrator literally: "The oxen of the gods plowed the *ishakku's* onion patches; the onion and cucumber patches of the *ishakku* were located in the god's best fields." In addition, the more important temple officials, particularly the *sanga's*, were deprived of many of their donkeys and oxen and of much of their grain.

Even death brought no relief from levies and taxes. When a dead man was brought to the cemetery for burial, a number of officials and parasites made it their business to be on hand to relieve the bereaved family of quantities of barley, bread, and beer, and various furnishings. From one end of the state to the other, our historian observes bitterly, "There were the tax collectors." No wonder the palace waxed fat and prosperous. Its lands and properties formed one vast, continuous, and unbroken estate. In the words of the Sumerian historian, "The houses of the *ishakku* and the fields of the *ishakku*, the houses of the palace harem and the fields of the palace harem, the houses of the palace nursery and the fields of the palace nursery crowded each other side to side."

At this low point in the political and social affairs of Lagash, our Sumerian historian tells us, a new and god-fearing ruler came to the fore, Urukagina by name, who restored justice and freedom to the long-suffering citizens. He removed the inspector of the boatmen from the boats. He removed the cattle inspector from the cattle, large and small. He removed the fisheries inspector from the fisheries. He removed the collector of the silver which had to be paid for the shearing of the white sheep. When a man divorced his wife, neither the *ishakku* nor his vizier got anything. When a perfumer made an oil preparation, neither the *ishakku*, nor the vizier, nor the palace steward got anything. When a dead man was brought to the cemetery for burial, the officials received considerably less of the dead man's goods than formerly, in some cases a good deal less than half. Temple property was now highly respected. From one end of the land to the other, our on-the-scene historian observes, "There was no tax collector." He, Urukagina, "established the freedom" of the citizens of Lagash.

But removing the ubiquitous revenue collectors and the parasitic officials was not Urukagina's only achievement. He also put a stop to the injustice and exploitation suffered by the poor at the hands of the rich. For example, "The house of a lowly man was next to the house of a 'big man,' and the 'big man' said to him, 'I want to buy it from you.' If, when he (the 'big man') was about to buy it from him, the lowly man said, 'pay me as much as I think fair,' and then he (the 'big man') did not buy it, that 'big man' must not 'take it out' on the lowly man."

Urukagina also cleared the city of usurers, thieves, and murderers. If, for instance, "a poor man's son laid out a fishing pond, no one would now steal its fish." No wealthy official dared trespass on the garden of a "poor man's mother," pluck the trees, and carry off their fruit, as had been their wont. Urukagina made a special covenant with Ningirsu, the god of Lagash, that he would not permit widows and orphans to be victimized by the "men of power."

How helpful and effective were these reforms in the struggle for power between Lagash and Umma? Unfortunately, they failed to bring about the expected strength and victory. Urukagina and his reforms were soon "gone with the wind." Like many another reformer, he seemed to have come "too late" with "too little." His reign lasted less than ten years, and he and his city were soon overthrown by Lugal-zaggisi, the ambitious ruler of nearby Umma, who succeeded in making himself the king of Sumer and the surrounding lands, at least for a very brief period.

The Urukagina reforms and their social implications made a profound impression on our ancient "historians." The text of the documents has been found inscribed in four more or less varying versions on three clay cones and an oval-shaped plaque. All of them were excavated by the French at Lagash in 1878. They were copied and first translated by François Thureau-Dangin, the . . . painstaking cuneiformist. . . . However, the interpretation of the Urukagina reforms in the present volume is based on a still unpublished translation of the document prepared by Arno Poebel, the leading Sumerologist of our time.

Freedom under law, it should now be evident, was a way of life not unknown to the Sumerians of the third millennium B.C. Whether laws had already been written down and promulgated in the form of codes in Urukagina's day is still uncertain; at least no law codes from that period have as yet been recovered. But that proves little. For a long time the oldest law code known was one dating back to about 1750 B.C., but only recently three earlier codes have come to light. The oldest of these is the code of the Sumerian ruler Ur-Nammu; it dates from the end of the third millennium B.C. It was excavated in 1889–1900, but it was not until 1952 that it was identified and translated, and even then more or less by accident.

Pa-ser was a reform mayor of Thebes near the end of Egypt's greatness
as a civilization. He could not prove his charges of graft and corruption
in the handling of tomb robberies, but the record of his attempt shows that
hypocrisy is not confined to the twentieth century. Here Professor Wilson
relates one of the consequences of the tyranny of corrupt government:
a military coup that results in another tyranny, a police state. Can you
give some recent examples?

Where Is the Glory?

John A. Wilson

When his rival Pa-wer-aa heard that Pa-ser had promised five new
accusations about tomb robbery, the Mayor of Western Thebes seized
the initiative and asked the Vizier for a new investigation: "I have
heard the words which this Mayor of Thebes spoke to the people of
the great and august necropolis . . . and I report them to my lord, for
it would be a crime for one in my position to hear something and conceal it. But I do not know the bearing of the very serious charges which
the Mayor of Thebes says that (his informants) made to him. I really
cannot understand them, but I report them to my lord, so that my lord
may get to the bottom of these charges." Pa-wer-aa then put Pa-ser
further in the wrong by pointing out that the latter had accepted information which ought to have gone directly to the Vizier.

The Vizier acted promptly on Pa-wer-aa's report. On the very next
day a new commission of inquiry sat in the Temple of Amon. The
Vizier himself presided, and the High Priest of Amon lent his dignity
to the court. Among the officials on the bench was Pa-ser himself, sitting on the hearing on his charges. Three wretched prisoners were
introduced, but before any testimony was heard, the Vizier made an
opening statement which was so heavy with authoritative indignation
that it choked off all debate: "This Mayor of Thebes (Pa-ser) made
certain charges to the supervisors and necropolis workers (day before
yesterday), in the presence of the Royal Butler and Secretary of
Pharaoh, Nes-Amon, making statements about the great tombs which
are in the Place of Beauty; even though, when I myself—the vizier
of the land—was there with the Royal Butler and Secretary of Pharaoh, Nes-Amon, we inspected the tombs . . . and found them unin-
jured, so that all that he has said was found to be false. Now, see, the

From *The Burden of Egypt: An Interpretation of Ancient Egyptian Culture*
by John A. Wilson (Chicago: University of Chicago Press, 1966), pp. 286–
288. © 1951 by the University of Chicago. All rights reserved. Published 1951.

coppersmiths stand before you. Let them tell all that happened."
Naturally, after so biased an opening statement, the coppersmiths felt
no obligation to support Pa-ser's charges. "They were questioned, but
the men were found to know no tomb in the Place of Pharaoh about
which the Mayor had spoken the words. He was placed in the wrong
about it. The great officials released the coppersmiths. . . . A report
was drawn up; it is deposited in the Vizier's archives."

One can imagine Pa-ser sitting on the bench and hearing his charges
swept aside by his superiors. He was completely outmaneuvered by
those who wanted no disturbance of the evil status quo. The aftermath of the case is interesting. After this trial, we never hear another
word about Pa-ser, the Mayor of Thebes. He drops out of the record.
On the other hand, his wily rival, Pa-wer-aa, was still Mayor and Chief
of Police in Western Thebes seventeen years later, seventeen years in
which the tomb robberies in his district continued in crescendo. Fifteen months after this trial, one of the tombs in the Queens' Valley was
found smashed to bits by robbers. In all the documents of investigation there was not a single defendant of high position. Only the little
men, the stonemasons and coppersmiths and farmers, were caught.
Why?

The deposition of the stonemason Amon-pa-nefer gives us the answer. He and his gang were the looters of the tomb of Sebek-em-saf.
He described the tunneling into the tomb and the exciting first view
of the jewel-laden "god lying at the rear of his burial-place." When
the mummies of the pharaoh and of his queen had been stripped of
the gold and silver and costly stones, the thieves set fire to the coffins.
"And we made the gold which we had found on these two gods—from
their mummies, amulets, ornaments, and coffins—into eight shares.
And twenty *deben* of gold fell to each one of the eight of us, making
160 *deben* of gold, without dividing the rest of the furniture(?)."
The total of gold from this tomb was nearly 40 lb. Troy, each robber
taking 5 lb., which was no small amount for a peasant.

Amon-pa-nefer continued: "Then we crossed over to Thebes. And
after some days, the agents of Thebes heard that we had been stealing
in the west, so they arrested me and imprisoned me at the Mayor of
Thebes' place. So I took the twenty *deben* of gold that had fallen to
me as (my) share, and gave them to Kha-em-Opet, the District Clerk
of the harbor at Thebes. He let me go, and I joined my companions,
and they made up for me another share. And I, as well as the other
robbers who are with me, have continued to this day in the practice of
robbing the tombs of the nobles and people of the land who rest in the

west of Thebes. And a large number of the men of the land rob them also."

Twenty *deben* of gold—nearly two kilograms or five Troy pounds—was a very large bribe. Not only did this stonemason walk out of imprisonment, but he was permitted to continue his robberies. What happpened to the records of his arrest? Probably that District Clerk of the Theban harbor did not retain all of the twenty *deben*; the bribe went on up high enough to choke off any inquisitiveness about the failure of legal procedure. The long and sorry record of the tomb robberies of the Twentieth Dynasty is a story of higher officials evading their duties because they were gaining personal advantage out of such evasion. It was a cynical rejection of the content of *maʿat* and a retention of so much of the form of *maʿat* as would make an impressive documentary show. The unimportant little people who were threatened and beaten and tortured by examining magistrates were the sacrifices for the responsible officers who were examining them. Here the Egyptian spirit reached bottom.

A century after these tomb robberies had come to their climax the state finally took action to protect the sacred persons of those gods who had once been kings. Furtively they took the royal mummies to a secret pit in the necropolis and there stacked them up like cordwood: thirty in one room. Since they were already stripped of treasure they rested undisturbed for nearly three thousand years. But the damage had already been done when the priest-kings of the Twenty-first Dynasty gave them this inglorious reburial.

In the struggle for power in the Egyptian state, the pharaoh never regained the ground lost by the Amarna heresy. But it was not the High Priest of Amon nor the Vizier who won out. It was not a member of the family which held the high priesthood, Ramses-nakht and Amen-hotep and their relatives, who took over the control of Upper Egypt. It was the army which snatched the power at the end of the Ramesside period. A certain Heri-Hor, of obscure parentage, served in the army and finally rose to the position of Viceroy of Nubia and Commander of the Army. Rather abruptly in the last years of Ramses XI, the final king of the Twentieth Dynasty, Heri-Hor appeared in Thebes as Vizier for Upper Egypt and High Priest of Amon. The implication is strong that there was an army coup to seize power from the ruling clique, and the ecclesiastical role of the new military dictator, Heri-Hor, was assumed by him in order to gather all the reins into his own hands. Very soon the Ramesside pharaohs faded out of sight, unwept and unhonored, the last of a line of true claimants to the dignity of god-emperor. After an interval Heri-Hor took to himself the crown, passing the viziership and the high priesthood to his son, but he was also scrupulous to make his son Commander of the Army, because the control of the state lay in the exercise of police power. Heri-Hor did not attempt to rule all of Egypt. Merchant princes at the northern capital, Tanis, set up a dynasty of their own, so that the rule was divided between Upper and Lower Egypt. Never again was ancient Egypt to enjoy a firmly united land for any length of time. The inner dynamic power was dead in the organism.

We owe to the Sumerians and the Egyptians at least part of our orientation
toward materialistic goals and the nation-state, and though much good
and beauty have come from these things they have also been the occasion
for endless violence. Hutchins, former president of the University of Chicago
and now president of the Center for the Study of Democratic Institutions
in Santa Barbara, Calif., has proposed a change in direction for mankind.
It is not a new suggestion—a delegate to the 1787 Constitutional
Convention in Philadelphia proposed that the new Constitution emphasize
the refinements of the intellect and knowledge. His was a lonely voice
in an atmosphere of "practicality." Hutchins, and some of the youth
participating in today's rebellion, protest the materialistic and nationalistic
myths and traditions that started in ancient Sumeria and Egypt.

Aims of Industrial Society No Longer Satisfying

Robert M. Hutchins

What most rebellious students are saying is that since they do not
want to lead trivial lives they would like some education.

Since few of them have had any, the noises they make can hardly
add up to an intelligible curriculum, but this is not their fault. They
know the institutions they are attending and the curricula they are
nominally pursuing are dedicated to other purposes than helping them
understand and cope with the contemporary world.

Some of those purposes are praiseworthy enough. Who can be
against research when it is defined as the pursuit of truth for its own
sake?

The pinnacles of higher education in the United States are occupied
by men and institutions largely devoted to serving the power of the
state and promoting its prosperity. There ought to be some connection
between knowledge and wisdom. How this connection can be formed
in a knowledge industry remains a mystery.

Since the war, the American university has geared itself up to serve
the industrial state and has now reached the pinnacle in this respect.
But the future of that state is not altogether clear.

A computerized, automated world is one in which the material
goods necessary for human existence can be supplied with very little
human labor. Already, if the war in Vietnam were stopped, $30 bil-
lion would be available annually for other purposes. This is roughly

From "Aims of Industrial Society No Longer Satisfying" by Robert M.
Hutchins, *Los Angeles Times*, August 10, 1969. Copyright, Los Angeles Times.
Reprinted with permission.

10 times what has been devoted to foreign aid and 15 times what has been spent in any year in the war on poverty.

The aim of an industrial society is material goods, with the power, prosperity and prestige they give. The concern is with "conquering" nature, with knowledge as power, with technical competence, with men as producers, consumers, statistical units and objects of propaganda, and with such welfare measures as tend toward the stability necessary for business.

We shall surely have a guaranteed annual income, because it will be good for General Motors. More cars will be sold if more people have the money to buy them, and besides, as Governor Reagan has said, riots are bad for business.

The nation state has been the sponsor of industralization and the engine of the rapacity and greed of the industrial society. Hence national systems of education have been designed to "process" the young for industry and to make them the willing victims of its claims.

But at the pinnacle of education's effectiveness in this regard, the taste of ashes is on the lips of the younger generation everywhere: in the West, in the Communist countries, and in the third world. This suggests the possibility that the aims of the industrial society may no longer satisfy the aspirations of the human animal.

In a postindustrial age it would obviously be stultifying to train the young in educational systems for industry. Already the rapidity of technological change has made such training ineffective. The only techniques that appear to have enduring value under all circumstances are those of language and mathematics, which are implicated in everything we do. These are the liberal arts, the arts of becoming human.

The alternative to liberal education in the future is one now being pursued with some vigor in parts of this country, and that is the effort to make the young into conventional well-tubbed Americans, conforming in matters tonsorial, sartorial, and political to the prejudices of their elders. This is of course ridiculous, but the possibility is not to be excluded on that ground. A more persuasive argument against this possibility is that the experience of all historical regimes shows it is hard to carry it out over any length of time.

Meanwhile the nation state is rapidly becoming an anachronism. No nation can now manage its own economy or protect its own people. Hence it can no longer carry out the only purpose it has had. All problems, as the gold crisis reminds us, are now world problems. The nation state is an obstacle to their solution.

The industrial system, as the multinational corporation shows, is now at odds with the nation state, which now stands in the way of its expansion over the globe and its claim to roam the world at will, free of geographical barriers politically imposed. The industrial system now makes the world state necessary.

In the postindustrial age, when science, an international commodity, will be the source of wealth and when industrial competition must fade, national systems of education, if they turn away, as they must, from preparing the young for industry, may also turn away from the nationalistic, imperialistic aspects of such preparation.

In the absence of industrial competition, the temptation may be to regard all men as neighbors in the sense in which that word was used of the Good Samaritan. Let us hope the temptation will prove irresistible. The postindustrial society, in short, could be one in which men set seriously to work to straighten out their relations with one another and in which they sought, not material goods, but moral, intellectual, or what might be called cultural goods.

Such a society could be a learning society. Its object could be to raise every community and every man to the highest cultural level attainable.

If we look far enough into the future we can see that as the technology becomes available the computer and other devices can make every home a learning unit. All members of the family could be continuously engaged in learning. Teachers might function as visiting nurses do today, and as physicians used to do.

Educational Institutions Would Not Award Degrees

In such a society the role of educational institutions would be to provide for what is notably missing from them today, and that is the interaction of minds. Eventually these institutions would not be "processing" anybody for anything or awarding certificates, diplomas or degrees. The search for what have been called sheepskins to cover our intellectual nakedness, which has been necessary to gain status in the industrialized society, has smothered learning for its own sake.

In a postindustrial age the university could be transformed into a contemporary version of the Platonic academy. It could be a center of independent thought and criticism, bringing the great intellectual disciplines together so that they might shed light on one another and on the major issues facing modern man.

The view of the future of education I have briefly sketched is not utopian, because it involves little dependence on the intelligence and character of the present residents of this planet. The industrial system has set in motion irreversible tendencies that will lead to its own extinction. It has dug its own grave.

World war is now impossible. The nation state, which is a war system, is now impossible. Manpower will be unnecessary. Therefore the aim of education has to be manhood. This change could ultimately eliminate institutions and institutional practices appropriate, if at all, to a superseded regime. Education could at last come into its own.

In the meantime, the frenzy for educational innovation that is sweeping the country suggests that people are becoming aware of the disparity between the drift of the society and the aims of education. In the general confusion nobody knows what to do next in education, but almost everybody has a vague feeling that we ought to be doing something different from what we have been doing. When anything can be done, we might as well do the right thing.

Well, what is the right thing?

Suppose we forget the multiversity, or what is sometimes called the multi-purpose university, a contradiction in terms if there ever was one. Suppose we let it die, as it is bound to do in the postindustrial age.

It cannot be saved from itself; for as long as the departments control teaching and research and as long as departmental prestige and budgets depend on the number of graduate students and the volume of publication, the multiversity will remain a series of technical schools rather than an educational institution and a base for academic careerism rather than a community of scholars.

But we ought to try to extricate from the multiversity those students who are interested in education, in learning for its own sake. They haven't much chance now, and as long as the universities are multiversities they can't have much. For them the only answer now is colleges.

What we have to have is many more independent colleges of liberal arts. I mean colleges that seriously undertake to help the student become human by helping to develop his mind. Civilization and culture cannot be preserved and expanded unless the rising generation can be civilized.

Civilization and culture cannot be preserved and expanded without another institution that is missing. Today we have no centers of independent thought and criticism. The multiversity is not independent. It is the result of the parallelogram of forces at work in the community.

It is not engaged as an institution in thought or criticism, though isolated members of it often are. It is dedicated to training and what is called service. It is not a center; it is compartmentalized both vertically and horizontally into departments and divisions that are in competition for money and students. A multipurpose institution can by definition have no unifying principle.

And so I come to my final proposition. It is hardly a proposition, for I cannot demonstrate it. It is rather a foreboding, or a presentiment. It seems fairly clear that the transition from the industrial to a postindustrial age will involve severe dislocations.

Who can tell what form the final spasms of the nation state may take or what kind of travail will mark the birth of the world community? Who can say whether political, social and economic institutions built by and for an industrial society will come crashing down or gradually fade away? What forces of reaction and repression may these changes set in motion?

This transition is of the most fundamental kind, involving the disruption, sudden and complete, of the habits and ideals by which a large part of the human race has lived for centuries. When 35 years ago John Maynard Keynes wrote about the postindustrial era that he saw coming in a century, he said he viewed the prospect with a certain dread. The Golden Age would lie before us, but could we summon the intelligence, the character, the wisdom to keep from blowing ourselves up out of sheer boredom and frustration?

Vast Difference Between Leisure and Vacant Time

The philosophers from Aristotle to Adler have taught us that leisure is supreme among human activities and that the resulting goods of self-improvement constitute the most important ingredient in a good life. But they have also taught us that there is a vast difference between leisure and vacant time, and that philosophy and politics, using that word to describe activity for the common good, are the two chief forms of leisure.

An educational system that gets us in shape to turn vacant time into leisure seems now beyond our power. The way to fortify ourselves is therefore to establish wherever we can colleges of liberal arts and those centers of independent thought and criticism for which I would prefer to reserve the name of university.

If these colleges and universities can become incandescent, if they can be points of light, then culture and civilization can be preserved and expanded as they have been by small groups during dark days in the past.

Questions

1 Gordon Childe speaks of copper-age villages of Mesopotamia turning into bronze-age cities in the great valley. He calls this the "urban revolution," with man beginning to specialize as weaver, potter, weaponmaker, merchant, and so on, and with power becoming concentrated in the hands of a few. Other than magnitude, what problems do our cities have today that Sumerian cities did not?

2 Childe also speaks of a great population explosion in the transitional era between the two early ages of copper and bronze. Compare the land problem then with the land problem in the thirty years between 1970 and 2000, when there will be an increase (in only one generation!) of world population from about 3.5 billion to over 7 billion.

3 Egypt was divided not only into nomes but also into two rather distinct cultures, north and south. It appears, in generalizing about many nations, that differences and conflicts are more marked north–south than they are east–west. What have been the north–south conflicts in China, Japan, Russia, Germany, Italy, Great Britain, the Sudan, The Congo (Leopoldville), and last, but not least, the United States? What have been the results? Does the north usually predominate?

4 What are the disadvantages of specialization in a democratic-type civilization? What are the disadvantages of a materialistic orientation of life in a free society?

5 There was a tax reform program in Lagash, Sumeria, 4500 years ago. What was the problem? What is the acute problem about taxes in America today?

6 Are Robert Hutchins' proposals practical ones? Is his voice a lonely one as was the voice nearly two hundred years ago at the Constitutional Convention?

7 What have been the problems of states' rights versus centralized government in the history of the United States?

3 Crime and Punishment in the Ancient Near East

This essay, on reassessing the relevance of the Code of Hammurabi and the Mosaic Code, asserts that the attitudes shown in Sophocles' "Antigone," Henry Thoreau's "Civil Disobedience," and Martin Luther King, Jr.'s "Letter From Birmingham Jail" are far more relevant to America's problems today than were the law codes of the ancient Near East.

Hammurabi, Moses, and Eldridge Cleaver

Melvin Steinfield

Early in 1969 Eldridge Cleaver, author of *Soul on Ice* and Minister of Information of the Black Panther Party, fled the United States in order to avoid being returned to jail. To his devoted followers and his many admirers, Cleaver was a political refugee unjustly oppressed by a racist power-structure seeking to destroy him; he fled to save his skin. To others, Cleaver was a dangerous criminal threatening the security of the country and deserving to be punished for his efforts to undermine law and order in America.

Throughout the course of history, many men have been considered heroes by some and criminals by others. Indeed the question of patriot or traitor, hero or rebel, is really a matter of who happens to be the judge. "Criminal" is defined by the society.

And look at some of the definitions! In the eighteenth century in some European countries the punishment for stealing a loaf of bread was death. In several seventeenth-century American colonies it was against the law *not* to carry a gun to church every Sunday. As recently as 1940 half the states in America ruled it a felony for white-black intermarriage; in some cases, the punishment was a lengthy prison sentence.

Faced with laws like these, men will naturally begin to inquire: Who makes these laws? Who determines what the punishment should be for a crime? How widely do laws vary from time to time and place to place?

It is not surprising that some even begin to flirt with the following kinds of such questions: Should unjust laws be obeyed? Should one harbor and shield a person who is fleeing the law if the law is unjust or cruel? Are disenfranchised citizens obligated to obey laws imposed by exploitative powers? Must one obey a law that he had no voice in shaping?

To put it on a quite personal basis, imagine yourself in the following situation: You are a Northerner in 1851. Would you help escaped slaves make their way to Canada? Or would you obey the Federal Fugitive Slave Law and return them to their Southern masters? The ultimate personalized query for the present is: Would you help Eldridge Cleaver leave the country?

A host of additional questions will undoubtedly occur to anyone giving this matter careful thought. Right now, the timely question to ask is: How did all this get started? When did Western man get hung-up on law and order?

As one might expect, man has always had to confront the law-and-order issue. The earliest civilizations in the ancient Near East developed the first codes of law, as a consequence of this concern. It is from those beginnings that the seeds of controversy about law and order have sprouted.

Two of the best-known codes of the ancient Near East are the Code of Hammurabi and the Mosaic Code of the Old Testament.

How relevant are they to today's world? Except as a historical curiosity, these codes are becoming increasingly less relevant, for several reasons.

It is true that the Code of Hammurabi is frequently cited as one of the major achievements of Western civilization. It is supposed to represent a step forward for man because for the first time it defined what a crime was and prescribed the punishment for it, thus removing crime and punishment from the arbitrary whim of the rulers.

But perhaps Hammurabi is overrated. Lest he be canonized undeservedly, let us examine certain myths. In the first place, Hammurabi was not the first person to establish a written code of laws. The earliest is that of Ur-Nammu, a Sumerian king of the twenty-first century B.C. In 1947 a clay tablet was discovered that contains thirty-seven laws preserved from an unknown larger number of laws. This tablet is now referred to as the Lipit-Ishtar Code and is another early code dating back to approximately 1850 B.C. Furthermore, scholars have known for some time now that Hammurabi (1728–1686 B.C.) codified many laws that had been written in Babylonia as early as 2250 B.C. We just do not have the records of the original laws in our possession.

Secondly, the birth of Western civil law is with Roman law, not the Code of Hammurabi. As Professor Cyrus Gordon notes in his *Hammurapi's Code: Quaint or Forward-Looking?*:

> We cannot speak of any direct influence of the code on subsequent history, because the code was of limited circulation and the stela [tablet] itself was carried off by the Elamites to Susa, where it was eventually forgotten and lay buried until French archaeologists unearthed it in 1901–1902.[1]

Thirdly, while it is true that the Hammurabic Code and the Old

Testament must be judged in the context of their own times, we must not be blind to the degree of cruel and unusual punishments they imposed by our standards today. Sometimes it is said that Hammurabi started a trend toward a more humane treatment of criminals. According to this version of criminological history, prehistoric men functioned with a bitter vengeance. If a villager raped, or stole, or killed, then a blood feud might develop, or the entire village be destroyed, to avenge the crime. Then along came Hammurabi, who set up the "eye for eye, tooth for tooth" concept, which was a softening of the preceding patterns of punishment. Ultimately, Hammurabi was replaced with an ideal even more humane: rehabilitation.

Actually, however, Hammurabi did not start much of a trend. The cruelty of the Old Testament punishments, written at least five centuries after Hammurabi, attests to the lack of improvement. Several examples illustrate this. In the Code of Hammurabi, adulterers were strangled to death and then thrown into the water. Strangulation is not very pleasant, but at least the whole show is over in a few minutes, with a relatively painless passing from this world to the next. Contrast the Hammurabic prescription for adultery with the Old Testament Code, which calls for stoning.

According to Hammurabic Law 129: "If a man's wife be caught lying with another, they shall be strangled and cast into the water. If the wife's husband would save his wife, the king can save his servant."[2] Thus there is some flexibility. Also, the punishment is not as bad as it sounds, for no one minds being drowned after he is strangled. But in the Old Testament there is a less flexible, more stringent code: "If there is a betrothed virgin, and a man meets her in the city and lies with her, then you shall bring them both out to the gate of that city, and you shall stone them to death with stones. . . ."[3]

If anything, the trend from Hammurabi to the Old Testament is toward more rigidity and more cruel punishments, rather than less, as sometimes alleged. This difference can be seen in the corresponding sections on the generation-gap. Hammurabic Law 195: "If a son has struck his father, his hands shall be cut off."[4] The Old Testament: "Whoever curses his father or his mother shall be put to death."[5]

Another example is in the corresponding sections on runaway farm animals. According to Hammurabic Laws 250 and 251:

> If a bull has gone wild and gored a man, and caused his death, there can be no suit against the owner. If a man's ox be a gorer, and has revealed its evil propensity as a gorer, and he has not blunted its horn, or shut up the ox, and then that ox has gored a

free man and caused his death, the owner shall pay half a mina of silver."[6]

Nothing happens to the ox, who is, after all, a dumb animal, and the owner, even in the most severe cases, is permitted to pay a fine. But in the Mosaic Code, the ox is to be punished by stoning, and the owner, in certain cases, could be killed as punishment:

If an ox gore a man or a woman, that they die: then the ox shall be surely stoned, and his flesh shall not be eaten; but the owner of the ox shall be clear. But if the ox has been accustomed to gore in the past, and its owner has been warned but has not kept it in, and it kills a man or a woman, the ox shall be stoned, and its owner also shall be put to death. If a ransom is laid on him, then he shall give for the redemption of his life whatever is laid upon him.[7]

Furthermore, we must not forget about the sins of the fathers being visited upon the sons unto the fourth and fifth generation. That aspect of the Mosaic Code resembles the curse-and-plague syndrome of Greek culture more than it does Hammurabi. Of course, Hammurabi did touch upon that type of punishment now and then, as Law 230 indicates: "If a builder has caused the son of the owner of the house to die [owing to the house's faulty construction], one shall put to death the son of that builder."[8]

The differential treatment before the law that the ancient Near Eastern law codes sanctioned is a prominent feature of the Code of Hammurabi. Note the different punishments given those of different status (Laws 196–199):

If a man has knocked out the eye of a patrician, his eye shall be knocked out. If he has broken the limb of a patrician, his limb shall be broken. If he has knocked out the eye of a plebeian or has broken the limb of a plebeian, he shall pay one mina of silver. If he has knocked out the eye of a patrician's servant, or broken the limb of a patrician's servant, he shall pay half his value.[9]

In this respect, the Old Testament did improve upon Hammurabi, seizing upon this opportunity to free the slave. Exodus 21:26: "When a man strikes the eye of his slave, male or female, and destroys it, he shall let the slave go free for the eye's sake."

There are other passages in Exodus that provide for the possibility of freedom for slaves, but the over-all tenor of the ordinances is to uphold slavery as a way of life, just as Hammurabi did.

Of course, there is a danger in relying exclusively upon a literal interpretation of the laws of a society. How the laws are applied and how strictly they are enforced needs to be considered lest one be misled. Nevertheless, the general orientation of laws does mirror most societies rather accurately. By these standards, the Code of Hammurabi was not the forerunner of more humane attitudes toward criminals.

The cruelty, the manifest injustice of punishing innocent relatives for someone else's wrongdoing, the differential treatment before the law, the support of slavery, these are among the more objectionable features of the Hammurabi Code and the Old Testament. They are features that are frequently glossed over as historians praise the unique and comprehensive achievements of early civilized man. Perhaps "an eye for an eye" is a little better than a blood feud involving an entire family, but we must also be aware of Hammurabic Law 205: "If a slave has struck a free man, they shall cut off his ear."[10] Except for the specific part of the anatomy involved, this type of mutilation resembles the treatment slaves in America received for defiant and unruly behavior.

Putting Hammurabi in perspective, then, we find that double standards are authorized and that equality before the law is not part of ancient Near Eastern law codes. But we live in an age in which equality before the law, both in theory and in practice, is one of the most relevant issues of our time. If Hammurabi is to shape our attitude, then law and order will be the number one goal, not justice. What room is there in our society for those who prefer to follow the heritage of the great dissenters, figures such as Antigone, Thoreau, and Martin Luther King, all of whom protested unjust laws?

With Antigone we come to the first major symbol of nonviolent dissent in Western civilization. She is the character in Sophocles' play *Antigone* who buries her brother in defiance of the decree of the leader of the city, Creon. Creon refuses to permit burial because Antigone's brother was a traitor. Antigone cannot accept the ban on his burial because burial meant so much to the Greeks and because she feels she has an unbreakable loyalty to her brother. Thus she becomes the spokesman for the law that is higher than man-made law. She disobeys civil authority because she believes in the justice of what she is doing and because, in her view, the man-made law is unjust.

Antigone became a much-talked about symbol of idealism through the years that Western civilization was busy bloodying up battlefields. But from the time the play was written (fifth century B.C.) to the middle of the nineteenth century, it was merely an academic symbol. Although there were many protests against established law before the mid-nineteenth century, none of them mentioned Antigone by name. However, about 1850 new vitality and relevance was breathed into

Sophocles' famous heroine. The issue which brought the matter to a head was slavery, the very same institution upheld in so many ways by the law codes of the ancient Near East.

The horrible injustice and cruelty of slavery stimulated many Americans to question the validity of the laws and of the government that upheld them. One questioner was Henry David Thoreau, who wrote a famous essay on civil disobedience, excerpts of which appear in the readings. Thoreau advocated defiance of unjust laws, and spent a day in jail for refusing to pay his poll tax as a protest against his government's support of slavery as an institution. As a measure of his defiance, there is the famous exchange between Thoreau and the essayist and poet Ralph Waldo Emerson: "What are you doing in jail, Henry?" "What are you doing *out* of jail, Ralph?"

Thoreau's life and essay exerted inestimable influence upon Mohandes Gandhi (1869–1948), the famous political, social, and religious leader of India. And Thoreau and Gandhi both were definite influences upon Martin Luther King, Jr. and the entire nonviolent protest movement of the American civil rights revolution. Lunchcounter sit-ins, for example, openly and nonviolently defied the unjust laws of the segregated society; other recent demonstrations protested the failure of government to end the disparity between the laws in theory and in application.

Since the end of the Second World War, American society has been undergoing the most serious and sustained challenges to the stability of its cultural canons and social institutions. A very important role in the protest movements against the established myths and traditions has been played by individuals and groups who show the influence of the spirit of Antigone, Thoreau, Gandhi, and King. Current events have thus created a need to reassess the relevance of such old Western civilization study-favorites as the law codes of the ancient Near East.

What do you think? Where does the relevance lie? Hammurabi or Antigone? The Mosaic Code or Eldridge Cleaver? Are you for law and order or do you have other views?

Notes

1 Cyrus Gordon, *Hammurapi's Code: Quaint or Forward-Looking?* (New York: Holt, 1957), p. 3.

2 Quoted in Harry J. Carroll, Jr., *et al.,* eds., The Development of Civilization, Vol. I (Palo Alto, Calif.: Scott Foresman, 1961), p. 27. From C. H. W. Johns, ed., "Library of Ancient Inscriptions," in *Babylonian and Assyrian Laws, Contracts and Letters* (New York: Scribner's, 1904).

3 Deuteronomy 22:23.

4 Carroll, *op. cit.*, p. 29.

5 Exodus 21:17.

6 Quoted in George H. Knoles and Rixford K. Snyer, eds., *Readings in Western Cilivilization*, 3rd ed., Vol. I (Philadelphia: Lippincott, 1960), p. 7. From C. H. W. Johns, ed., *Babylonian and Assyrian Laws, Contracts and Letters* (New York: Scribner's, 1904).

7 Exodus 21:28-30.

8 John Louis Beatty and Oliver A. Johnson, eds., *Heritage of Western Civilization*, 2nd ed. (Englewood Cliffs, N.J.: Prentice-Hall, 1966), p. 12.

9 Carroll, *op cit.*, p. 29.

10 There are several different renditions of this law: Carroll, *op. cit.*, p. 30, renders it: "If the slave of anyone has smitten the privates of a free-born man, his ear shall be cut off." Gordon, *op. cit.*, p. 21, renders it: If a man's slave has struck the cheek of a patrician, they shall cut off his ear."

The following excerpts from the Code of Hammurabi reveal several interesting features of the Mesopotamian empire that Hammurabi forged in the early seventeenth century B.C. Note the severity of the punishments and the differential treatment before the law. Law 26 provides for draft-dodgers and Law 218 helps explain why there were no heart transplants in ancient Babylon.

The Birth of Law and Order

The Code of Hammurabi

8. If a patrician has stolen ox, sheep, ass, pig, or ship, whether from a temple, or a house, he shall pay thirtyfold. If he be a plebeian, he shall return tenfold. If the thief cannot pay, he shall be put to death.

. . . .

14. If a man has stolen a child, he shall be put to death.

15. If a man has induced either a male or female slave from the house of a patrician, or plebeian, to leave the city, he shall be put to death.

21. If a man has broken into a house he shall be killed before the breach and buried there.

22. If a man has committed highway robbery and has been caught, that man shall be put to death.

23. If the highwayman has not been caught, the man that has been robbed shall state on oath what he has lost, and the city or district governor in whose territory or district the robbery took place shall restore to him what he has lost.

25. If a fire has broken out in a man's house and one who has come to put it out has coveted the property of the householder and appropriated any of it, that man shall be cast into the self-same fire.

26. If a levy-master, or warrant-officer, who has been detailed on the king's service, has not gone, or has hired a substitute in his place, that levy-master, or warrant-officer, shall be put to death and the hired substitute shall take his office.

. . . .

From *Babylonian and Assyrian Laws, Contracts and Letters* by C. H. W. Johns (New York: Scribner's, 1904), pp. 44–66.

The heart of the Mosaic Code is contained in Chapters 20–23 of the second book of the Old Testament. Written at least five centuries after the Hammurabic Code, it borrowed heavily from the other codes of the Near East yet added some refinements of its own. Can you find examples of improvements in the law that were not indicated in the essay?

The Word of God

Exodus

Chapter 20

And God spoke all these words, saying,

"I am the Lord your God, who brought you out of the land of Egypt, out of the house of bondage.

"You shall have no other gods before me.

"You shall not make yourself a graven image, or any likeness of anything that is in heaven above, or that is in the earth below, or that is in the water under the earth; you shall not bow down to them or serve them; for I the Lord your God am a jealous God, visiting the iniquity of the fathers upon the children to the third and fourth generation of those who hate me, but showing steadfast love to thousands of those who love me and keep my commandments.

"You shall not take the name of the Lord your God in vain; for the Lord will not hold him guiltless who takes his name in vain.

"Remember the sabbath day, to keep it holy. Six days you shall labor and do all your work; but the seventh day is a sabbath to the Lord your God; in it you shall not do any work, you, or your son, or your daughter, your manservant, or your maidservant, or your cattle, or the sojourner who is within your gates; for in six days the Lord made heaven and earth, the sea, and all that is in them, and rested the seventh day; therefore the Lord blessed the sabbath day and hallowed it.

"Honor your father and your mother, that your days may be long in the land which the Lord your God gives you.

"You shall not kill.

"You shall not commit adultery.

"You shall not steal.

"You shall not bear false witness against your neighbor.

"You shall not covet your neighbor's house; you shall not covet your neighbor's wife, or his manservant, or his maidservant, or his ox, or his ass, or anything that is your neighbor's."

Now when all the people perceived the thunderings and the

lightnings and the sound of the trumpet and the mountain smoking, the people were afraid and trembled; and they stood afar off, and said to Moses, "You speak to us, and we will hear; but let not God speak to us, lest we die."

And Moses said to the people, "Do not fear; for God has come to prove you, and that the fear of him may be before your eyes, that you may not sin."

And the people stood afar off, while Moses drew near to the thick cloud where God was. And the Lord said to Moses, "Thus you shall say to the people of Israel: 'You have seen for yourselves that I have talked with you from heaven. You shall not make gods of silver to be with me, nor shall you make for yourselves gods of gold. An altar of earth you shall make for me and sacrifice on it your burnt offerings and your peace offerings, your sheep and your oxen; in every place where I cause my name to be remembered I will come to you and bless you. And if you make me an altar of stone, you shall not build it of hewn stones; for if you wield your tool upon it you profane it. And you shall not go up by steps to my altar, that your nakedness be not exposed on it.'

Chapter 21

"Now these are the ordinances which you shall set before them. When you buy a Hebrew slave, he shall serve six years, and in the seventh he shall go out free, for nothing. If he comes in single, he shall go out single; if he comes in married, then his wife shall go out with him. If his master gives him a wife and she bears him sons or daughters, the wife and her children shall be her master's and he shall go out alone. But if the slave plainly says, 'I love my master, my wife, and my children; I will not go out free,' then his master shall bring him to God, and he shall bring him to the door or the doorpost; and his master shall bore his ear through with an awl; and he shall serve him for life.

"When a man sells his daughter as a slave, she shall not go out as the male slaves do. If she does not please her master, who has designated her for himself, then he shall let her be redeemed; he shall have no right to sell her to a foreign people, since he has dealt faithlessly with her. If he designates her for his son, he shall deal with her as with a daughter. If he takes another wife to himself, he shall not diminish her food, her clothing, or her marital rights. And if he does not do these three things for her, she shall go out for nothing, without payment of money.

"Whoever strikes a man so that he dies shall be put to death. But if he did not lie in wait for him, but God let him fall into his hand, then I will appoint for you a place to which he may flee. But if a man wilfully attacks another to kill him treacherously, you shall take him from my altar, that he may die.

"Whoever strikes his father or his mother shall be put to death.

"Whoever steals a man, whether he sells him or is found in possession of him, shall be put to death.

"Whoever curses his father or his mother shall be put to death.

"When men quarrel and one strikes the other with a stone or with his fist and the other man does not die but keeps his bed, then if the man rises again and walks abroad with his staff, he that struck him shall be clear; only he shall pay for the loss of his time, and shall have him thoroughly healed.

"When a man strikes his slave, male or female, with a rod and the slave dies under his hand, he shall be punished. But if the slave survives a day or two, he is not to be punished; for the slave is his money.

"When men strive together, and hurt a woman with child, so that there is a miscarriage, and yet no harm follows, the one who hurt her shall be fined, according as the woman's husband shall lay upon him; and he shall pay as the judges determine. If any harm follows, then you shall give life for life, eye for eye, tooth for tooth, hand for hand, foot for foot, burn for burn, wound for wound, stripe for stripe.

"When a man strikes the eye of his slave, male or female, and destroys it, he shall let the slave go free for the eye's sake. If he knocks out the tooth of his slave, male or female, he shall let the slave go free for the tooth's sake.

"When an ox gores a man or a woman to death, the ox shall be stoned, and its flesh shall not be eaten; but the owner of the ox shall be clear. But if the ox has been accustomed to gore in the past, and its owner has been warned but has not kept it in, and it kills a man or a woman, the ox shall be stoned, and its owner also shall be put to death. If a ransom is laid on him, then he shall give for the redemption of his life whatever is laid upon him. If it gores a man's son or daughter, he shall be dealt with according to this same rule. If the ox gores a slave, male or female, the owner shall give to their master thirty shekels of silver, and the ox shall be stoned.

"When a man leaves a pit open, or when a man digs a pit and does not cover it, and an ox or an ass falls into it, the owner of the pit shall make it good; he shall give money to its owner, and the dead beast shall be his.

"When one man's ox hurts another's, so that it dies, then they shall sell the live ox and divide the price of it; and the dead beast also they shall divide. Or if it is known that the ox has been accustomed to gore in the past, and its owner has not kept it in, he shall pay ox for ox, and the dead beast shall be his.

Chapter 22

"If a man steals an ox or a sheep, and kills it or sells it, he shall pay five oxen for an ox, and four sheep for a sheep. He shall make restitution; if he has nothing, then he shall be sold for his theft. If the stolen beast is found alive in his possession, whether it is an ox or an ass or a sheep, he shall pay double.

"If a thief is found breaking in, and is struck so that he dies, there shall be no bloodguilt for him; but if the sun has risen upon him, there shall be bloodguilt for him.

"When a man causes a field or vineyard to be grazed over, or lets his beast loose and it feeds in another man's field, he shall make restitution from the best in his own field and in his own vineyard.

"When fire breaks out and catches in thorns so that the stacked grain or the standing grain or the field is consumed, he that kindled the fire shall make full restitution.

"If a man delivers to his neighbor money or goods to keep, and it is stolen out of the man's house, then, if the thief is found, he shall pay double. If the thief is not found, the owner of the house shall come near to God, to show whether or not he has put his hand to his neighbor's goods.

"For every breach of trust, whether it is for ox, for ass, for sheep, for clothing, or for any kind of lost thing, of which one says, 'This is it,' the case of both parties shall come before God; he whom God shall condemn shall pay double to his neighbor.

"If a man delivers to his neighbor an ass or an ox or a sheep or any beast to keep, and it dies or is hurt or is driven away, without any one seeing it, an oath by the Lord shall be between them both to see whether he has not put his hand to his neighbor's property; and the owner shall accept the oath, and he shall not make restitution. But if it is stolen from him, he shall make restitution to its owner. If it is torn by beasts, let him bring it as evidence; he shall not make restitution for what has been torn.

"If a man borrows anything of his neighbor, and it is hurt or dies, the owner not being with it, he shall make full restitution. If the owner was with it, he shall not make restitution; if it was hired, it came for its hire.

"If a man seduces a virgin who is not betrothed, and lies with her, he shall give the marriage present for her, and make her his wife. If her father utterly refuses to give her to him, he shall pay money equivalent to the marriage present for virgins.

"You shall not permit a sorceress to live.

"Whoever lies with a beast shall be put to death.

"Whoever sacrifices to any god, save to the Lord only, shall be utterly destroyed.

"You shall not wrong a stranger or oppress him, for you were strangers in the land of Egypt. You shall not afflict any widow or orphan. If you do afflict them, and they cry out to me, I will surely hear their cry; and my wrath will burn, and I will kill you with the sword, and your wives shall become widows and your children fatherless.

"If you lend money to any of my people with you who is poor, you shall not be to him as a creditor, and you shall not exact interest from him. If ever you take your neighbor's garment in pledge, you shall restore it to him before the sun goes down; for that is his only covering, it is his mantle for his body; in what else shall he sleep? And if he cries to me, I will hear, for I am compassionate.

"You shall not revile God, nor curse a ruler of your people.

"You shall not delay to offer from the fulness of your harvest and from the outflow of your presses.

"The first-born of your sons you shall give to me. You shall do likewise with your oxen and with your sheep: seven days it shall be with its dam; on the eighth day you shall give it to me.

"You shall be men consecrated to me; therefore you shall not eat any flesh that is torn by beasts in the field; you shall cast it to the dogs.

Chapter 23

"You shall not utter a false report. You shall not join hands with a wicked man, to be a malicious witness. You shall not follow a multitude to do evil; nor shall you bear witness in a suit, turning aside after a multitude, so as to pervert justice; nor shall you be partial to a poor man in his suit.

"If you meet your enemy's ox or his ass going astray, you shall bring it back to him. If you see the ass of one who hates you lying under its burden, you shall refrain from leaving him with it, you shall help him to lift it up.

"You shall not pervert the justice due to your poor in his suit.

Keep far from a false charge, and do not slay the innocent and righteous, for I will not acquit the wicked. And you shall take no bribe, for a bribe blinds the officials, and subverts the cause of those who are in the right.

"You shall not oppress a stranger; you know the heart of a stranger, for you were strangers in the land of Egypt.

"For six years you shall sow your land and gather in its yield; but the seventh year you shall let it rest and lie fallow, that the poor of your people may eat; and what they leave the wild beasts may eat. You shall do likewise with your vineyard, and with your olive orchard.

"Six days you shall do your work, but on the seventh day you shall rest; that your ox and your ass may have rest, and the son of your bondmaid, and the alien, may be refreshed . . . ."

Sophocles, one of the world's greatest dramatists, produced a lasting symbol of the superiority of divine law to man-made law. Antigone voices her feelings in a sharp exchange with Creon, who represents the State, in the selection below. Do you find the issues relevant today? With whom do you tend to identify, Antigone or Creon?

The Unwritten Statutes of Heaven

Sophocles

CREON: And thy prisoner here—how and whence hast thou taken her?

GUARD: She was burying the man; thou knowest all.

CREON: Dost thou mean what thou sayest? Dost thou speak aright?

GUARD: I saw her burying the corpse that thou hadst forbidden to bury. Is that plain and clear?

CREON: And how was she seen? how taken in the act?

GUARD: It befell on this wise. When we had come to the place,—with those dread menaces of thine upon us,—we swept away all the dust that covered the corpse, and bared the dank body well; and then sat us down on the brow of the hill, to windward, heedful that the smell from him should not strike us; every man was wide awake, and kept his neighbor alert with torrents of threats, if any one should be careless of this task.

So went it, until the sun's bright orb stood in mid-heaven, and the heat began to burn: and then suddenly a whirlwind lifted from the earth a storm of dust, a trouble in the sky, and filled the plain, marring all the leafage of its woods; and the wide air was choked therewith: we closed our eyes, and bore the plague from the gods.

And when, after a long while, this storm had passed, the maid was seen; and she cried aloud with the sharp eye of a bird in its bitterness,—even as when, within the empty nest, it sees the bed stripped of its nestlings. So she also, when she saw the corpse bare, lifted up a voice of wailing, and called down curses on the doers of that deed. And straightway she brought thirsty dust in her hands; and from a shapely ewer of bronze, held high, with thrice-poured drink-offering she crowned the dead.

We rushed forward when we saw it, and at once closed upon our quarry, who was in no wise dismayed. Then we taxed her with her past and present doings; and she stood not on denial of aught,—at

From *The Antigone* by Sophocles, translated by Richard C. Jebb (Cambridge: Cambridge University Press, 1891).

once to my joy and to my pain. To have escaped from ills one's self is a great joy; but 'tis painful to bring friends to ill. Howbeit, all such things are of less account to me than mine own safety.

CREON: Thou—thou whose face is bent to earth—dost thou avow, or disavow, this deed?

ANTIGONE: I avow it; I make no denial.

CREON: (*To* GUARD) Thou canst betake thee whither thou wilt, free and clear of a grave charge. (*Exit* GUARD.)

(*To* ANTIGONE) Now, tell me thou—not in many words, but briefly—knewest thou that an edict had forbidden this?

ANTIGONE: I knew it: Could I help it? It was public.

CREON: And thou didst indeed dare to transgress that law?

ANTIGONE: Yes; for it was not Zeus that had published me that edict; not such are the laws set among men by the Justice who dwells with the gods below; nor deemed I that thy decrees were of such force, that a mortal could override the unwritten and unfailing statutes of heaven. For their life is not of to-day or yesterday, but from all time, and no man knows when they were first put forth.

Not through dread of any human pride could I answer to the gods for breaking *these*. Die I must,—I know that well (how should I not?)—even without thy edicts. But if I am to die before my time, I count that a gain: for when any one lives, as I do, compassed about with evils, can such an one find aught but gain in death?

So for me to meet this doom is trifling grief; but if I had suffered my mother's son to lie in death an unburied corpse, that would have grieved me; for this, I am not grieved. And if my present deeds are foolish in thy sight, it may be that a foolish judge arraigns my folly.

CHORUS: The maid shows herself passionate child of passionate sire, and knows not how to bend before troubles.

CREON: Yet I would have thee know that o'er-stubborn spirits are most often humbled; 'tis the stiffest iron, baked to hardness in the fire, that thou shalt oftenest see snapped and shivered; and I have known horses that show temper brought to order by a little curb; there is no room for pride, when thou art thy neighbor's slave.—This girl was already versed in insolence when she transgressed the laws that had been set forth; and, that done, lo, a second insult,—to vaunt of this, and exult in her deed.

Now verily I am no man, she is the man, if this victory shall rest with her, and bring no penalty. No! be she sister's child, or nearer to me in blood than any that worships Zeus at the altar of our house, —she and her kinsfolk shall not avoid a doom most dire; for indeed I charge that other with a like share in the plotting of this burial.

And summon her—for I saw her e'en now within,—raving and not mistress of her wits. So oft, before the deed, the mind stands self-convicted in its treason, when folks are plotting mischief in the dark. But verily this, too, is hateful,—when one who hath been caught in wickedness then seeks to make the crime a glory.

ANTIGONE: Wouldst thou do more than take and slay me?

CREON: No more, indeed; having that, I have all.

ANTIGONE: Why then dost thou delay? In thy discourse there is nought that pleases me,—never may there be!—and so my words must needs be unpleasing to thee. And yet, for glory—whence could I have won a nobler, than by giving burial to mine own brother? All here would own that they thought it well, were not their lips sealed by fear. But royalty, blest in so much besides, hath the power to do and say what it will.

CREON: Thou differest from all these Thebans in that view.

ANTIGONE: These also share it; but they curb their tongues for thee.

CREON: And art thou not ashamed to act apart from them?

ANTIGONE: No; there is nothing shameful in piety to a brother.

CREON: Was it not a brother, too, that died in the opposite cause?

ANTIGONE: Brother by the same mother and the same sire.

CREON: Why, then, dost thou render a grace that is impious in his sight?

ANTIGONE: The dead man will not say that he so deems it.

CREON: Yea, if thou makest him but equal in honour with the wicked.

ANTIGONE: It was his brother, not his slave, that perished.

CREON: Wasting this land; while *he* fell as its champion.

ANTIGONE: Nevertheless, Hades desires these rites.

CREON: But the good desires not a like portion with the evil.

ANTIGONE: Who knows but this seems blameless in the world below?

CREON: A foe is never a friend—not even in death.

ANTIGONE: 'Tis not my nature to join in hating, but in loving.

CREON: Pass, then, to the world of the dead, and, if thou must needs love, love them. While I live, no woman shall rule me.

Written in 1849, "On Civil Disobedience," from which the following
selection was taken, represents the distillation of a lifetime of critical
thinking by a famous American, who is also known for his "Walden."
Thoreau says that justice, rather than power, is the state's reason for being.
Is his argument about revolution and civil disobedience logical? Is it workable?

Casting Your Whole Vote

Henry David Thoreau

How does it become a man to behave toward this American government to-day? I answer, that he cannot without disgrace be
associated with it. I cannot for an instant recognize that political
organization as *my* government which is the *slave's* government also.

All men recognize the right of revolution; that is, the right to
refuse allegiance to, and to resist, the government, when its tyranny
or its inefficiency are great and unendurable. But almost all say that
such is not the case now. But such was the case, they think, in the
Revolution of '75. If one were to tell me that this was a bad government because it taxed certain foreign commodities brought to its
ports, it is most probable that I should not make an ado about it,
for I can do without them. All machines have their friction, and
possibly this does enough good to counterbalance the evil. At any rate,
it is a great evil to make a stir about it. But when the friction comes
to have its machine, and oppression and robbery are organized, I
say, let us not have such a machine any longer. In other words, when
a sixth of the population of a nation which has undertaken to be
the refuge of liberty are slaves, and a whole country is unjustly
overrun and conquered by a foreign army, and subjected to military
law, I think it is not too soon for honest men to rebel and revolu-
tionize. What makes this duty the more urgent is the fact, that the
country so overrun is not our own, but ours is the invading army. . . .

It is not a man's duty, as a matter of course, to devote himself
to the eradication of any, even the most enormous wrong; he may
still properly have other concerns to engage him; but it is his duty,
at least, to wash his hands of it, and, if he gives it no thought longer,
not to give it practically his support. If I devote myself to other
pursuits and contemplations, I must first see, at least, that I do not
pursue them sitting upon another man's shoulders. I must get off
him first, that he may pursue his contemplations too. . . .

From *Writings* by Henry D. Thoreau (Boston: Houghton Mifflin, 1906),
Vol. IV.

Unjust laws exist: shall we be content to obey them, or shall we endeavor to amend them, and obey them until we have succeeded, or shall we transgress them at once? Men generally, under such a government as this, think that they ought to wait until they have persuaded the majority to alter them. They think that, if they should resist, the remedy would be worse than the evil. But it is the fault of the government itself that the remedy *is* worse than the evil. *It* makes it worse. Why is it not more apt to anticipate and provide for reform? Why does it not cherish its wise minority? Why does it cry and resist before it is hurt? Why does it not encourage its citizens to be on the alert to point out its faults, and *do* better than it would have them? Why does it always crucify Christ, and excommunicate Copernicus and Luther, and pronounce Washington and Franklin rebels? . . .

Under a government which imprisons any unjustly, the true place for a just man is also a prison. The proper place to-day, the only place which Massachusetts has provided for her freer and less desponding spirits, is in her prisons, to be put out and locked out of the State by her own act, as they have already put themselves out by their principles. It is there that the fugitive slave, and the Mexican prisoner on parole, and the Indian come to plead the wrongs of his race, should find them; on that separate, but more free and honorable ground, where the State places those who are not *with* her, but *against* her,—the only house in a slave State in which a free man can abide with honor. If any think that their influence would be lost there, and their voices no longer afflict the ear of the State, that they would not be as an enemy within its walls, they do not know by how much truth is stronger than error, nor how much more eloquently and effectively he can combat injustice who has experienced a little in his own person. Cast your whole vote not a strip of paper merely, but your whole influence. A minority is powerless while it conforms to the majority; it is not even a minority then; but it is irresistible when it clogs by its whole weight. If the alternative is to keep all just men in prison, or give up war and slavery, the State will not hesitate which to choose. . . .

From Antigone to Thoreau to Gandhi to Martin Luther King, Jr., there is a
common spiritual bond: the belief that unjust laws must be defied
nonviolently. Is this idea beginning to exert a greater influence upon Western
man in the twentieth century than in earlier times? As you think about
the following passages from Dr. King's 1963 letter, some questions to keep
in mind are: Do you think Dr. King's letter is the high point of the Antigone
tradition? Is the civil rights movement the beginning of the end for
Hammurabi-type rigidity in laws?

Letter From Birmingham Jail

Martin Luther King, Jr.

You may well ask: "Why direct action? Why sit-ins, marches
and so forth? Isn't negotiation a better path?" You are quite right in
calling for negotiation. Indeed, this is the very purpose of direct
action. Nonviolent direct action seeks to create such a crisis and
foster such a tension that a community which has constantly refused
to negotiate is forced to confront the issue. It seeks so to dramatize
the issue that it can no longer be ignored. My citing the creation
of tension as part of the work of the nonviolent-resister may sound
rather shocking. But I must confess that I am not afraid of the word
"tension." I have earnestly opposed violent tension, but there is a
type of constructive, nonviolent tension which is necessary for
growth. Just as Socrates felt that it was necessary to create a tension
in the mind so that individuals could rise from the bondage of myths
and half-truths to the unfettered realm of creative analysis and
objective appraisal, so must we see the need for nonviolent gadflies
to create the kind of tension in society that will help men rise from
the dark depths of prejudice and racism to the majestic heights of
understanding and brotherhood.

The purpose of our direct-action program is to create a situation
so crisis-packed that it will inevitably open the door to negotiation. I
therefore concur with you in your call for negotiation. Too long has
our beloved Southland been bogged down in a tragic effort to live
in monologue rather than dialogue.

*   *   *   *

We have waited for more than 340 years for our constitutional and God-given rights. The nations of Asia and Africa are moving with jetlike speed toward gaining political independence, but we still creep at horse-and-buggy pace toward gaining a cup of coffee at a lunch counter. Perhaps it is easy for those who have never felt the stinging darts of segregation to say, "Wait." But when you have seen vicious mobs lynch your mothers and fathers at will and drown your sisters and brothers at whim; when you have seen hate-filled policemen curse, kick and even kill your black brothers and sisters; when you see the vast majority of your twenty million Negro brothers smothering in an airtight cage of poverty in the midst of an affluent society; when you suddenly find your tongue twisted and your speech stammering as you seek to explain to your six-year-old daughter why she can't go to the public amusement park that has just been advertised on television, and see tears welling up in her eyes when she is told that Funtown is closed to colored children, and see ominous clouds of inferiority beginning to form in her little mental sky, and see her beginning to distort her personality by developing an unconscious bitterness toward white people; when you have to concoct an answer for a five-year-old son who is asking: "Daddy, why do white people treat colored people so mean?"; when you take a cross-country drive and find it necessary to sleep night after night in the uncomfortable corners of your automobile because no motel will accept you; when you are humiliated day in and day out by nagging signs reading "white" and "colored"; when your first name becomes "nigger," your middle name becomes "boy" (however old you are) and your last name becomes "John," and your wife and mother are never given the respected title "Mrs."; when you are harried by day and haunted by night by the fact that you are a Negro, living constantly at tiptoe stance, never quite knowing what to expect next, and are plagued with inner fears and outer resentments; when you are forever fighting a degenerating sense of "nobodiness"—then you will understand why we find it difficult to wait. There comes a time when the cup of endurance runs over, and men are no longer willing to be plunged into the abyss of despair. I hope, sirs, you can understand our legitimate and unavoidable impatience.

*   *   *   *

I must make two honest confessions to you, my Christian and Jewish brothers. First, I must confess that over the past few years I have been gravely disappointed with the white moderate. I have almost reached the regrettable conclusion that the Negro's great stumbling block in his stride toward freedom is not the White Citizen's Counciler or the Ku Klux Klanner, but the white moderate, who is more devoted to "order" than to justice; who prefers a negative peace which is the absence of tension to a positive peace which is the presence of justice; who constantly says: "I agree with you in the goal you seek but I cannot agree with your methods of direct action"; who paternalistically believes he can set the timetable for another man's freedom; who lives by a mythical concept of time and who constantly advises the Negro to wait for a "more convenient season." Shallow understanding from people of good will is more frustrating than absolute misunderstanding from people of ill will. Lukewarm acceptance is much more bewildering than outright rejection.

I had hoped that the white moderate would understand that law and order exist for the purpose of establishing justice and that when they fail in this purpose they become the dangerously structured dams that block the flow of social progress. I had hoped that the white moderate would understand that the present tension in the South is a necessary phase of the transition from an obnoxious negative peace, in which the Negro passively accepted his unjust plight, to a substantive and positive peace, in which all men will respect the dignity and worth of human personality. Actually, we who engage in nonviolent direct action are not the creators of tension. We merely bring to the surface the hidden tension that is already alive. We bring it out in the open, where it can be seen and dealt with. Like a boil that can never be cured so long as it is covered up but must be opened with all its ugliness to the natural medicines of air and light, injustice must be exposed, with all the tension its exposure creates, to the light of human conscience and the air of national opinion before it can be cured. . . .

*   *   *

Before closing I feel impelled to mention one other point in your statement that has troubled me profoundly. You warmly commended the Birmingham police force for keeping "order" and "preventing violence." I doubt that you would have so warmly commended the police force if you had seen its dogs sinking their teeth into unarmed, nonviolent Negroes. I doubt that you would so quickly commend the policemen if you were to observe their ugly and inhumane treatment of Negroes here in the city jail; if you were to watch them push and curse old Negro women and young Negro girls; if you were to see them slap and kick old Negro men and young boys; if you were to observe them, as they did on two occasions, refuse to give us food because we wanted to sing our grace together. I cannot join you in your praise of the Birmingham police department.

It is true that the police have exercised a degree of discipline in handling the demonstrators. In this sense they have conducted themselves rather "nonviolently" in public. But for what purpose? To preserve the evil system of segregation. Over the past few years I have consistently preached that nonviolence demands that the means we use must be as pure as the ends we seek. I have tried to make clear that it is wrong to use immoral means to attain moral ends. But now I must affirm that it is just as wrong, or perhaps even more so, to use moral means to preserve immoral ends. Perhaps Mr. Conner and his policemen have been rather nonviolent in public, as was Chief Pritchett in Albany, Georgia, but they have used the moral means of nonviolence to maintain the immoral end of racial injustice. As T. S. Eliot has said: "The last temptation is the greatest treason: To do the right deed for the wrong reason."

Questions

1 How does one define an unjust law?

2 Can each man define the law for himself?

3 Does a person living in a free society have the right to disobey a law? Is his right limited to working legally to change or abolish it?

4 What if everyone used the methods of Antigone and Thoreau?

5 Can you cite some examples of laws being more humane than the people who apply them?

6 What laws that are in effect today do you consider unjust or inhumane? What are you planning to do about this situation?

4 Self-Fulfillment in Ancient Greece

The following essay tries to show that the culturally conditioned classical
Greek was hampered in his efforts to realize personal ambitions because of
two significant taboos. Do you see any interesting parallels or contrasts
between the realities of self-fulfillment in ancient Athens and
contemporary America?

Polis and Hubris: Two Greek Hangups

Melvin Steinfield

If residents of most large cities in America were asked to indicate
the tallest buildings in the downtown section, they would have to
point to the pathetic clusters of bank and insurance buildings that
scratch the clouds like a conspiracy of King Kongs. They could not
even imagine the huge chunk of pride most Athenian citizens of the
Golden Age felt when they guided a visitor to their Acropolis. For
though the Greeks built no skyscrapers, they possessed a sense of
community that was reflected in the quality of their public buildings.
They had an identification with the *polis* (city) that is rarely attained
in the typical American metropolis or megalopolis.

Men of every succeeding civilization have admired with awe what
the Greeks accomplished in their Golden Age. Again and again they
have returned to study the Greek achievement in order to gain insight
into solving the problems of their own time. But they never recap-
tured quite the degree of identification with the city-state possessed
by Greeks, particularly the Athenians.

Nor was man ever again haunted as much as the Athenians were
by the strange taboo known as *hubris* (pride). For it was in the
environment of the city-state, and the many demands it imposed,
that the concept of hubris functioned to hinder individual self-
fulfillment. The relationship of both hubris and polis to the Greek
achievement will be discussed later. Here it is important to note that
individual self-fulfillment was a vital part of the Greek vision of
happiness. It was an especially important goal for the Athenian of the
fifth century B.C.

It is also an important goal for Americans of the twentieth century
A.D. In fact, one of the most relevant questions a student can ask
himself today is: What kinds of obstacles will the society I live in
place before my goals of self-fulfillment? Looking at the world less
cynically, he might ask such questions as: How much will I be
permitted to develop my potential as a complete human being with

my own distinct personality?, or, How free am I to express myself in words and actions? He might wonder: Are we as free as the Athenians of the Golden Age?

To some, America is the land of freedom and unlimited opportunity in which a "rugged individualist" who dedicates himself to hard work is practically assured of success at whatever he attempts. This attitude is based upon a traditional faith in America as the land of golden opportunity, which goes back to the days of the Puritan settlers. It is reinforced by the Horatio Alger stories of rags-to-riches and with slogans such as "the sky's the limit."

But not everyone shares this optimism. Many of the student-protest movements of the past few years have stressed the dehumanizing and impersonal nature of our society. It is not just the war in Vietnam or racism at home, they say, but a society that has gone mad in the pursuit of power and materialistic things while ignoring the human values of our Western heritage. According to this view, America is on the verge of committing the same kind of hubris that the ancient Athenians did. Furthermore, claim those who are not impressed with the Puritan concept, the individual is being overwhelmed by a massive, technologically oriented society that has undergone unprecedented change in a short time. His individuality and his humanity are not cultivated in a polis-type atmosphere. Rather, they are buried at the bottom of a mass society. Many individuals are wondering about their role in an overpopulated world.

Where does this leave historians and others who are trying to make an intelligent study of the past in order to add to their understanding of the present and of ourselves? If students of the same college generation can differ so markedly in their interpretations of the opportunities and limitations of their own society, is it so surprising that historians find themselves challenged by the enormous difficulty of describing accurately the way people of a previous era lived? How much do we really know about the Greeks after all? And particularly, what percentage of that is relevant to the critical issues of today?

Another challenge to understanding the past or the present is the unfortunate fact that the stated values of a society do not always correspond to the actual reality of that society. Practices tend to fall short of values (see the article by Levine following this essay). Because there is often a disparity between the proud claims of public officials and the way it really is for many of the people in a society, students of history must be alert to the danger of being deluded into judging a society merely by taking at face value its claims and ideals.

This caution is especially important to the student of ancient

Greek history. If one were to judge only by the claims of its leaders, Athens during the Golden Age was a model society for individual self-fulfillment. Most historians today agree that individualism was treasured as a major value of the Greek heritage. Mottoes such as *Know thyself,* or *Man is the measure of all things* symbolize the great attention focused by the Greeks on the question of individuality. Aristotle wrote about "actualizing one's potentiality" and his teacher, Plato, pondered the issue of a just society in which every individual can play his proper and just role.

One of the most important sources of belief in the cult of individualism in classical Greece is Thucydides' *History of the Peloponnesian War.* Thucydides warns his readers not to regard the speeches he reports as verbatim accounts, but rather "while keeping as closely as possible to the general sense of the words that were actually used, to make the speakers say what, in my opinion, was called for by each situation." The following statements by Pericles, the leader of Athens, are excerpted from his Funeral Oration, which is reprinted in its entirety in the readings.

> Our constitution is called a democracy because power is in the hands not of a minority but of the whole people. When it is a question of settling private disputes, everyone is equal before the law; when it is a question of putting one person before another in positions of public responsibility, what counts is not membership of a particular class, but the actual ability which the man possesses. No one, so long as he has it in him to be of service to the state, is kept in political obscurity because of poverty. . . . Taking everything together then, I declare that our city is an education to Greece, and I declare that in my opinion each single one of our citizens, in all the manifold aspects of life, is able to show himself the rightful lord and owner of his own person, and do this, moreover, with exceptional grace and exceptional versatility.[1]

But Pericles' boast about Athens must not hide the fact that in the middle of the fifth century B.C. one-third of the population of Athens consisted of slaves; women did not vote, serve on juries, or hold office; and the privileges of "democracy" were confined to an aristocracy of adult males. As in other countries, there was a democracy of the few and the claims of universal democracy were simply not true.

Apart from the obvious omissions in Pericles' speech, there were two cultural patterns of classical Greece that inhibited the individual's desire for unrestrained freedom of expression and development. One of these was the taboo against immoderate success, and, what is worse, immoderate boasting about that success (hubris). Hubris, and the punishment that goes along with it, nemesis, is a recurring theme in Greek thought from Homer to the Golden Age.

According to the doctrine of hubris, excessive pride or arrogance will be punished by nemesis, a vindictive type of revenge. Thus if a man brags arrogantly about his wealth, he can expect to encounter financial disaster before long. To boast about one's success in life is an unpardonable sin to ancient Greeks because it carries the presumption that man entirely controls his own destiny and that he alone is completely responsible for his success. This ignores the importance of fate, moderation, and polis in Greek life. As C.M. Bowra states, in *The Greek Experience*:

> Unbridled arrogance shocked the Greeks morally, politically, and aesthetically. It was, in their view, quite different from legitimate ambition, since this was possible only with a large degree of self-control and even of self-sacrifice. At all periods from the Heroic Age to the fourth century, arrogance was regarded as the worst of evils, because it made chaos of all attempts to achieve balance and harmony in the self and because it scorned the social obligations on which the city-state depended.[2]

There are many examples in Greek literature of individuals committing the sin of hubris and suffering as a consequence some sort of nemesis. For example, the god Prometheus defies Zeus and gives man fire. Because he refused to accept a limitation on what he might do, because his actions went beyond the bounds of restraint and moderation, Prometheus, even though he is a god, must suffer retribution. In this particular case, the nemesis was to be bound to a rock while vultures ate away at his liver by day. (Since he was immortal, he could not die; his liver grew back at night so that the process could be repeated daily.)

Why was Prometheus bound to the rock? He defied Zeus by giving man fire and other means of increasing his freedom and his conquest of nature. The Chorus of *Prometheus Bound,* by Aeschylus, sings a warning to the Athenians in the Amphitheatre:

> But thee, Prometheus, racked
> With anguish infinite,
> I shudder to behold:
> For Zeus thou dost defy—self-willed—
> Revering overmuch the sons of men.
> For tell me, O my friend,
> How, rendering unto them

> This thankless service, art thou helped?
> Can short-lived mortals mend thy plight?
> Seest thou not the feeble helpless state,
> Shadowy as a dream, whereto are bound
> The purblind race of men?
> No human counsels shall avail
> To pass the bounds of that great harmony
> Which Zeus ordains.
> So am I taught, Prometheus, by the sight
> Of this thy ruined state.[3]

The message is clear: "No human counsels shall avail to pass the bounds of that great harmony which Zeus ordains."[4] For the individual to overstep his bounds is to invite disaster.

Another example of hubris in Greek thought can be found in Homer's *Odyssey*. After Odysseus kills his wife's suitors, his old nurse is about to gloat over his success, but he is aware of the sin of boasting. He chides her with: "It is an unholy thing to boast over slain men."

Odysseus is not the only major character in the Homeric poems who deals with hubris. Achilles, the hero of the *Iliad*, arrogantly asserts that the Greeks will beg him to fight for them as soon as they realize his importance on the battlefield: ". . . the day is coming when Achaeans one and all will miss me sorely, and you in your despair will be powerless to help them as they fall in their hundreds to Hector killer of men. Then, you will tear your heart out in remorse for having treated the best man in the expedition with contempt." Achilles had just committed hubris—he dared think of himself as the best in the expedition. As fans of the *Iliad* know, it is Achilles who starts tearing his own heart out with remorse over the death of his best friend, Patrocles. Patrocles' death was Achilles' punishment for having committed hubris.

Both Herodotus and Thucydides, famous Greek historians of the fifth century B.C., are conscious of hubris and its importance in the Greek scheme of values. Herodotus tells of the rich and powerful Lydian King Croesus who supposes that he is the happiest of men, thus bringing into play the forces of nemesis that will destroy the basis for his arrogance. (This is powerfully and explicitly described in Herodotus' *History of the Persian War*. The famous section on Croesus and Solon is included in the readings.)

Thucydides also devotes considerable space to listing and analyzing instances of hubris. For example, during the War Debate at Sparta, he has one of the Spartan kings say:

"Slow" and "cautious" can equally well be "wise" and "sensible." Certainly it is because we possess these qualities that we are the only people who do not become arrogant when we are successful and who in times of stress are less likely to give in than others. We are not carried away by the pleasure of hearing ourselves praised. . . .[5]

The Athenians, however, had become arrogant after the Persian Wars, according to Thucydides. The Melian Dialogue is a clear example of the growing imperialistic sentiment in Athens and how it corrupted the older values of moderation. The powerful Athenians inform the Melians that they must become their allies or face destruction. The Melians plead to be allowed to remain neutral, but the Athenians say they cannot afford to allow this because their prestige would suffer and it would create the appearance of weakness on their part. This hard line was typical of the attitude that had infected the Athenians after they let their success in the Persian Wars go to their heads. And as it turned out, there was a nemesis—the Athenians lost the Greek civil war, known as the Peloponnesian War.

Pericles' Funeral Oration came at the peak of Athenian power and glory, the end of the first year of the Peloponnesian War. He commits hubris by arrogantly boasting about Athens' preeminence in the Greek world of 431 B.C.: "Mighty indeed are the marks and monuments of our empire which we have left. Future ages will wonder at us, as the present age wonders at us now."

Poor Pericles failed to abide by the rules of restraint. He committed hubris by virtue of his immoderate boasting. He failed to act humbly to set limits to what Athens should hope to achieve, allowing himself freedom from restraint. His nemesis was not long in coming. Within a few weeks, the plague broke out in Athens, Pericles died, and there followed a long series of disasters for the hubris-committing Athenians.

The examples could continue almost indefinitely, but the point should be amply illustrated by now: a Greek was faced each day with the culturally ingrained attitude that he must not allow himself to be carried away with his own success. He must remember that there are forces beyond his control that are responsible for his success. To brag about great achievement, or even to strive too far, is to defy the will of the gods, to flaunt fate, to commit hubris.

Polis is the second of the two Greek hangups that have the effect of limiting self-development and expression. It is, like hubris, a major element of the Greek life-style. Polis means city-state, but it is much more; it is a way of life. When Aristotle opened his *Politics* with "Man is a political animal," he meant it as only classical Greeks could mean it: man is an animal who by nature lives in a polis.

The individual Greek citizen must never forget his relationship to the community; that is the pervasive meaning of polis. That is why Plato and Aristotle always dealt with the subject of justice for the individual in the context of the polis. The two simply could not be separated. That is why exile was such a severe punishment in ancient Greece. For to be cut off from one's community meant that his fellow citizens held him in low regard, and that was a fate worse than death. Death with honor, especially if it occurred while fighting on behalf of one's city-state, was one of the greatest blessings that could befall a man. But dishonor was worse than death. Thus we find that a public burial with full state honors is at one end of the spectrum, and exile is at the other end. These are the extremes of reward and punishment in Greek polis life. Polis was a hangup, then, because it imposed a continuous responsibility on every Greek citizen to think and act with the best interests of the community always as a main consideration. Individual aspirations were frequently dampened by the pressure of this concept, though it did inspire men to make great sacrifices on behalf of the state.

Consider the behavior of Hector in the *Iliad* when he realized that he was no match for Achilles and that he faced imminent death: "But now my death is upon me. Let me at least not die without a struggle, inglorious, but do some big thing first, that men to come shall know of it."

Or listen to the reasons that Solon offers to explain why a relatively obscure Athenian by the name of Tellus was considered one of the happiest persons in the world: "First, his city was prosperous and he had fine sons, and lived to see children born to each of them, and all these children surviving . . . ."[6] In other words, he lived in a prosperous community and he contributed to the prosperity of the community. An individual's happiness is always related to the condition of his community as well as to the manner of his death: ". . . and secondly, after a life, which by our standards was a good one, he had a glorious death. In a battle with the neighboring town of Eleusis, he fought for his countrymen, routed the enemy, and died like a soldier; and the Athenians paid him the high honor of a public funeral on the spot where he fell."[7]

Thus the concept of polis embodied a sense of community identification that the individual never lost. Nor could he ever escape it.

A prosperous city was something to be happy about. Conversely, no matter how well one's personal fortunes might be going, if his polis were in trouble, he could not be content.

How much freedom did the typical aristocratic Athenian of the Golden Age enjoy? How much of a dampening effect did his sense of awareness of hubris and polis exert on his enthusiasm for individual achievement? Did he willingly accept or grudgingly observe these restraints? It is difficult to answer these questions. On the whole, it would appear that polis and hubris were two values that exerted a tremendous influence upon the daily lives of ancient Greeks. Whether the Greeks themselves were fully conscious of the extent to which their actions were shaped and conditioned and restricted by these values is impossible to ascertain.

What is certain is that every society has its particular hangups. The individual who wants to gather some extra dimensions of comparison with his own life-style would be wise to consider the restraints upon self-fulfillment in ancient Greece. What is truly remarkable is that, despite these restraints, the Greek achievement was phenomenal. Or maybe because of them?

Notes

1 Thucydides, *History of the Peloponnesian War*, translated by Rex Warner (Baltimore, Md.: Penguin, 1956), pp. 117, 119.

2 C. M. Bowra, *The Greek Experience* (New York: New American Library, 1959), p. 102.

3 Aeschylus, *Prometheus Bound*, translated by Robert Whitelaw, in Lane Cooper, ed., *Fifteen Greek Plays* (New York: Oxford University Press, 1943), p. 17.

4 Homer, *The Iliad*, translated by E. V. Rieu (Baltimore, Md.: Penguin, 1954), p. 29.

5 Thucydides, *op. cit.*, p. 59.

6 Herodotus, *The Histories*, translated by Aubrey de Selincourt (Baltimore, Md.: Penguin, 1954), p. 24.

7 *Ibid.*

The following commencement address was delivered at Harvard University in June 1969. It is a valuable source for pinpointing the clash of values in contemporary America. It also underscores the difficulty of accurately interpreting a society's character. Pericles made certain statements about the nature of Athenian values and the possibilities for individual self-fulfillment. Does this mean that the values were actually realized? What about self-fulfillment of American ideals? Do you share Levine's concern?

The Disparity Between Ideals and Practices

Meldon E. Levine

> The streets of our country are in turmoil. The universities are filled with students rebelling and rioting. Communists are seeking to destroy our country. Russia is threatening us with her might. And the republic is in danger. Yes, danger from within and without. We need law and order! . . . without law and order our nation cannot survive. . . .

These words were spoken in 1932 by Adolf Hitler.

We have heard almost every one of those assertions used this year in this country as justifications for repressing student protests. Instead of adjudicating the legitimate causes of the dissatisfaction, our political and social leaders have searched for explanations which deny either the validity or the pervasiveness of the dissent.

Our society cannot afford to deny this conflict any longer. You cannot expect it to go away by suppressing it. For it is a conflict inherent in our consciences—one which exists because you have taught us what America should stand for.

What is this protest all about?

It is not a protest to subvert institutions or an attempt to challenge values which have been affirmed for centuries. We are *not*—as we have been accused—conspiring to destroy America. We are attempting to do precisely the reverse: we are affirming the values which you have instilled in us and which you have taught us to respect.

Confidence and Respect Gone

You have told us repeatedly that trust and courage were standards to emulate. You have convinced us that equality and justice were inviolable concepts. You have taught us that authority should be guided by reason and tempered by fairness. *And we have taken you seriously.*

From "Affirming Values You Taught Us" by Meldon E. Levine, *Los Angeles Times,* July 2, 1969. Copyright, Los Angeles Times. Reprinted with permission.

115

We have accepted your principles—and have tried to implement them. But we have found this task to be less than easy. Almost every one of us has faced the inflexibility and the insensitivity of our system.

To those who would argue that the system has been responsive, there is a one-word answer: Vietnam. It is not a weakness but a strength of American education that enables us to understand the absurdity of the premises which control our policy in Vietnam and which threaten to embroil us elsewhere.

We have tried every possible peaceful means to change our disastrous course. We have signed petitions. We have written to our congressmen. We have had teach-ins. We have marched. We have reasoned with anyone who would listen. And, in 1968, after years of peaceful protest and after the American people had spoken in primary after primary in favor of a change, we were not even given a choice on Vietnam.

We have grown weary of being promised a dialogue. What we urgently need is a meaningful response.

Our experience with Vietnam reflects the type of frustration we face every time we press for change. We are told to follow "the system." But when I look at that "system," I see rules—but not understanding. I see standards—but no compassion.

And although our complaints are more with society than with the university, the university itself is not an illogical target. Some students believe it contributes to oppressive social policies and most of us feel that it has become, in an unresponsive system, the only means whereby we can focus attention on the most serious injustices which continue to infect our nation.

And the university too has tenaciously resisted change. Six years ago, I was elected president of the student body at Berkeley. I ran on a moderate platform—one calling for educational reform, increased university involvement in the community, and student participation in academic decision-making.

Since that time, I have received degrees at Berkeley, at Princeton, and at Harvard. And I have heard my fellow students raise the same issues—time and again. And time and again, I have witnessed the university's response: A committee will be formed, and the issues will be discussed.

Year after year, the result is the same. And eventually the tactic of setting up committees is discredited. They come to be seen as a device to buy time rather than to make changes; an opportunity to stall until another class of undergraduates leaves the school, removing that particular thorn from the university's side as they go.

Thus, the university and the society respond the same way to our appeals for change: A direct confrontation of ideas is refused and the issues raised are avoided. But explaining the issues away won't make them go away. And the frustration which comes both from the issues themselves and from the continual denial of their existence touches all segments of the campus.

If anyone still doubts the depth of the conviction, I ask him to witness the intensity with which it is felt. I ask him to review the efforts of my classmates. These efforts were pursued not as a sacrifice, though sacrifices were made; not as a risk, though risks were involved; not to gain praise, though praise they deserve, but because this was *necessary* to achieve the ideals which you have held forth for us.

They chose to work with poor people in Appalachia and with black people in Mississippi and in urban ghettos. They persevered in calling attention to the injustices in Vietnam, despite accusations of disloyalty to their country. And when the price was raised to include physical danger, they exhibited courage and did not waver—in Chicago, in Berkeley, and in Cambridge.

Now, for attempting to achieve the values which you have taught us to cherish, your response has been astounding. It has escalated from the presence of police on the campuses to their use of clubs and of gas. At Berkeley in May, the state ordered a helicopter to gas the campus from the sky and ordered the police to shoot protesters from the street. Whether the victims had themselves engaged in violence seems to have made little difference.

When this type of violent repression replaces the search for reasonable alternatives, Americans are allowing their most fundamental ideals to be compromised.

What do you think that response does to students?

It drives the wedge even deeper. It creates solidarity among a previously divided group, committing the uncommitted and radicalizing the moderates.

"You Have Convinced Us"

I have asked many of my classmates what they wanted me to say in this address. "Talk with them about hypocrisy," most of them said. "Tell them they have broken the best heads in the country, embittered the most creative minds, and turned off their most talented scholars. Tell them they have destroyed our confidence and lost our respect. Tell them that, as they use the phrase, 'law and order' is merely a substitute for reason and an alternative to justice."

Continuing to explain the conflict away will only serve to heighten the frustration. It can no longer be denied. Once you recognize that it pervades the campuses—that it affects more than a discontented few—how will you respond?

So far, we have been unable to understand your response. You have given us our visions and then asked us to curb them. You have offered us dreams and then urged us to abandon them. You have made us idealists and then told us to go slowly.

We have been asking for no more than what you have taught us is *right*. We can't understand why you have been so offended. But as the repression continues, as the pressure increases, as the stakes become higher and the risks greater, we can do nothing but resist more strongly and refuse more adamantly. For it would be unthinkable to abandon principle because we were threatened or to compromise ideals because we were repressed.

We are asking that you allow us to realize the very values which you have held forth. And we think you should be *with us* in our quest.

The following excerpt from Herodotus' "History of the Persian War" contains significant statements about Greek values. Solon personifies the wise Greek philosopher who expounds with great wisdom the nature of true happiness. He stands in sharp contrast with Croesus, who violates many Greek rules of good behavior. Observe carefully how Croesus commits hubris and notice the vindictive nature of the nemesis that befalls him as a consequence.

Defining the Good Life

Herodotus

Solon left home and, after a visit to the court of Amasis in Egypt, went to Sardis to see Croesus.

Croesus entertained him hospitably in the palace, and three or four days after his arrival instructed some servants to take him on a tour of the royal treasuries and point out the richness and magnificence of everything. When Solon had made as thorough an inspection as opportunity allowed, Croesus said: "Well, my Athenian friend, I have heard a great deal about your wisdom, and how widely you have traveled in the pursuit of knowledge. I cannot resist my desire to ask you a question: who is the happiest man you have ever seen?"

The point of the question was that Croesus supposed himself to be the happiest of men. Solon, however, refused to flatter, and answered in strict accordance with his view of the truth. "An Athenian," he said, "called Tellus."

Croesus was taken aback. "And what," he asked sharply, "is your reason for this choice?"

"There are two good reasons," said Solon, "first, his city was prosperous, and he had fine sons, and lived to see children born to each of them, and all these children surviving; and, secondly, after a life which by our standards was a good one, he had a glorious death. In a battle with the neighboring town of Eleusis, he fought for his countrymen, routed the enemy, and died like a soldier; and the Athenians paid him the high honor of a public funeral on the spot where he fell."

All these details about the happiness of Tellus, Solon doubtless intended as a moral lesson for the king; Croesus, however, thinking he would at least be awarded second prize, asked who was the next happiest person whom Solon had seen.

"Two young men of Argos," was the reply; "Cleobis and Biton.

From *The Histories* by Herodotus, translated by Aubrey de Selincourt (Baltimore, Md.: Penguin, 1954), pp. 23–29. Reprinted by permission.

They had enough to live on comfortably; and their physical strength is proved not merely by their success in athletics, but much more by the following incident. The Argives were celebrating the festival of Hera, and it was most important that the mother of the two young men should drive to the temple in her ox-cart; but it so happened that the oxen were late in coming back from the fields. Her two sons therefore, as there was no time to lose, harnessed themselves to the cart and dragged it along, with their mother inside, for a distance of nearly six miles, until they reached the temple. After this exploit, which was witnessed by the assembled crowd, they had a most enviable death—a heaven-sent proof of how much better it is to be dead than alive. Men kept crowding round them and congratulating them on their strength, and women kept telling the mother how lucky she was to have such sons, when, in sheer pleasure at this public recognition of her sons' act, she prayed the goddess Hera, before whose shrine she stood, to grant Cleobis and Biton, who had brought her such honor, the greatest blessing that can fall to mortal man.

"After her prayer came the ceremonies of sacrifice and feasting; and the two lads, when all was over, fell asleep in the temple—and that was the end of them, for they never woke again.

"The Argives had statues made of them, which they sent to Delphi, as a mark of their particular respect."

Croesus was vexed with Solon for giving the second prize for happiness to the two young Argives, and snapped out: "That's all very well, my Athenian friend; but what of my own happiness? Is it so utterly contemptible that you won't even compare me with mere common folk like those you have mentioned?"

"My lord," replied Solon, "I know God is envious of human prosperity and likes to trouble us. . . . You can see from that, Croesus, what a chancy thing life is. You are very rich, and you rule a numerous people; but the question you asked me I will not answer, until I know that you have died happily. Great wealth can make a man no happier than moderate means, unless he has the luck to continue in prosperity to the end. Many very rich men have been unfortunate, and many with a modest competence have had good luck. The former are better off than the latter in two respects only, whereas the poor but lucky man has the advantage in many ways; for though the rich have the means to satisfy their appetites and to bear calamities, and the poor have not, the poor, if they are lucky, are more likely to keep clear of trouble, and will have besides the blessings of a sound body, health, freedom from trouble, fine children, and good looks.

"Now if a man thus favored dies as he has lived, he will be just the one you are looking for: the only sort of person who deserves to be called happy. But mark this: until he is dead, keep the word 'happy' in reserve. Till then, he is not happy, but only lucky.

"Nobody of course can have all these advantages, any more than a country can produce everything it needs: whatever it has, it is bound to lack something. The best country is the one which has most. It is the same with people: no man is ever self-sufficient—there is sure to be something missing. But whoever has the greatest number of the good things I have mentioned, and keeps them to the end, and dies a peaceful death, that man, my lord Croesus, deserves in my opinion to be called happy.

"Look to the end, no matter what it is you are considering. Often enough God gives a man a glimpse of happiness, and then utterly ruins him."

These sentiments were not of the sort to give Croesus any pleasure; he let Solon go with cold indifference, firmly convinced that he was a fool. For what could be more stupid than to keep telling him to look at the "end" of everything, without any regard to present prosperity?

After Solon's departure Croesus was dreadfully punished, presumably because God was angry with him for supposing himself the happiest of men. It began with a dream he had about a disaster to one of his sons: a dream which came true. He had two sons: one with a physical disability, being deaf and dumb; the other, named Atys, as fine a young man as one can fancy. Croesus dreamt that Atys would be killed by a blow from an iron weapon. He woke from the dream in horror, and lost no time in getting his son a wife, and seeing to it that he no longer took the field with the Lydian soldiers, whom he used to command. He also removed all the weapons—javelins, spears and so on—from the men's rooms, and had them piled up in the women's quarters, because he was afraid that some blade hanging on the wall might fall on Atys' head.

The arrangements for the wedding were well in hand, when there came to Sardis an unfortunate stranger who had been guilty of manslaughter. He was a Phrygian, and related to the Phrygian royal house. This man presented himself at the palace and begged Croesus to cleanse him from blood-guilt according to the laws of the country (the ceremony is much the same in Lydia as in Greece): and Croesus did as he asked. When the formalities were over, Croesus, wishing to know who he was and where he came from, said: "What is your name, stranger, and what part of Phrygia have you come from, to take refuge with me? What man or woman did you kill?"

"Sire," the stranger replied, "I am the son of Gordias, and Midas was my grandfather. My name is Adrastus. I killed my brother by accident, and here I am, driven from home by my father and stripped of all I possessed."

"Your family and mine," said Croesus, "are friends. You have come to a friendly house. If you stay in my dominions, you shall have all you need. The best thing for you will be not to take your misfortune too much to heart." Adrastus, therefore, took up his residence in the palace.

Now it happened just at this time that Mount Olympus in Mysia was infested by a monstrous boar. This tremendous creature used to issue from his mountain lair and play havoc with the crops, and many times the Mysians had taken the field against him, but to no purpose. The unfortunate hunters received more damage than they were able to inflict. As a last resource the Mysians sent to Croesus. "Sire," the messengers said, "a huge beast of a boar has appeared amongst us, and is doing fearful damage. We want to catch him, but we can't. Please, my lord, send us your son with a party of young men, and some dogs, so that we can get rid of the brute."

Croesus had not forgotten his dream, and in answer to this request forbade any further mention of his son.

"I could not send him," he said; "he is just married, and that keeps him busy. But I will certainly send picked men, with a complete hunting outfit, and I will urge them to do all they can to help rid you of the animal."

This answer satisfied the Mysians; but at that moment Atys, who had heard of their request, entered the room. The young man, finding that Croesus persisted in his refusal to let him join the hunting party, said to his father: "Once honor demanded that I should win fame as a huntsman and fighter; but now, father, though you cannot accuse me of cowardice or lack of spirit, you won't let me take part in either of these admirable pursuits. Think what a figure I must cut when I walk between here and the place of assembly! What will people take me for? What must my young wife think of me? That she hasn't married much of a husband, I fear! Now, father, either let me join this hunt, or give me an intelligible reason why what you're doing is good for me."

"My son," said Croesus, "of course you are not a coward or anything unpleasant of that kind. That is not the reason for what I'm doing. The fact is, I dreamt that you had not long to live—that you would be killed by an iron weapon. It was that dream that made me hasten your wedding; and the same thing makes me refuse to let you join in this enterprise. As long as I live, I am determined to protect you, and to rob death of his prize. You are my only son, for I do not count that wretched cripple, your brother."

"No one can blame you, father," Atys replied, "for taking care of me after a dream like that. Nevertheless there is something which you have failed to observe, and it is only right that I should point it out to you. You dreamt that I should be killed by an iron weapon. Very well: has a boar got hands? Can a boar hold this weapon you fear so much? Had you dreamt that I should be killed by a boar's tusk or anything of that sort, your precautions would be justified. But you didn't: it was a weapon which was to kill me. Let me go, then. It is only to hunt an animal, not to fight against men."

"My boy," said Croesus, "I own myself beaten. You interpret the dream better than I did. I cannot but change my mind, and allow you to join the expedition."

The king then sent for Adrastus the Phrygian, and said to him: "Through no fault of your own, Adrastus, you came to me in great distress and with an ugly stain on your character. I gave you ritual purification, welcomed you to my house, and have spared no expense to entertain you. Now I expect a fair return for my generosity: take charge of my son on this boar-hunt; protect him from footpads and cut-throats on the road. In any case it is your duty to go where you can distinguish yourself: your family honor demands it, and you are a stalwart fellow besides."

"Sire," Adrastus answered, "under ordinary circumstances I should have taken no part in this adventure. A man under a cloud has no business to associate with those who are luckier than himself. Indeed I have no heart for it, and there are many reasons to prevent my going. But your wishes make all the difference. It is my duty to gratify you in return for your kindness; so I am ready to do as you ask. So far as it lies in my power to protect your son, you may count on his returning safe and sound."

When Adrastus had given his answer, the party set out, men, dogs, and all. They made their way to Olympus and kept their eyes open for the boar. As soon as they spotted him, they surrounded him and let fly with spears—and then it was that the stranger—Adrastus, the very man whom Croesus had cleansed from the stain of blood— aimed at the boar, missed him, and struck the king's son. Croesus' dream had come true.

A messenger hurried off to Sardis, and Croesus was told of the encounter with the boar and the death of his son. The shock of the news was dreadful; and the horror of it was increased by the fact that the weapon had been thrown by the very man whom the king had cleansed from the guilt of blood. In the violence of his grief Croesus prayed to Zeus, calling on him as God of Purification to witness what he had suffered at the hands of his guest; he invoked him again under his title of Protector of the Hearth, because he had unwittingly entertained his son's murderer in his own house; and yet again as God of Friendship, because the man he had sent to guard his son had turned out to be his bitterest enemy.

Before long the Lydians arrived with the body, followed by the unlucky killer. He took his stand in front of the corpse, and stretching out his hands in an attitude of submission begged the king to cut his throat there and then upon the dead body of his son.

"My former trouble," he said, "was bad enough. But now that I have ruined the man who absolved me of my guilt, I cannot bear to live."

In spite of his grief Croesus was moved to pity by these words.

"Friend," he said, "as you condemn yourself to death, there is nothing more I can require of you. Justice is satisfied. This calamity is not your fault; you never meant to strike the blow, though strike it you did. Some God is to blame—some God who long ago warned me of what was to happen."

Croesus buried his son with all proper ceremony; and as soon as everything was quiet after the funeral, Adrastus—the son of Gordias, the grandson of Midas: the man who had killed his brother and ruined the host who gave him purification—convinced that he was the unluckiest of all the men he had ever known, stabbed himself and fell dead upon the tomb.

In this famous passage from Thucydides' History of the Peloponnesian War, Pericles, the ruler of Athens, delivers his Funeral Oration. For the most part, the speech recounts the blessings of living in Athens as perceived by the Athenians themselves. Strong claims are made for the advantages to the individual and for the superiority of Athens over Sparta as far as the general way of life is concerned,and other insights into the mind of the Athenians are given. The arrogant tone of boasting was an act of immoderation and was destined to bring suffering upon the proud Athenians. One wonders whether the Athenian youth shared Pericles' description of the Great Society. Maybe they noticed wide disparities between the claims and the realities, as did Levine in his speech on American ideals and practices.

Athens, the School of Hellas

Thucydides

Many of those who have spoken here in the past have praised the institution of this speech at the close of our ceremony. It seemed to them a mark of honor to our soldiers who have fallen in war that a speech should be made over them. I do not agree. These men have shown themselves valiant in action, and it would be enough, I think, for their glories to be proclaimed in action, as you have just seen it done at this funeral organized by the state. Our belief in the courage and manliness of so many should not be hazarded on the goodness or badness of one man's speech. Then it is not easy to speak with a proper sense of balance, when a man's listeners find it difficult to believe in the truth of what one is saying. The man who knows the facts and loves the dead may well think that an oration tells less than what he knows and what he would like to hear: others who do not know so much may feel envy for the dead, and think the orator over-praises them, when he speaks of exploits that are beyond their own capacities. Praise of other people is tolerable only up to a certain point, the point where one still believes that one could do oneself some of the things one is hearing about. Once you get beyond this point, you will find people becoming jealous and incredulous. However, the fact is that this institution was set up and approved by our forefathers, and it is my duty to follow the tradition and do my best to meet the wishes and the expectations of every one of you.

I shall begin by speaking about our ancestors, since it is only right

From *History of the Peloponnesian War* by Thucydides, translated by Rex Warner (Baltimore, Md.: Penguin, 1956), pp. 116–123. Reprinted by permission.

and proper on such an occasion to pay them the honor of recalling what they did. In this land of ours there have always been the same people living from generation to generation up till now, and they, by their courage and their virtues, have handed it on to us, a free country. They certainly deserve our praise. Even more so do our fathers deserve it. For to the inheritance they had received they added all the empire we have now, and it was not without blood and toil that they handed it down to us of the present generation. And then we ourselves, assembled here today, who are mostly in the prime of life, have, in most directions, added to the power of our empire and have organized our State in such a way that it is perfectly well able to look after itself both in peace and in war.

I have no wish to make a long speech on subjects familiar to you all: so I shall say nothing about the warlike deeds by which we acquired our power or the battles in which we or our fathers gallantly resisted our enemies, Greek or foreign. What I want to do is, in the first place, to discuss the spirit in which we faced our trials and also our constitution and the way of life which has made us great. After that I shall speak in praise of the dead, believing that this kind of speech is not inappropriate to the present occasion, and that this whole assembly, of citizens and foreigners, may listen to it with advantage.

Let me say that our system of government does not copy the institutions of our neighbors. It is more the case of our being a model to others, than of our imitating anyone else. Our constitution is called a democracy because power is in the hands not of a minority but of the whole people. When it is a question of settling private disputes, everyone is equal before the law; when it is a question of putting one person before another in positions of public responsibility, what counts is not membership of a particular class, but the actual ability which the man possesses. No one, so long as he has it in him to be of service to the state, is kept in political obscurity because of poverty. And, just as our political life is free and open, so is our day-to-day life in our relations with each other. We do not get into a state with our next-door neighbor if he enjoys himself in his own way, nor do we give him the kind of black looks which, though they do no real harm, still do hurt people's feelings. We are free and tolerant in our private lives; but in public affairs we keep to the law. This is because it commands our deep respect.

We give our obedience to those whom we put in positions of authority, and we obey the laws themselves, especially those which are for the protection of the oppressed, and those unwritten laws which it is an acknowledged shame to break.

And here is another point. When our work is over, we are in a position to enjoy all kinds of recreation for our spirits. There are various kinds of contests and sacrifices regularly throughout the year; in our own homes we find a beauty and a good taste which delight us every day and which drive away our cares. Then the greatness of our city brings it about that all the good things from all over the world flow in to us, so that to us it seems just as natural to enjoy foreign goods as our own local products.

Then there is a great difference between us and our opponents, in our attitude toward military security. Here are some examples: Our city is open to the world, and we have no periodical deportations in order to prevent people observing or finding out secrets which might be of military advantage to the enemy. This is because we rely, not on secret weapons, but on our own real courage and loyalty. There is a difference, too, in our educational systems. The Spartans, from their earliest boyhood, are submitted to the most laborious training in courage; we pass our lives without all these restrictions, and yet are just as ready to face the same dangers as they are. Here is a proof of this: When the Spartans invade our land, they do not come by themselves, but bring all their allies with them; whereas we, when we launch an attack abroad, do the job by ourselves, and, though fighting on foreign soil, do not often fail to defeat opponents who are fighting for their own hearths and homes. As a matter of fact none of our enemies has ever yet been confronted with our total strength, because we have to divide our attention between our navy and the many missions on which our troops are sent on land. Yet, if our enemies engage a detachment of our forces and defeat it, they give themselves credit for having thrown back our entire army; or, if they lose, they claim that they were beaten by us in full strength. There are certain advantages, I think, in our way of meeting danger voluntarily, with an easy mind, instead of with a laborious training, with natural rather than with state-induced courage. We do not have to spend our time practicing to meet sufferings which are still in the future; and when they are actually upon us we show ourselves just as brave as these others who are always in strict training. This is one point in which, I think, our city deserves to be admired. There are also others:

Our love of what is beautiful does not lead to extravagance; our love of the things of the mind does not make us soft. We regard wealth as something to be properly used, rather than as something to boast about. As for poverty, no one need be ashamed to admit it: the real shame is in not taking practical measures to escape from it. Here each individual is interested not only in his own affairs but in the affairs of the state as well: even those who are mostly occupied with their own business are extremely well-informed on general politics—

this is a peculiarity of ours: we do not say that a man who takes no interest in politics is a man who minds his own business; we say that he has no business here at all. We Athenians, in our own persons, take our decisions on policy or submit them to proper discussions: for we do not think that there is an incompatibility between words and deeds; the worst thing is to rush into action before the consequences have been properly debated. And this is another point where we differ from other people. We are capable at the same time of taking risks and of estimating them beforehand. Others are brave out of ignorance; and, when they stop to think, they begin to fear. But the man who can most truly be accounted brave is he who best knows the meaning of what is sweet in life and what is terrible, and then goes out undeterred to meet what is to come.

Again, in questions of general good feeling there is a great contrast between us and most other people. We make friends by doing good to others, not by receiving good from them. This makes our friendship all the more reliable, since we want to keep alive the gratitude of those who are in our debt by showing continued goodwill to them: whereas the feelings of one who owes us something lack the same enthusiasm, since he knows that, when he repays our kindness, it will be more like paying back a debt than giving something spontaneously. We are unique in this. When we do kindnesses to others, we do not do them out of any calculations of profit or loss: we do them without afterthought, relying on our free liberality. Taking everything together then, I declare that our city is an education to Greece, and I declare that in my opinion each single one of our citizens, in all the manifold aspects of life, is able to show himself the rightful lord and owner of his own person, and do this, moreover, with exceptional grace and exceptional versatility. And to show that this is no empty boasting for the present occasion, but real tangible fact, you have only to consider the power which our city possesses and which has been won by those very qualities which I have mentioned. Athens, alone of the states we know, comes to her testing time in a greatness that surpasses what was imagined of her. In her case, and in her case alone, no invading enemy is ashamed at being defeated, and no subject can complain of being governed by people unfit for their responsibilities. Mighty indeed are the marks and monuments of our empire which we have left. Future ages will wonder at us, as the present age wonders at us now. We do not need the praises of a Homer, or of anyone else whose words may delight us for the moment, but whose estimation of facts will fall short of what is really true. For our adventurous spirit has forced an entry into every sea and into every land; and everywhere we have left behind us everlasting memorials of good done to our friends or suffering inflicted on our enemies.

This, then, is the kind of city for which these men, who could not bear the thought of losing her, nobly fought and nobly died. It is only natural that every one of us who survive them should be willing to undergo hardships in her service. And it was for this reason that I have spoken at such length about our city, because I wanted to make it clear that for us there is more at stake than there is for others who lack our advantages; also I wanted my words of praise for the dead to be set in the bright light of evidence. And now the most important of these words has been spoken. I have sung the praises of our city; but it was the courage and gallantry of these men, and of people like them, which made her splendid. Nor would you find it true in the case of many of the Greeks, as it is true of them, that no words can do more than justice to their deeds.

To me it seems that the consummation which has overtaken these men shows us the meaning of manliness in its first revelation and in its final proof. Some of them, no doubt, had their faults; but what we ought to remember first is their gallant conduct against the enemy in defense of their native land. They have blotted out evil with good, and done more service to the commonwealth than they ever did harm in their private lives. No one of these men weakened because he wanted to go on enjoying his wealth: no one put off the awful day in the hope that he might live to escape his poverty and grow rich. More to be desired than such things, they chose to check the enemy's pride. This, to them, was a risk most glorious, and they accepted it, willing to strike down the enemy and relinquish everything else. As for success or failure, they left that in the doubtful hands of Hope, and when the reality of battle was before their face, they put their trust in their own selves. In the fighting, they thought it more honorable to stand their ground and suffer death than to give in and save their lives. So they fled from the reproaches of men, abiding with life and limb the brunt of battle; and, in a small moment of time, the climax of their lives, a culmination of glory, not of fear, were swept away from us.

So and such they were, these men—worthy of their city. We who remain behind may hope to be spared their fate, but must resolve to keep the same daring spirit against the foe. It is not simply a question of estimating the advantages in theory. I could tell you a long story (and you know it as well as I do) about what is to be gained by beating the enemy back. What I would prefer is that you should fix your eyes every day on the greatness of Athens as she really is, and should fall in love with her. When you realize her greatness, then reflect that what made her great was men with a spirit of adventure, men who knew their duty, men who were ashamed to fall below a certain standard. If they ever failed in an enterprise, they made up their minds that at any rate the city should not find their courage lacking to her, and they gave to her the best contribution that they could. They gave her their lives, to her and to all of us, and for their own selves they won praises that never grow old, the most splendid of sepulchers— not the sepulcher in which their bodies are laid, but where their glory remains eternal in men's minds, always there on the right occasion to stir others to speech or to action. For famous men have the whole earth as their memorial: it is not only the inscriptions on their graves in their own country that mark them out; no, in foreign lands also, not in any visible form but in people's hearts, their memory abides and grows. It is for you to try to be like them. Make up your minds that happiness depends on being free, and freedom depends on being courageous. Let there be no relaxation in face of the perils of the war. The people who have most excuse for despising death are not the wretched and unfortunate, who have no hope of doing well for themselves, but those who run the risk of a complete reversal in their lives, and who would feel the difference most intensely, if things went wrong for them. Any intelligent man would find a humiliation caused by his own slackness more painful to bear than death, when death comes to him unperceived, in battle, and in the confidence of his patriotism.

For these reasons I shall not commiserate with those parents of the dead, who are present here. Instead I shall try to comfort them. They are well aware that they have grown up in a world where there are many changes and chances. But this is good fortune—for men to end their lives with honor, as these have done, and for you honorably to lament them: their life was set to a measure where death and happiness went hand in hand. I know that it is difficult to convince you of this. When you see other people happy you will often be reminded of what used to make you happy too. One does not feel sad at not having some good thing which is outside one's experience: real grief is felt at the loss of something which one is used to. All the same, those of you who are of the right age must bear up and take comfort in the thought of having more children. In your own homes these new children will prevent you from brooding over those who are no more, and they will be a help to the city, too, both in filling the empty places, and in assuring her security. For it is impossible for a man to put forward fair and honest views about our affairs if he has not, like everyone else, children whose lives may be at stake. As for those of you who are now to old to have children, I would ask you to count as gain the greater part of your life, in which you have been happy, and remember that what remains is not long, and let your hearts be lifted up at the thought of the fair fame of the dead. One's sense of honor is the only thing that does not grow old, and the last pleasure, when one is worn out with age, is not, as the poet said, making money, but having the respect of one's fellow men.

As for those of you here who are sons or brothers of the dead, I can see a hard struggle in front of you. Everyone always speaks well of the dead, and, even if you rise to the greatest heights of heroism, it will be a hard thing for you to get the reputation of having come near, let alone equalled, their standard. When one is alive, one is always liable to the jealousy of one's competitors, but when one is out of the way, the honor one receives is sincere and unchallenged.

Perhaps I should say a word or two on the duties of women to those among you who are now widowed. I can say all I have to say in a short word of advice. Your great glory is not to be inferior to what God has made you, and the greatest glory of a woman is to be least talked about by men, whether they are praising you or criticizing you. I have now, as the law demanded, said what I had to say. For the time being our offerings to the dead have been made, and for the future their children will be supported at the public expense by the city, until they come of age. This is the crown and prize which she offers, both to the dead and to their children, for the ordeals which they have faced. Where the rewards of valor are the greatest, there you will find also the best and bravest spirits among the people. And now, when you have mourned for your dear ones, you must depart.

Questions

1 What kinds of restraints do you face each day?

2 How reasonable are the values of moderation and community identification?

3 To what extent do you agree or disagree with Levine's analysis of student protest?

4 How wide a gap is there in America between ideals and realities?

5 The Greeks are often praised for their achievements in rational thought. Do you consider hubris-nemesis a rational concept?

6   Which societies seemed to place greatest emphasis upon well-rounded development of individual capacities? Are you judging by what was said or by what was actually accomplished?

7   What clues to understanding the Greek mind can you find in the selections by Herodotus and Thucydides?

8   Imagine that you are Herodotus or Thucydides viewing the present condition of world affairs. What countries would you use as examples of how not to behave? Which ones are the most overt and glaring hubris-committers?

9   Was there a greater disparity between the ideals and practices of ancient Athens or of present-day America? Which society was more hypocritical?

10 No Greek would have dared operate an industry for his own enrichment if the industry had polluted the air or water of his community. Is this restraint so bad? Would it have been swept aside if Greece had gone through an industrial revolution or an overpopulation challenge?

5 Law and Order, Protest and Violence, Roman Style

We have heard much of the protest and violence in America and little of
the protest and violence in ancient Rome. But Rome's problems were in
many ways similar to our own. Both republics offered hope for liberty and
justice for all; both even offered hope for political and economic equality,
so far as humanly possible. Rome's Republic, 509–27 B.C., failed to
live up to its promises. America, despite its problems, still offers hope for
all mankind, for there is the hope that America, with its many races,
religions, and nationalities, can demonstrate to a divided world
that peoples of diverse backgrounds can live in relative harmony with
progress toward liberty and justice for all. This is the promise of America.
Some myths, canons, and hangups will be factors in determining
the answer to the promise.

With Liberty and Justice for Some

Frederick Gentles

There were fires in the sky . . . there was a violent earthquake
and a cow talked—there was a rumor that a cow talked the
previous year, but nobody believed it: this year they did. Nor
was that all: it rained lumps of meat. Thousands of birds (we
are told) seized and devoured the pieces in mid-air, while what
fell to the ground lay scattered about for several days without
going putrid. The Sybilline Books were consulted by two officials, who found in them the prediction that danger threatened
from a "concourse of alien men," who might attack "the high
places of the City, with the shedding of blood." There was also
found, amongst other things, a warning to avoid factious politics. This annoyed the tribunes, who swore the prophecies were
a fake, deliberately invented to stop the passage of the proposed
law. A dangerous clash was imminent, and only avoided by—
would you believe it?—a report from the Hernici that the
Volscians and the Aequians, in spite of their recent losses, were
on the warpath again. The old cycle was being repeated.[1]

The year was just the other side of 450 B.C. and the place was
Rome, where the Establishment, represented by the Patricians, was
being challenged—challenged by the Plebeians, whose tribunes were
demanding changes. According to the Roman historian Livy, the
tribunes of the Plebeians had suggested that the laws be codified to
curb the powers of tyrannical consuls. The suggestion was really a
demand, and the Patricians were so disturbed at this threat to their
power that they declared war on the nearby tribes to distract the
people from domestic troubles. The Plebeians rioted. They actually

protested the war—a war, they said, that was not necessary. As violence took hold in the Forum and on the streets, uncompromising partisans arose on both sides. One young conservative, the champion of the Patrician cause, hounded the tribunes out of the Forum and scattered the mob by threats and beatings. An equally uncompromising liberal tribune brought this young nobleman to trial for intemperate, lawless, and violent acts, and thereby succeeded in paving the way for the passage of the famous Twelve Tables, Rome's first written law.

This is the story of the Roman Republic. It is the story of the haves being challenged with protest and violence by the have-nots. It is a story remarkably like that of nineteenth and twentieth-century Europe and America, where laboring men, farmers, immigrants, and women struggled for political and economic rights against those with business and property interests. In Rome and America an establishment class creates the myths, and makes the canons—or laws—which become settled in the minds of many as the way of life. But the Roman and American establishments were unique. They were usually willing to compromise, especially if there were threats to the general welfare.

The willingness of conservative and liberal factions to compromise their differences in a republican form of government breathed life into both Roman and Western civilizations for many generations. The American Republic, not yet two hundred years old, is one of the oldest in the Western world, and, except for four years of the Civil War, change has been made within the framework of constitutional government. The Roman Republic, 509–27 B.C., lived nearly four hundred years before crumbling into civil strife, civil war, and Julius Caesar. This is not to say, however, that during that four centuries of prevailing law and order there was peace and harmony in the Roman world. The evolution of liberty and justice for all was often mutated by protest, agitation, and even violence.

After their success in codifying the law, the Plebeians next agitated for the right to intermarry with the Patrician class. Livy tells of the bitterness of the common people and of the violence of the Establishment. The tribune Canuleius, addressing the Assembly of citizens, declared:

> Men of Rome, the violence with which the Senate has been opposing our programme of reform has made me realize more vividly than ever before the depth of the contempt in which you are held by the aristocracy. I have often suspected it, but now I know; they think you are unworthy of living with them

within the walls of the same town. Yet what is the object of our proposals? It is merely to point out that we are their fellow-citizens—that we have the same country as they, even though we have less money. We seek the right of intermarriage, a right commonly granted to other nations on our borders—indeed, before now Rome has granted citizenship, which is more than intermarriage, even to a defeated enemy. We propose that a man of the people may have the right to be elected to the consulship: is that the same as saying some rogue who was, or is, a slave? Such is their contempt for you that they would rob you, if they could, of the very light you see by; they grudge you the air you breathe, the words you speak, the very fact that you have the shape of men.[2]

Indeed, the Romans too had their ghettos, their upper-crust society with uncontaminated blood living in uncontaminated neighborhoods, and violent methods to keep people in their place.

But the Plebs persisted. Canuleius continued:

One could hardly offer a more signal insult to one section of the community than to consider it unfit to marry with, as if it were too dirty to touch: it is like condemning it to exile and banishment within the city walls. They take every precaution against the dreadful risk of becoming related by blood to us poor scum. We expect to gain nothing from marrying into your class except to be considered as human beings and citizens of Rome; and your opposition is wholly unreasonable—unless you take pleasure merely in humiliating and insulting us.[3]

Any parallels in twentieth-century Europe and America?

But the Plebs continued their fight to become part of the Haves. One exasperated Patrician consul finally called a meeting to protest to the people their constant demands. His heart-rending appeal is an exhibit of sheer frustration over the continuing ferment. He emphasizes the extreme flexibility and generosity of the conservatives in granting one reform after another, though he does admit, indirectly, that the lower class does not have full civil liberty:

The truth is that our communal life is poisoned by political discord and party strife, and it was that which raised his [the enemy] hopes of destroying us, seeing as he did, your lust for liberty in perpetual conflict with our lust for power, and each party's loathing of the representative magistracies of the other. What, in God's name, do you want now? Once it was tribunes, and to preserve the peace we let you have them; then it was *decemvirs,* and we permitted their appointment. Soon you were

sick of them; we forced them to resign. . . . Again you wanted
tribunes—and got them. . . . You have your tribunes to protect you, your right of appeal to the people, your popular decrees
made binding on the Senate, while in the empty name of justice
all our privileges are trampled under foot: all this we have borne,
and are still bearing. How is it all to end? Will the time ever
come when we can have a united city, a united country? You
have beaten us, and we accept our defeat with more equanimity
than you your victory.[4]

The consul seems to be asking, what more do you Plebeians want,
blood? And that was it. The Plebs wanted blood, and they eventually
got the right to intermarry into Patrician families.

In forcing the Patricians to share their power, the Plebs at one
time threatened to bring the economy to a halt by walking out of
the city and letting the Patricians do the dirty work; this early
example of the general strike was effective, though the Plebs resorted
to such extreme measures only on occasion. The Plebeians continued
to gain more rights as the Republic continued on down through the
years, because the system was flexible enough. But at last a new aristocracy of leading Patrician and Plebeian families came to rule Rome,
and the earlier promise of the Republic to provide a legislature responsive to the needs of the people gave way to the tyranny of the
new elite and a legislature and executive responsive to its special
needs. There was to be liberty and justice only for those who had
made it, not for all.

Two major factors that led to the tragedy of the Roman Republic
were the acquisition of an empire, starting with the Punic wars, and
the creation of a military-commercial complex, which resulted from
conquest and trade. The idea of a federal republic, which at its beginnings gave citizens of the Italian states rights equal to or nearly
equal to the rights of the citizens of Rome, was not extended to the
Greek, Spanish, and African colonies the Republic had taken. Rather,
the colonies were treated as sources of loot, slaves, and tribute by
the proconsuls and by the carpetbaggers who followed them south—
and east and west. The colonies were exploited, as colonies were to
be exploited on into the twentieth century. The wealth and slaves
flowing back to Rome on all the roads leading to that great city
undermined the morals and the simple life-style of a predominantly
agricultural community. Old ways were changed as farming became
commercial and absentee landlords bought up huge estates to be
worked by slaves. Leases on the public lands were acquired by the
wealthy. The small farmer was frequently in trouble with Rome's

stringent debtor laws passed by the Establishment and finally he found himself in Rome to compete with other farmers and the multiplying slave population for jobs. He became one of the motley mob of the idle, the hungry, the illiterate, and the unwashed. As part of the mob, he became fair game for ambitious politicians and military men who needed popular support as consuls and generals.

As wealthy Patrician and Plebeian families turned to commerce, and as a new middle class of prosperous businessmen, contractors, bankers, and government bureaucrats rose to political influence, great tenement blocks were constructed to house the poor in ghettos described by one historian as no better than rabbit warrens. The rich became richer, the poor became poorer, and urban conditions deteriorated to a point that threatened all, though not all could see the threat. However, Tiberius Gracchus, tribune for the year 133 B.C., saw the need for resettling the surplus population on the land. He proposed that leases on the public lands be limited in size and that the landless be given government subsidies to start private enterprises. This was a program of poor-relief, and, as usual, there was opposition from the wealthy, especially from those who had leases on thousands of acres of the public lands that had been acquired as Rome conquered Italy.

Tiberius pushed his law through despite political maneuvers by the Senate, and he appointed a land commission composed of himself, his brother, and his father-in-law to carry out the reform. However, when he ran for an unprecedented second term as tribune to carry out this and other reforms, the conservative extremists took the law into their own hands, gathered a force, and made for the Forum, where some three hundred fell, including Tiberius, who was clubbed to death with a footstool. This date, 133 B.C., is taken as the beginning of the breakdown of law and order in the Republic: compromise and reform gave way to a century of bloody battles between gangs of liberal and conservative hoodlums and, finally, to civil war and dictatorship.

Ten years later, the brother of Tiberius, Gaius Gracchus, became tribune and introduced a new deal that provided for resumption of the land commission, a dole of wheat to every resident citizen who applied in person, road and bridge building for commercial purposes, and the settlement of the surplus population in colonies favorably placed for trade. Gracchus planned to reform the government entirely by taking ultimate power from the Senate and giving it to the tribunes, who would have sole executive power, and to the Assembly of people. But when he planned to extend Roman citizenship with its many fringe benefits to several other Italian communities, the mob, upon whom he depended for votes in the Assembly, reacted against this measure that would have brought greater peace and unity to Italy. Romans were jealous of their material privileges as citizens, and they were not about to share the wheat dole, the special accommodation at spectacles, and the bribes they received for votes at election time. There was a backlash, a Roman citizens' backlash. The Senate feared Gracchus, too, and declared a state of emergency when mobs gathered. In the melee, Gracchus, surrounded by his enemies, had his slave run him through. People in the streets had seen him running from his pursuers but did nothing to help him—they did not want to get involved. His head was cut off and taken to the consul Opimius, who then ordered the slaying of three thousand of Gaius' followers without trial.

The next hundred years were the years of the professional soldier, although the Republic continued on in name. With the acquisition of empire and the commercial spirit, Rome was unable to keep the military subordinate to civilian control. The consul as chief executive was also a general. Marius, Sulla, Pompey, Caesar, Crassus, Antony, and Augustus were generals who dominated the political scene after the time of the Gracchi. They were all connected, directly and indirectly, with banking, commercial, and huge property interests. And it is fatal for a country with democratic aspirations to place its military men in a position to exercise primary political power. The army is not a democratic institution, and generals, when given political power, are inclined to direct civilians as they direct soldiers— which means giving orders and no back-talk allowed.

The historian Sallust, who lived during these shaky times, says that Marius was consumed by ambition to become consul and was qualified in every way except by his red blood and his country-style grammar. He curried the favor of the people, however, won success as a general against Jugurtha in Africa, and through sheer doggedness was elected consul an unprecedented six times between 107 and 100 B.C. By recruiting soldiers from the common people of Rome, Marius made them more loyal to him than to Rome. (Some twenty-one centuries later, Mussolini and Hitler made new use of this old idea.) Democracy was as good as dead when left to generals of the army such as Sulla, Marius, and their successors. The first century before Christ was a witches' Sabbath of rival military and commercial factions conspiring and murdering for political control of the wealthy city, its Italian colonies, and its Mediterranean empire. The people were pawns in the struggle, used by politician-generals to further their selfish ambitions. (The idea of a military state is well known to people living in twentieth-century Czechoslovakia, Russia, Spain, Greece, Paraguay, Portugal, to mention only a few.)

Tacitus, another historian, who lived a century after Sallust, blamed the decline and fall of the Republic on man's love of wealth and power, and he found this behavior instinctive in all men:

> From time immemorial, man has had an instinctive love of power. With the growth of our empire, this instinct has become a dominant and uncontrollable force. It was easy to maintain equality when Rome was weak. World-wide conquest and the destruction of all rival communities or potentates opened the way to the secure enjoyment of wealth and an overriding appetite for it. This was how the smouldering rivalry between senate and people was first fanned into a blaze. Unruly tribunes alternated with powerful consuls. Rome and the Roman forum had a foretaste of what civil war means. Then Gaius Marius, whose origin was of the humblest, and Lucius Sulla, who outdid his fellow nobles in ruthlessness, destroyed the republican constitution by force of arms. In its place they put despotism. After them came Gnaeus Pompey, who, though more secretive, was not better, and from then on the one and only aim was autocracy. Roman legions did not shrink from civil war at Pharsalia or Philippi. . . .[5]

Did Tacitus have the clue to the causes of man's problems down through the ages? Or is his observation too simple? He called the age degenerate.

Janus (now January), was an ancient Italian deity who presided over doors and gates and over beginnings and endings and was usually represented with two faces turned in opposite directions. Closed doors symbolized peace. Open doors symbolized war.

But the gates of the temple of Janus were closed for the first time in two hundred years in January of 29 B.C. This meant the end of civil strife and foreign war and a time of universal peace. The gates were not to be opened again for two hundred years, when the *Pax Romana* came to an end and Rome once again, this time the Empire, started on a long period of decline and decay.

Rome fell; will we?

In Rome, as in America, there was excessive spending on the military establishment. There was the philosophy among many of eat, drink, and be merry for tomorrow we die. Rome became, at least in part, a hedonistic society. Law and order broke down and violence took over as the selfish undermined both government and culture. The quality of life deteriorated, and one can only guess what the violence and trivia might have been had the Romans invented TV. President Nixon is concerned with the quality of life in America. What is quality?

Dante pointed out that Augustus Caesar and Jesus Christ were contemporaries. Both were princes of peace, one for the universal state and the other for the universal brotherhood of man. Neither prevailed. Christ did not even prevail among Christians, in Ireland or in many other places in the Christian world. Tacitus suggests the fault is in the instinctive behavior of man; Ashley Montagu would disagree, believing man to be a product of his environment, conditioned to behave in certain ways. Based on what you have read in this essay, with which man do you agree?

Notes

1 Livy, *The Early History of Rome*, translated by Aubrey de Selincourt (London: Penguin, 1960), p. 178.

2 *Ibid.*, pp. 255–256.

3 *Ibid.*, p. 258.

4 *Ibid.*, p. 243.

5 Tacitus, *The Histories*, translated by Kenneth Wellesley (London: Penguin, 1964), pp. 103–104.

The Roman upperclass was hung-up on the fear of their pure and superior blood being contaminated by lower-class blood. The myth was not a new one, for the Egyptians and Mesopotamians of a much earlier day had their lines of "pure" blood also. This myth was not to die but rather to continue into Europe and the two Americas, where Hitler, the Spanish aristocrats in the new world, and the KKK, along with many other groups, seized on to the idea of racial supremacy. In the selection that follows, the Tribune Canuleius protests vigorously the discrimination against common citizens and makes a strong case for an integrated society with liberty and justice for all. Livy, a contemporary of Augustus and of Christ, lived from 59 B.C. to 17 A.D. The reading is from his Book Four, "War and Politics."

The Civil Rights Problem, 450 B.C.

Livy

The next consuls were Marcus Genucius and Caius Curtius. War and political dissension made the year a difficult one. Hardly had it begun, when the tribune Canuleius introduced a bill for legalizing intermarriage between the nobility and the commons. The senatorial party objected strongly on the grounds not only that the patrician blood would thereby be contaminated but also that the hereditary rights and privileges of the *gentes,* or families, would be lost. Further, a suggestion, at first cautiously advanced by the tribunes, that a law should be passed enabling one of the two consuls to be a plebeian, subsequently hardened into the promulgation, by nine tribunes, of a bill by which the people should be empowered to elect to the consulship such men as they thought fit, from either of the two parties. The senatorial party felt that if such a bill were to become law, it would mean not only that the highest office of state would have to be shared with the dregs of society but that it would, in effect, be lost to the nobility and transferred to the commons. It was with great satisfaction, therefore, that the Senate received a report, first that Ardea had thrown off her allegiance to Rome in resentment at the crooked practice which had deprived her of her territory; secondly, that troops from Veii had raided the Roman frontier, and, thirdly, that the Volscians and Aequians were showing uneasiness at the fortification of Verrugo. In the circumstances it was good news, for the nobility could look forward even to an unsuccessful war with greater complacency than to an ignominious peace. Accordingly they made the most of the situation; the Senate ordered an immediate raising of troops and a general

From *The Early History of Rome* by Livy, translated by Aubrey de Selincourt (London: Penguin, 1960), pp. 253–256, 258–259.

mobilization on the largest possible scale and with even greater urgency than in the previous year, in the hope that the revolutionary proposals which the tribunes were bringing forward might be forgotten in the bustle and excitement of three imminent campaigns. Canuleius replied with a brief but forceful statement in the Senate to the effect that it was useless for the consuls to try to scare the commons from taking an interest in the new proposals, and, declaring that they should never, while he lived, hold a levy until the commons had voted on the reforms which he and his colleagues had introduced, immediately convened an assembly. The battle was on: the consuls and the Senate on the one side, Canuleius and the populace on the other, were in the full flood of mutual recriminations. The consuls swore that the lunatic excesses of the tribunes were past endurance, that it was the end of all things, that war was being deliberately provoked far more deadly than any with a foreign enemy. "The present situation," they said, "is not, we admit, the fault of one party only: the senate is not less guilty than the people, or the consuls than the tribunes. In all communities the qualities or tendencies which carry the highest reward are bound to be most in evidence and to be most industriously cultivated—indeed it is precisely that which produces good statesmen and good soldiers; unhappily here in Rome the greatest rewards come from political upheavals and revolt against the government, which have always, in consequence, won applause from all and sundry. Only recall the aura of majesty which surrounded the Senate in our father's day, and then think what it will be like when we bequeath it to our children! Think how the laboring class will be able to brag of the increase in its power and influence! There can never be an end to this unhappy process so long as the promoters of sedition against the government are honored in proportion to their success. Do you realize, gentlemen, the appalling consequences of what Canuleius is trying to do? If he succeeds, bent, as he is, upon leaving nothing in its original soundness and purity, he will contaminate the blood of our ancient and noble families and make chaos of the hereditary patrician privilege of taking the auspices to determine, in the public or private interest, what Heaven may will—and with what result? that, when all distinctions are obliterated, no one will know who he is or where he came from! Mixed-marriages forsooth! What do they mean but that men and women from all ranks of society will be permitted to start copulating like animals? A child of such intercourse will never know what blood runs in his veins or what form of worship he is entitled to practice; he will be nothing—or six of one and half a dozen of the other, a very monster!

"But even this is not enough: having made hay of the dictates of religion and the traditions of our country, these revolutionary fire-eaters are now out for the consulship. They began merely by suggesting that one of the two consuls might be a plebeian, but now they have brought in a bill which would enable the people to elect consuls as it pleased, from either party—plebeian or patrician. And whom are they likely to elect? Obviously, men of their own class, and the most turbulent demagogues at that. We shall have men like Canuleius and Icilius in the highest office of state. God forbid that an office invested with an almost kingly majesty should fall so low! We should rather die a thousand times than allow such a shameful thing to happen. We are very sure that our forefathers too, had they guessed that by wholesale concessions they would exacerbate, rather than appease, the hostility of the commons and lead them to make further demands each more exaggerated than the last, would have faced at the outset any struggle, however fierce and embittered, rather than permit such laws to be imposed upon them. The concession in the matter of tribunes only led to another, and so it goes on. It is impossible to have tribunes side by side with a governing class in the same community; either the nobility or the tribunate must go. Now—better late than never—we must make a firm stand against their reckless and unprincipled conduct. Are we to take no action when they first deliberately embroil us, thus inviting a foreign invasion, and then prevent us from arming for defense against the danger for which they were themselves responsible? Or when, having more or less invited an enemy to attack us, they refuse to allow us to raise troops—nay, worse, when Canuleius has the audacity to declare in the Senate that unless the members of the House permit his proposals to be accepted as law, as if he were a conquering hero, he will rescind the order for mobilization? What is such a statement but a threat to betray his country, to submit passively to the storming and capture of Rome? It is indeed a timely word of encouragement to the Volscians, to the Aequians, to the men of Veii— but hardly to the common people of Rome. The enemy may well be confident in their ability to climb, with Canuleius in command, to the Citadel on the heights of the Capitol! Gentlemen, unless the tribunes, when they robbed you of your dignity and privileges, robbed you of your courage too, we are ready to put first things first: we will lead you against criminal citizens of Rome before we lead you against an enemy in arms."

While opinions of this sort were being vented in the Senate, Canuleius was defending his proposed reforms and attacking the consuls elsewhere. "Men of Rome," he said, "the violence with which the

Senate has been opposing our program of reform has made me realize more vividly than ever before the depth of the contempt in which you are held by the aristocracy. I have often suspected it, but now I know: they think you are unworthy of living with them within the walls of the same town. Yet what is the object of our proposals? It is merely to point out that we are their fellow-citizens—that we have the same country as they, even though we have less money. We seek the right of intermarriage, a right commonly granted to other nations on our borders—indeed, before now Rome has granted citizenship, which is more than intermarriage, even to a defeated enemy. By our other proposal we intend no innovation, but merely seek the recovery and enjoyment of the popular right to elect whom we will to positions of authority. What is there in this to make them think that chaos is come again? Is this enough to justify what came near to being a personal assault upon me in the Senate, or their threat to use violence against the sacrosanct office of the tribunes? If the people of Rome are allowed to vote freely for the election to the consulship of whom they please—if even a man of their own class, provided that he is worthy of it, may hope to rise to this high honor—does that mean that our country's stability and power are necessarily done for? We propose that a man of the people may have the right to be elected to the consulship: is that the same as saying some rogue who was, or is, a slave? Such is their contempt for you that they would rob you, if they could, of the very light you see by; they grudge you the air you breathe, the words you speak, the very fact that you have the shape of men. They declare—if I may say so without irreverence—that a plebeian consul would be a sin in the sight of heaven. . . .

" . . . One could hardly offer a more signal insult to one section of the community than to consider it unfit to marry with, as if it were too dirty to touch: it is like condemning it to exile and banishment within the city walls. They take every precaution against the dreadful risk of becoming related by blood to us poor scum. Come, come, my noble lords—if such a connection is a blot on your fine escutcheon—though I would mention that many of you were originally Albans or Sabines, not of noble birth at all, and got your present rank as a reward for services either at the hands of the kings or, later, of the people—could you not keep your precious blood pure simply by determining, on your own initiative, not to marry plebeian wives and not to let your sisters and daughters marry out of the patricate? No patrician girl need, I assure you, fear for her virtue so far as any of us are concerned: rape is a patrician habit. No one would have forced a marriage contract upon an unwilling party—but to set up a legal ban upon the right of intermarriage, *that,* I repeat, is the final insult to the commons. Why not go further and propose a ban on marriages between rich and poor? Marriages have always been a matter of private arrangement between families, and now you propose to subject them to the restraint of a law which is the very reflection of your own arrogant conceit, for the purpose, I presume, of splitting society in two and of turning united Rome into two separate communities. I wonder you do not pass a law to stop a plebeian living next door to a nobleman, or walking in the same street, or going to the same party, or standing by his side in the Forum. What difference does it make if a patrician marries a plebeian wife, or a plebeian a patrician one? There is no loss of privilege whatever, as children admittedly take the rank of the father; we expect to gain nothing from marrying into your class except to be considered as human beings and citizens of Rome; and your opposition is wholly unreasonable—unless you take pleasure merely in humiliating and insulting us.

"Finally tell me this: does the ultimate power in the state belong to you or to the Roman people? When we finished with the monarchy, was it to put supreme authority into your hands or to bring political liberty to all alike? Have the people, or have they not, the right to enact a law, if such is their will? Or are you to quash every proposal of ours by proclaiming a levy of troops immediately it is brought up, and as soon as I, in my capacity as tribune, begin to call upon the tribes to vote, is the consul to reply by administering the military oath and ordering mobilization, with threats against me and my office and the commons in general? Do not forget that twice already you have learned by experience the value of your threats in face of our united resolution—do you wish to pretend that on those occasions you abstained from actual physical conflict purely out of tender feelings toward us? or was the reason, perhaps that the stronger party happened to be the one to exercise restraint?"

Sallust (86–35 B.C.) became a tribune of the Plebeians in 52 B.C.,
after serving Caesar as an officer in the campaigns of the Civil War.
His histories of the Jugurthine War and the Catiline Conspiracy show his
bias against the arrogance of the Roman aristocracy. In this preface
to his "Catiline," he relates the sordid side of Roman politics and gives
several reasons for the decline and fall of the Republic.

Growing Love of Money and Lust for Power

Sallust

Every man who wishes to rise superior to the lower animals should
strive his hardest to avoid living all his days in silent obscurity, like
the beasts of the field, creatures which go with their faces to the
ground and are the slaves of their bellies. We human beings have
mental as well as physical powers; the mind, which we share with
gods, is the ruling element in us, while the chief function of the
body, which we have in common with the beasts, is to obey. Surely,
therefore, it is our intellectual rather than our physical powers that
we should use in the pursuit of fame. Since only a short span of life
has been vouchsafed us, we must make ourselves remembered as
long as may be by those who come after us. Wealth and beauty can
give only a fleeting and perishable fame, but intellectual excellence
is a glorious and everlasting possession.

Yet it was long a subject of hot dispute among men whether physical strength or mental ability was the more important requirement
for success in war. Before you start on anything, you must plan; when
you have made your plans, prompt action is needed. Thus neither
is sufficient without the aid of the other.

Accordingly the world's first rulers, who were called kings, adopted
one or other of two different policies, seeking either to make the
most of their intellectual endowment or to develop their bodily
strength. In those days men had not yet learnt to be covetous: each
was content with what he had. It was only when Cyrus[1] in Asia and
the Spartans and Athenians in Greece began to bring cities and nations into subjection, and to engage in wars because they thirsted for
power and thought their glory was to be measured by the extent of
their dominions, that the test of experience decided the ancient controversy: brains were shown to be more important than brawn. It is
a pity that kings and rulers do not apply their mental powers as

From *The Conspiracy of Catiline by Sallust,* translated by S. A. Hanford
(London: Penguin, 1963), pp. 175–179, 181–183.

effectively to the preservation of peace as to the prosecution of war. If they did, human life would be less chequered and unstable than it is: we should not see everything drifting to and fro in change and confusion. Sovereignty can easily be maintained by the same qualities as enable a man to acquire it. But when idleness replaces industry, when self-restraint and justice give place to lust and arrogance, the moral deterioration brings loss of station in its train. A degenerate ruler is always supplanted by a better man than himself.

Success in agriculture, seafaring, or building always depends on human excellence. But many are the men who, slaves of gluttony and sloth, have gone through life ignorant and uncivilized, as if they were mere sojourners in a foreign land, reversing, surely, the order of nature by treating their bodies as means of gratification and their souls as mere encumbrances. It makes no odds, to my mind, whether such men live or die; alive or dead, no one ever hears of them. The truth is that no man really lives or gets any satisfaction out of life, unless he devotes all his energies to some task and seeks fame by some notable achievement or by the cultivation of some admirable gift.

The field is wide, and men follow their natural bent in choosing this path or that. It is noble to serve the state by action, and even to use a gift of eloquence on its behalf is no mean thing. Peace, no less than war, offers men a chance of fame: they can win praise by describing exploits as well as by achieving them. And although the narrator earns much less renown than the doer, the writing of history is, in my opinion, a peculiarly difficult task. You must work hard to find words worthy of your subject. And if you censure misdeeds, most people will accuse you of envy and malice. When you write of the outstanding merit and glory of good men, people are quite ready to accept what they think they could easily do themselves; but anything beyond that is dismissed as an improbable fiction.

My earliest inclinations led me, like many other young men, to throw myself wholeheartedly into politics. There I found many things against me. Self-restraint, integrity, and virtue were disregarded; unscrupulous conduct, bribery, and profit-seeking were rife. And although, being a stranger to the vices that I saw practiced on every hand, I looked on them with scorn, I was led astray by ambition and, with a young man's weakness, could not tear myself away. However much I tried to dissociate myself from the prevailing corruption, my craving for advancement exposed me to the same odium and slander as all my rivals.

After suffering manifold perils and hardships, peace of mind at last returned to me, and I decided that I must bid farewell to politics for good. But I had no intention of wasting my precious leisure in idleness and sloth, or of devoting my time to agriculture or hunting—tasks fit only for slaves. I had formerly been interested in history, and some work which I began in that field had been interrupted by my misguided political ambitions. I therefore took this up again, and decided to write accounts of some episodes in Roman history that seemed particularly worthy of record—a task for which I felt myself the better qualified inasmuch as I was unprejudiced by the hopes and fears of the party man.

It is my intention to give a brief account, as accurate as I can make it, of the conspiracy of Catiline, a criminal enterprise which I consider specially memorable as being unprecedented in itself and fraught with unprecedented dangers to Rome. I must preface my narrative by a short description of Catiline's character.

Lucius Catiline was of noble birth. He had a powerful intellect and great physical strength, but a vicious and depraved nature. From his youth he had delighted in civil war, bloodshed, robbery, and political strife, and it was in such occupations that he spent his early manhood. He could endure hunger, cold, and want of sleep to an incredible extent. His mind was daring, crafty, and versatile, capable of any pretense and dissimulation. A man of flaming passions, he was as covetous of other men's possessions as he was prodigal of his own; an eloquent speaker, but lacking in wisdom. His monstrous ambition hankered continually after things extravagant, impossible, beyond his reach. After the dictatorship of Lucius Sulla, Catiline had been possessed by an overmastering desire for despotic power, to gratify which he was prepared to use any and every means. His headstrong spirit was tormented more and more every day by poverty and a guilty conscience, both of which were aggravated by the evil practices I have referred to. He was incited also by the corruption of a society plagued by two opposite but equally disastrous vices—love of luxury and love of money.

Since I have had occasion to mention public morality, it seems appropriate to go back further and briefly describe the principles by which our ancestors guided their conduct in peace and war, their method of governing the state which they made so great before bequeathing it to their successors, and the gradual degeneration of its noble character into vice and corruption.

The city of Rome, as far as I can make out, was founded and first inhabited by Trojan exiles who, led by Aeneas, were wandering without a settled home, and by rustic natives who lived in a state of anarchy uncontrolled by laws or government. When once they had come to live together in a walled town, despite different origins, languages, and habits of life, they coalesced with amazing ease, and before long what had been a heterogeneous mob of migrants was welded into a united nation.

When, however, with the growth of their population, civilization, and territory, it was seen that they had become powerful and prosperous, they had the same experience as most people have who are possessors of this world's goods: their wealth aroused envy. Neighboring kings and peoples attacked them, and but few of their friends aided them; the rest were scared at the prospect of danger and held aloof. The Romans, however, were alert both at home and abroad. They girded themselves in haste and with mutual encouragement marched forth to meet their foes, protecting by force of arms their liberty, country, and parents. Then, after bravely warding off the dangers that beset them, they lent aid to their allies and friends, and made new friends by a greater readiness to render services than to accept help from others. . . .

Thus by hard work and just dealing the power of the state increased. Mighty kings were vanquished, savage tribes and huge nations were brought to their knees; and when Carthage, Rome's rival in her quest for empire, had been annihilated,[2] every land and sea lay open to her. It was then that fortune turned unkind and confounded all her enterprises. To the men who had so easily endured toil and peril, anxiety and adversity, the leisure and riches which are generally regarded as so desirable proved a burden and a curse. Growing love of money, and the lust for power which followed it, engendered every kind of evil. Avarice destroyed honor, integrity, and every other virtue, and instead taught men to be proud and cruel, to neglect religion, and to hold nothing too sacred to sell. Ambition tempted many to be false, to have one thought hidden in their hearts, another ready on their tongues, to become a man's friend or enemy not because they judged him worthy or unworthy but because they thought it would pay them, and to put on the semblance of virtues that they had not. At first these vices grew slowly and sometimes met with punishment; later on, when disease had spread like a plague, Rome changed: her government, once so just and admirable, became harsh and unendurable. . . .

As soon as wealth came to be a mark of distinction and an easy way to renown, military commands, and political power, virtue began to decline. Poverty was now looked on as a disgrace and a blameless life as a sign of ill nature. Riches made the younger generation a prey to luxury, avarice, and pride. Squandering with one hand what they grabbed with the other, they set small value on their own property while they coveted that of others. Honor and modesty, all laws divine and human, were alike disregarded in a spirit of recklessness and intemperance. To one familiar with mansions and villas reared aloft on such a scale that they look like so many towns, it is instructive to visit the temples built by our godfearing ancestors. In those days piety was the ornament of shrines; glory, of men's dwellings. When they conquered a foe, they took nothing from him save his power to harm. But their base successors stuck at no crime to rob subject peoples of all that those brave conquerors had left them, as though oppression were the only possible method of ruling an empire. I need not remind you of some enterprises that no one but an eyewitness will believe —how private citizens have often levelled mountains and paved seas for their building operations. Such men, it seems to me, have treated their wealth as a mere plaything: instead of making honorable use of it, they have shamefully misused it on the first wasteful project that occurred to them. Equally strong was their passion for fornication, guzzling, and other forms of sensuality. Men prostituted themselves like women, and women sold their chastity to every comer. To please their palates they ransacked land and sea. They went to bed before they needed sleep, and instead of waiting until they felt hungry, thirsty, cold, or tired, they forestalled their bodies' needs by self-indulgence. Such practices incited young men who had run through their property to have recourse to crime. Because their vicious natures found it hard to forgo sensual pleasures, they resorted more and more recklessly to every means of getting and spending.

Notes

1 King of Persia 559–529 B.C.
2 In 146 B.C.

Professor Durant and his wife, Ariel, are authors and co-authors of many books on Western civilization and philosophy. In this selection, written in 1969, Durant speaks of causes once sponsored by Canuleius and the Gracchi and now sponsored by many of the youth around the world. He has seen many gains for liberty and equality in his life, and he holds out hope for continued gains in our American republic. Law, order, and protest are important in a democratic society. Is violence civilized?

Continue Dissent but Stay Civilized

Will Durant

It is good that the young should rebel and the old should resist; it is essential that minorities shall be heard; and one of the admirable aspects of the contemporary scene is the patient maintenance of free speech and minority rights by democracies tempted to answer force with superforce, joining in the martial march of authoritarian governments.

But the time has come for old and young to realize that civilization is endangered in its very foundations, that the social order that tamed us from savages into citizens is weakened in all it supports, and that the fruits of democratic progress may in a generation be lost in a contest between permissive anarchy and a police state.

What can we oldsters do about it? We can listen to the cries of the disadvantaged and dispossessed, and open the ways to controlled experiment with new ideas. We can check our racial antipathies by realizing that whichever side wins in a violent clash of races or classes democracy, humanity and security will disappear.

We can try to cleanse the avenues and halls of politics so that one need not be a millionaire to be eligible for the Presidency. We can join the young in restraining our government from undertaking to police the world instead of bringing hope and health to the poor.

If we can check our rush into imperialism we have the resources to educate every American for profitable employment even in our ever more automated and computerized society. We have been clever and generous enough to spread the benefits of our inventiveness, enterprise and skill to 80% of our people—the greatest achievement in economic history; we are learning to let consumption keep up with production.

From "Continue Dissent but Stay Civilized" by Will Durant, Los Angeles Times, June 29, 1969. Copyright, Los Angeles Times. Reprinted with permission.

Two more generations, given enlightened leadership in government and industry, may reduce the impoverished 20% to 15%, to 10%, to 5%, to zero. That would be the fulfillment of Amos and Isaiah; it would be the resurrection of Christ.

And what can you privileged youngsters do? First, continue to study. It is not true that education will merely plunge you into a coarsening race for material rewards; it will enlarge your understanding and make you more patient with complex problems and the shortcomings of men.

Study the roots of our crime and corruption, our economic inequities and our political failures; see how strong those roots are in the processes of biology, in the nature of man and in the centuries of history.

Reconcile yourselves to modest and gradual improvements after your proposals have faced the necessary test of conservative resistance. Continue to express your dissent and your needs but remember to remain civilized for you will sorely miss civilization if it is sacrificed in the turbulence of change.

Beware of those who take their vocabularies from privies; they are trying to cover up their lack of confidence in their own manhood by leveling you with themselves. Wear your hair and your feet as you like, but keep them clean, and do not add to the pollution of the air.

Watch your sexual freedom that it should bring no hurt to others or yourself. Lasting affection—the most precious gift of life—is rarely won by hasty accommodation to irresponsible desire.

Do not let the pessimism of contemporary thought darken your spirits; this is the passing mood of a transitional age, when we have waged a shamefully barbarous war, when the blackest sins of our history demand atonement and when some of our fairest myths have faded and left a somber emptiness where once they chastened our conduct and warmed our hearts.

Do not yield to the mechanistic philosophy that grew from a physics long since rejected by physicists; man can make marvelous machines, but he is not a machine; let not the work of your hands conceal the miracle of your minds. Every one of you is a mystery of rational consciousness; every girl among you is a temple and glory of creative life.

Do not believe those dispirited spirits who call progress a delusion; progress is intermittent but it is real. A hundred advances that I pled for in my youth—like higher wages, more humane employment, governmental checks on private industry, the partial redistribution of wealth through the welfare state, the spread of comfort and leisure, the extension of education, the multiplication of colleges and universities, the freedom of speech, assemblage, and the press, the access of every American to the ballot, to public office, to the professions, to the Supreme Court—all these have become accepted parts of the American system since Ariel and I agitated for them in our political puberty.

If the founders of our republic could return from their graves they would marvel at our advances, and would brand our pessimists as ingrates whining because perfection has not been laid at their feet.

I believe that we shall solve, or dissolve, within the limits of our nature, one after another of the problems that harass us today. Already our government, through a maze of difficulties, is seeking to end a disastrous war.

Our ethnic minorities will enter in ever greater number into our high schools, colleges and universities; they will get the courses that their pride may claim, and those that their adjustment to technology requires; they will rise in industry, in the professions, in the arts and sciences and in public office; they will become established parts of the American scene as did our German-Americans, our Irish-Americans, our Italian-Americans, our Polish-Americans, our Jewish-Americans, even a French-Canadian-American like me.

And, like their predecessors, they will lower their birth rate as they raise their income; and the urban ghettos will relieve their pressure and their poverty by following a hundred outlets into American life. It will take more time and patience than before, but it will come, or America will lose its meaning in the history and aspirations of humanity.

Richard J. Krickus, who is of Lithuanian extraction, is a consultant to the Institute for Resources Management on a project funded by the Office of Economic Opportunity. In this selection, written in 1968, originally for the "Washington Post," he describes the ethnic Europeans in America who are recently elevated to middle-class status. They are fearful of the blacks, who have not yet been accepted into labor unions, motels, and restaurants, and into white-dominated society in general, as fully accredited Americans. Is it fair to suggest that the position is similar to that of the Romans in Gaius Gracchus' time who did not want the benefits of their citizenship shared with other Italians? Are there some parallels with the Patrician-Plebeian conflict described by Livy?

Ethnics: A View From the Storm Center

Richard J. Krickus

If the myriad problems that are tearing our society asunder are to be resolved, we must listen to the disillusioned lower-middle-class white worker who lives in the midst of our urban crisis.

The largest and most strategically located group of white workers in America is found in our industrial Midwestern and Northeastern cities. The most prominent segment of this group is some 40 million ethnics who include the foreign-born and the first-, second- and third-generation Americans of European ancestry.

Today the ethnics have largely eschewed Old World customs in favor of the mainstream culture, yet a distinct group outlook has evolved. Differences between Poles and Italians exist but their perceptions of crucial domestic and foreign issues are similar. For example, even though antiblack feeling may be stronger in Polish than in Italian communities, both tend to view the black revolution with more alarm than nonethnic Northern whites do. Support for U.S. involvement in Vietnam is also stronger among the ethnics than is true of the white population at large.

The "ethnic position" on these issues explains why the left, as a whole, views them as contemptible racists, Vietnam Hawks, and political enemies who are providing the right with widespread popular support. The ethnics' hostility toward black militants, student radicals and dissident intellectuals is grounded in economic, social and political insecurity.

This condition is exacerbated by their proximity to smoldering black ghettos and the fear that the radicals are bent upon destroying the very institutions that have provided the ethnics with a way out of poverty and into the middle class.

Student Radicals, Blacks Anger Blue-Collar Workers

The activities of student radicals and black militants, in particular, have angered blue-collar workers. The liberals' attempts to explain, and some cases apologize for, the excesses of radicals and militants have alienated them from the working class urban whites. The growing frustration, anger and alienation that exists in lower-income white communities represents an explosive political force.

As things stand now, the radical and liberal left are dreaming if they think they can exploit this political resource. Indeed, it is precisely because they have ignored the legitimate fears of the white worker that a right-wing counterreaction is gaining momentum in the United States.

Years of toil and cautious saving have permitted a growing number of ethnic workingmen to buy homes in the center city or in nearby suburbs. But high taxes, inflation, the threat of automation, a rising cost of living, installment buying, and varied needs of large families explain why they are not secure in their recently acquired affluence.

Although a majority of ethnics enjoy a higher standard of living than their parents, a significant number, especially the older ones, earn only a few thousand dollars above OEO poverty guidelines.

A large number who barely subsist are caught in a web of inner-city hopelessness like their black neighbors.

White Workers Excluded From Studies by Liberals

Liberal political leaders, scholars and professional analysts have excluded the white industrial worker from their agenda for social change. The blacks, Puerto Ricans and Mexican-Americans command their attention.

Because these groups suffer disproportionately from poverty, they, like all poor people, deserve priority attention. It is, nonetheless, a political and planning mistake to disregard the plight of the white blue-collar workers. Without their support, the left cannot hope to forge a meaningful multiracial, multiclass political alliance. Should the right mobilize the white workers, the prospects for a peaceful and just solution to our domestic ills appear grim.

Although most ethnics continue to vote for the Democratic Party, they have in recent years deserted the party in growing numbers for more conservative political organizations and candidates. However, they do not reject all facets of economic liberalism such as unemployment insurance, Social Security or Medicare.

Indeed, they generally support progressive bread-and-butter legislation that affects the welfare of the workingman. At the same time, their rising standard of living testifies to what they believe is the free enterprise system. Even though their newly obtained economic status is precarious, America has produced for them. Thus, industrial white workers are among the most zealous proponents of hard work, individualism and decentralized government.

It matters little to point out that the ethnics' perception of capitalism does not conform to reality or that their tendency to accept certain noncapitalistic principles while rejecting others is inconsistent. In their eyes, "capitalism" is responsible for their improved economic condition. In addition, the American economic and political systems are evaluated by them as a single entity. To castigate one is to downgrade the other.

Attacks against our institutions by student radicals and intellectuals are deemed absurd. Unlike middle-class youths and intellectuals, the ethnic laborer is not bored with affluence. Student rioting, moreover, infuriates him because he must make great sacrifices to give his children a college education that was denied him.

Assertions that workers are being exploited in America do not jibe with the ethnics' perception of the facts. This matter is important, for it explains in large part why the ethnics give little credence to the many charges that the radicals are making against American institutions.

Another element explains the ethnics' hostility to the "peace movement." Today, a disproportionate number of white soldiers comes from the ethnic community. Casualties caused by the Vietnam war, therefore, are keenly relevant to the machinist in Gary and the truck driver in Newark. They deem any tacit effort or overt pronouncement that supports the enemy or his cause as treasonous.

When the white resident of a lower-class urban community is depicted on television, he is often shown in one dimension. His crass racism and anti-intellectualism are emphasized while his thinking and motives are lightly dismissed or never confronted.

In this connection, the apparent growing political affluence of the black community has exacerbated the ethnics' fear that their political influence is on the decline. Their desire for easy answers to our domestic ills, their craving for guidance and new leadership, and not white racism per se, explains the appeal of George C. Wallace and other conservatives to the ethnics.

In marked contrast to the liberal academic intellectuals and student radicals, the ethnics have rejected the Kerner Commission report's charge that white racism was the root cause of the riots that have erupted in America's black ghettos since Watts in 1965. The ethnics expressed disbelief and outrage that the charge was leveled against them.

The average ethnic's answer to the charge of white racism may be summed up as follows:

"Listen, my grandfather was born in Europe where he lived like a slave. He was no better off there than the slaves in the United States. When he came to America he lived in an overcrowded slum. He was poor, as were most of his friends and family. He didn't finish high school and he couldn't get a white-collar job. But hell, his poverty didn't lead to crime; he didn't riot; he didn't demand handouts or threaten to destroy his neighborhood if he didn't get his way.

"Why should I feel guilty? I didn't have anything to do with bringing colored people to this country nor am I responsible for their problems today. If they would get a job, work hard, save their money, they, too, could solve their own problems."

Is this an exaggerated account of the ethnic's perception of the black revolution? I think not. Most ethnics do not feel guilty or responsible for the plight of the black man, and they do not believe that they are racists. On the contrary, there is a prevailing view among them that many blacks are. The racial epithets that black militants toss around on national TV reinforce the ethnic's charge.

Unlike the guilt-ridden white liberal who accepts these epithets without rancor, the ethnics, who feel guiltless, are naturally angered by such racial slurs as honkie.

If the ethnics underestimate the relationship between skin color and black poverty, white reformers are mistaken when they explain the ethnics' racial posture as merely prejudice. The ethnics have reason to fear the black revolution.

They live close to the blacks. They often compete with blacks for the same jobs. Their neighborhoods and work places are centers of racial tension.

The middle-class reformer occupies a secure place in the United States socially, politically and economically. His contact with the average ghetto black is marginal and his knowledge of the black revolution is intellectual, detached. He does not feel directly threatened by mounting black militancy.

This existential difference—that the reformer can view the black revolution as an observer or sympathetic ally while the ethnic in center city sees himself as a participant (or victim)—is a crucial distinction. The implications of this existential difference can be illuminated by considering the most controversial issue in America today—law and order.

The tendency on the part of the left to discount well-founded fear of street crime is a costly mistake. Everybody who lives in our industrial cities has good cause to be alarmed by urban crime. To play down street crime is to jeopardize legitimate radical demands for social change.

To understand the ethnics' view of crime as it pertains to the black revolution demands candor. To wit, there is ample data that demonstrates a higher incidence of crime among blacks than whites. Criminologists explain this by citing the correlation between poverty, social disorganization and institutionalized racism with black pathology.

The ethnics who live in the inner cities and read about black crime in their newspapers are incapable of viewing this data with the social scientists' detachment.

The rising tide of frustration and widespread alienation that exists in the ethnic communities has reached crisis proportions. The specter of white backlash that has haunted America for the last five years is now gaining momentum. Demagogs on the right and political opportunists are now harvesting the fruit that the radicals have sown.

On the basis of their numbers and location, the ethnics are destined to play a pivotal role in the elimination of racism in the United States and the restoration of our cities. To ignore them is to allow the forces of reaction to mobilize them and to exploit their power to preclude a peaceful and just solution to our nation's domestic problems.

Questions

1 What are some modern applications of Canuleius' speech about the Plebeians being considered scum of the earth?

2 Besides black and brown protest movements of the present, can you detail other protest movements in nineteenth- and twentieth-century Europe and America?

3 How do the reforms of the Gracchi compare with reforms bringing about the welfare state?

6 Spiritual Light From the East

We see ourselves through seeing others; it is a means of gaining perspective and understanding. By taking a brief look at Eastern civilization—best seen not through stories of rulers, dates, and events but through its philosophies and religions—we hope to gain new insights into our Western civilization. The myths, the canons, and the hangups are quite different from the West. It is the venerable Asia that down through the ages has advised law and order and the leading of the good and moral life. The Eastern philosophies have an important message for the West in today's hectic world. The message is peace and quiet. The message is love and understanding of life.

From Asia With Love

Frederick Gentles

> The student learns by daily increment.
> The Way is gained by daily loss,
> Loss upon loss until
> At last comes rest.
>
> By letting go, it all gets done;
> The world is won by those who let it go!
> But when you try and try,
> The world is then beyond the winning.*

You students of life and history, don't be blind! Find the way through the Tao; the Tao is the way. Learn and you cannot succeed; unlearn until you have emptied your heads of everything—then you have learned. Become a born loser, and after you have lost everything, you cannot lose. Then you will be a success.

Lao Tzu, a contemporary of Confucius, developed this philosophy of life—a philosophy that was to guide and influence the lives of millions of Chinese. One must be content with nothing. This is the Way. Only stupid men laugh at the Tao. If they did not laugh, it would not be the Tao.

The good ruler undoes everything, and then there will be nothing to do. Good. Discard profit and there will be no thieves. Nothing is preferable to Something. Desire only leads to trouble and failure. Get rid of Desire. This is the Way. This is the Tao, the uncarved block. But once you carve the block with writing, the block is no longer the

*From *The Way of Life*, Leo Te Ching, a new translation by R. B. Blakney. Copyright © 1955 by Raymond B. Blakney. By arrangement with The New American Library, Inc., New York.

Tao. Words only confuse; they do not convey one's thoughts accurately. Better to not say anything.

Every society has a particular world view, and Chinese cosmology, based on the *I Ching,* or *Book of Changes,* considers the universe as one great unified mechanism. Within this view, the Tao makes use of the ancient idea of Yin and Yang—the duality of life. Unity is represented by a circle that is divided in two by an S-line: one side of the circle is the Yin, the Female principle in the universe, representing the negative side of life—darkness (the dark earth), cold, weakness, evil, error; the other side of the circle is the Yang, the Male principle in the universe, representing the positive side of life—light (the red sun), warmth, strength, good, truth. The constant interaction between the Yin and the Yang produces universal or cosmic harmony. One complements the other, and, indeed, they may even transform into each other. Contrary to the belief of many people, the two sides are not mutually exclusive; that is, within the black Yin side is a red circle representing the Yang, and within the red Yang is a black circle representing the Yin. Thus there is no purity in life; there is no absolute. In weakness there is strength, and in strength there is weakness; in all evil there is good and in all good there is evil; in all truth there is error and in all error there is truth.

In life and in Oriental and Occidental history one finds duality, paradoxes, contradictions, call them what you will. Mao Tse-tung has an essay on contradiction in which he says that every society, every mode of thought has its own contradictions and quality. There is nothing that does not contain contradiction, he says. There would be no world without plus and minus factors in things and in each of us, contradictory factors. The law of the unity of opposites, as Mao terms the phenomenon in life, is basic to Marx's dialectical materialism of thesis, antithesis, synthesis, though he admits that tracing contradictions can get exceedingly complex. He admits contradictions in Chinese Communism, and he sees contradictions in American life. There are contradictions in the Christian Church, liberty, equality, war, peace, victory, and defeat. Mao's victory was a defeat. In victory there is defeat.

We have heard of Oriental despotism and tortures, the Black Hole of Calcutta, the Huns, Genghiz Khan, the Mongols, and to the Westerner these things conjure up images of a mysterious and dangerous East. And it is true that there have been great wars—civil, racial, and national—and cruelty and bloodshed in the East, very largely for the same reasons as in the West: that is, to gain power and wealth. Statistics for the number killed must run into the hundreds of millions for both civilizations, East and West, and a historian studying the enormous slaughter on the two sides of the planet would be hard put to determine which was the more bloodstained. E is E and W is W, and on this particular trait of killing their fellow man, the two meet.

But there has been love, a lot of it, in Oriental civilization. The emphasis is on love in Hindu, Buddhist, Confucianist, and Mohist (not Maoist) institutions, and, according to one historian of Far Eastern civilization, love has been practiced to a high degree among the faithful hundreds of millions. The East can learn production methods from the West to increase the standard of living for its hungry masses, and the West can learn from the East, if it will, the great philosophy of love and wisdom.

> The sage must distinguish between knowledge and wisdom. Knowledge is of things, acts, and relations. But wisdom is of Brahman alone; and, beyond all things, acts, and relations, he abides forever. To become one with him is the only wisdom.[1]

Two great faiths began in India. Hinduism remained; Buddhism spread. Hinduism is the most complex and diverse of faiths with its uncounted gods and tolerance of all sorts of beliefs, including the Christian. There is no one church, there are no aggressive missionaries, and there is no compulsion to follow one form of worship, because all is divine, even the Creator's mountains, streams, trees, stones, insects, and animals of all kinds, especially the holy cow, which symbolizes the whole dumb creation of God. Yet within this diversity is unity; all mankind is in that great sea of the cosmic soul. This is the unity that only some are able to realize.

In Hinduism, the individual is immersed in God, who is everywhere and in all things. The roots of this belief are in the animism of simple people everywhere who wonder about the miracle of earth and life and who believe God or gods are responsible for all creation and everything that happens. (There is something of animism in the Holy Spirit of the Trinity.) In the Hindu, the individual soul or Atman must yoke itself, through meditation and concentration, to the universal soul or Brahma. When this yoke (yoga) is made, one realizes he is part of the great unending universe or cosmos and that there is no death, there is only a changing and a returning. There is an everlasting becoming until one reaches Nirvana, a blissful state that cannot be explained in words or by human experience, except to say that in it one is reunited with Brahma. If one has lived the good life, his karma (or fate) is to be reincarnated into a better life next time around, and if one lives a life of sin, he has suffered illusion and his karma is to be reincarnated in a lower form. When one finally reaches Nirvana, he is no longer chained to the wheel of life, he need not be reincarnated again; he has reached eternal bliss.

According to the *Upanishads,* one of the great scriptural books of the Hindu faith, the divine is in each of us, in each of us there is a breath of the eternal. "As a lump of salt when thrown into water melts away and the lump cannot be taken out, but wherever we taste the water it is salty, even so, O Maitreyi, the individual self, dissolved, is the Eternal."[2] Man suffers only because of his unwillingness to realize his ties to the divine:

> The Self, Maitreyi, is to be known. Hear about it, meditate upon it. By knowing Self, my beloved, through hearing, reflection, and meditation, one comes to know all things. . . .
>
> Let the gods ignore him who thinks that the gods are different from the Self.[3]

Another of the Hindu scriptures, the *Bhagavad-Gita,* emphasizes a positive morality of doing good unto others since others are a part of Self. By injuring others one injures Self. Due to the ignorance of the wicked, there is bloodshed and terror in the world. The wicked take pride in themselves and in the goods they possess. The wise man, the man of knowledge and wisdom, avoids violence, pride, hate, and anger; the wise man is patient and generous and has control of himself at all times.

The tradition of nonviolence, being harmless to others, has probably played a larger part in Indian culture than in any other major civilization. This tradition appealed to Henry David Thoreau, whose nineteenth-century transcendentalism was greatly influenced by Eastern thought and religion. It inspired him to protest the tyranny of the United States' government in starting the Mexican War and recognizing the institution of slavery. In the twentieth century, Mahatma Gandhi inherited the tradition of nonviolence and passive resistance, which he used with such phenomenal success to free India from its status as an English colony. The Reverend Martin Luther King, Jr. was also inspired by the tradition of love and nonviolence of the Hindus. And although he was hated by many, he did not reciprocate the hate, nor did Gandhi in his time. They suffered, as Christ suffered, because of the ignorance of the wicked. It takes a very strong and a very lovely person not to hate.

One who is nonviolent in thought and in deed is close to the world spirit, which is far along the road from matter. An Indian scholar has suggested that matter may be thought of as a block at the lower left corner of a page—this one, for instance—and the world spirit as a block in the upper right corner. It is the purpose of the individual to move from matter toward spirit. Plants, such as trees and flowers, are a step up from matter, exhibiting what is termed life. Animals are farther along and exhibit consciousness, while man is farther along still and shows intelligence. The more intelligent persons will be heading up toward the world spirit while those of lesser intelligence will be closer to the material block. Most Indians consider themselves somewhere between the saintly men on the way up and the evil men on the way down. They have been a practical people, say the historians, interested in their daily rice; they have deplored evil ways and revered virtue and virtuous men.

For several centuries prior to 1857, much of Hindu India was dominated by Muslims, whose faith was in many ways opposite to the Hindu. The Muslim believed in one god and only one; the Hindu had countless deities. The Muslim forbade images; the Hindu had hundreds of them. The Muslim believed in the brotherhood of man while the Hindu had a caste system in which some men were considered untouchable. The Muslim was somewhat intolerant of other faiths and spread across whole continents on missions to convert the heathen; the Hindu had the most tolerant of religious faiths and was not aggressively missionary. Yet the two faiths managed to exist for centuries side by side, until the modern spirit of nationalism produced such lingering distrust and lack of understanding that in 1947 the Muslim country of Pakistan was born out of India by way of civil war. The bitterness, hatred, and distrust linger on.

Siddhartha Gautama, the Buddha, the Enlightened One, shows the way, shows the light. The eternal law is love. Buddha (563?–?483 B.C.), born a prince and possessing all the good things of this earth, in his early manhood left his family and his kingdom to search for enlightenment. After many years of poverty and struggle, he found what he was looking for, while sitting under the famous Bo (fig) tree. What he discovered there are the Four Noble Truths:

1. All life is filled with suffering.
2. Suffering is caused by a desire for impermanent things.
3. Suffering can be ended by ending the desire for impermanent things.
4. The Eightfold Path that ends suffering is: right view, right thought, right speech, right action, right livelihood, right effort, right mindfulness, and right concentration.

Through correct mind-control and correct meditation or serenity, love is gained by turning away every selfish thought. These are the last two steps of Buddha's Eightfold Path to eliminate suffering in this world.

171

Buddha's own life exemplified his teaching of the Golden Mean—a middle road between the extremes of asceticism (where one may not be of use to others) and self-indulgence (where one may do injury to others as well as to self). Buddhism has succeeded so well as a practical day-to-day religion that today, 2500 years after its founding, about twenty percent of the world's population has been directly influenced by the faith.

In his book on Buddhism, Christmas Humphries suggests that civilization and progress, if carried too far, may be antagonistic to love:

> Civilization is inseparable from competition, which produces and implies antagonism. Man against man, business firm against business firm, nation against nation and race against race, such is the ceaseless cry. Competition has its uses, but when its usefulness is past it becomes a fetter in the path of progress, and must give way in time to cooperation based on mutual understanding and respect. One of the greatest pronouncements ever made in the field of morality is contained in the Dhammapada: "Hatred ceaseth but by love. This is the eternal law."[4]

As Christianity, five hundred years later, was to move westward from the land of its birth, Buddhism began to move eastward from India. In time and place the faith fragmented into many interpretations of the mind of Buddha. To the southeast in Asia, Ceylon, Burma, Thailand, Cambodia, and, to a lesser extent, in Vietnam, the Lesser Vehicle of Buddhism, the Hinayana or Thervada school, predominates with its simple and single emphasis on the sending out of lovingkindness to all mankind. In the *Discourse on Universal Love,* the Buddha said:

> As a mother, even at the risk of her own life, protects and loves her child, her only child, so let a man cultivate love without measure toward the whole world, above, below, and around, unstinted, unmixed with any feeling of differing or opposing interests. Let a man remain steadfastly in this state of mind all the while he is awake, whether he be standing, walking, sitting, or lying down. This state of mind is the best in the world.[5]

The Thervada school has been described by Christmas Humphries as the finest moral philosophy in the world today:

> It is reasonable, making no appeal to dogmatic assumption; it is objective, and will stand the criticism of logic and science. It is self-reliant, claiming assistance from neither God nor gods, saviours or priestly men; it is the most tolerant creed on earth and expresses compassion not only for all men, but for all animals and the least living thing. By the ignorant it is described

as pessimistic. If this were true, and it is quite untrue, it is strange that its adherents today, the Sinhalese, Burmese, Siamese and Cambodians, are among the merriest, happiest people on earth.[6]

North in Asia is the Greater Vehicle, the Mahayana, which is practiced in many forms in the Himalayas, Tibet, China, Japan, and Korea.

One of the most significant types of behavior, and explanations of behavior, coming out of Asia belongs to the Zen school of Buddhism, which flowered first in China as Ch'an and developed later in Japan in several forms. Zen has its background in the paradoxes of the Tao and in the void of Nirvana, in the nonconceptual world of the Hindu and of Mahayana Buddhism. There is duality and conflict in the world because there is language, and language is not of the real world. Language and thought are invented, and we think and speak with these symbols. The nonverbal world of no-thought does not have symbols and classes; hence, there can be no conflict, no duality. The direct way to truth is not through symbols but through getting rid of symbols.

The Tao of Lao Tzu and the *Book of Changes* describe the Yin and Yang, the diversity within the unity, and the interaction between good and evil, truth and error, and so forth. Zen recognizes conflict in the world of words; indeed, so often it is a war of words. It is as impossible for man to achieve harmony in this world as it is for a thermostat to maintain a constant seventy degrees, says Alan W. Watts in his thoughtful little book *The Way of Zen*. There must be variation for the man to operate, and there must be variation for the thermostat to operate. Where there is love, there must also be hate. Where there is evil, there must also be good. Of course, the degree of variation is important. There are dangers inherent in any body of ideas if they are used in the extreme.

> Since the world points up beauty as such,
> There is ugliness too.
> If goodness is taken as goodness,
> Wickedness enters as well.
>
> For is and is-not come together;
> Hard and easy are complementary;
> Long and short are relative;
> High and low are comparative;
> Pitch and sound make harmony;
> Before and after are a sequence.[7]

This is life. Accept it. Calmly.

However, Dr. Watts reports that one San Francisco politician hates the left wing so much he will not, when driving, make a left turn. Though he must go 'round in circles, the left is still there. And so is the right for those on the left. The mind is bound in this dualistic pattern, and it is difficult to think in any other terms or in a mixture of the two, says Dr. Watts.

Yet Zen is a liberation from this pattern, and its apparently dismal starting point is to understand the absurdity of choosing, of the whole feeling that life may be significantly improved by a constant selection of the "good." One must start by "getting the feel" of relativity, and by knowing that life is not a situation from which there is anything to be grasped or gained—as if it were something which one approaches from outside, like a pie or a barrel of beer. To succeed is always to fail—in the sense that the more one succeeds in anything, the greater is the need to go on succeeding. To eat is to survive to be hungry.[8]

One does not have a choice. There is a well-known saying by Ch'ing-yuan:

Before I had studied Zen for thirty years, I saw mountains as mountains, and waters as waters. When I arrived at a more intimate knowledge, I came to the point where I saw that mountains are not mountains, and waters are not waters. But now that I have got its very substance, I am at rest. For it's just that I see mountains once again as mountains, and waters once again as waters.[9]

Aristotle perpetuated a lot of trouble by classifying things. Man is proud to be of this or that classification, and he is now numbered, stamped, labeled, communized, propagandized, capitalized, sterilized, Anglicized, homogenized, and bamboozled by government, company, school, church, club, newspaper, and TV. Forever, and words, words, words. All is artificial, because words are artificial, says the Zen Buddhist. Zen is meditation and a release from duality and conflict. Zen cannot be explained in words. Zen is an experience.

Zen is the quiet life. One does not necessarily improve the world by doing something. One may do his part in improving the world by doing nothing. If more people did nothing there wouldn't be so much conflict. Cats, dogs, tigers, and pigs do a lot of lying around; people lie about also—on the beach, in the mountains, and at bars, where only a minimum amount of conflict takes place. The United States is making a start on a guaranteed annual income for everyone. With increasing automation and cybernation (computers giving birth to more computers), we are heading toward a civilization based on use of leisure time. How will man behave when he has more leisure? Perhaps it will be a more peaceful world.

But Zen Buddhists do not withdraw from the world. They eat, breathe, sleep, defecate, walk, jog, and even love. They also work, and they believe in work:

> The insight which lies at the root of Far Eastern culture is that opposites are relational and so fundamentally harmonious. Conflict is always comparatively superficial, for there can be no ultimate conflict when the pairs of opposites are mutually interdependent. Thus our stark divisions of spirit and nature, subject and object, good and evil, artist and medium are quite foreign to this culture.[10]

Zen and Confucianism complemented one another in both China and Japan. They were both oriented on man rather than on god, on love rather than hate, on things being relative rather than on things being absolute. Confucius, who lived in the sixth century B.C., was a this-worldly man who believed in law and order from the nation down through the feudal domains to family and individual.

But Confucius' world was out of order. The Chou-dynasty emperors had been losing power to those who feared a big and centralized government. Rather than big-government tyranny, there was local-government tyranny, with large provinces conquering small provinces, feudal lords conquering and losing territory, armies marching up and down and across China fighting, fighting, fighting. Taxes were high to support the growing armies, crops were destroyed, peasants were poor, and there was graft and corruption at all levels. What to do about this chaos and anarchy?

Confucius was really a behavioral scientist. He said that man has seven natural instincts of joy, anger, sorrow, fear, love, hate, and desire. One must bring these natural emotions under control and see that they work for the common good. Let us have "correct thoughts" appears time and again in the works of Confucius. "Correct thoughts" is the "Know thyself" of Socrates, the "Do unto others" of Christians, the "love" of Buddha, and the "peace" of the hippies.

Correct thinking means bringing the world into harmony by having humility, being loyal to family, obeying the law, worshipping whatever gods have to be worshipped, respecting knowledge, and being patient, gentle, and kind. Patience is particularly important. Patience is basic to the conservatism of the Chinese in the 2500 years since Confucius. But patience finally led to exasperation as the Chinese saw British, French, Russians, Germans, Portuguese, and Japanese overrunning their land in the nineteenth and twentieth centuries. Confucius and the conservative spirit of believing in the past were blamed for the backwardness of China in the new world. Mao Tse-tung has his "Mao-think" as the new correct thinking, and Confucius is dead. After more than 2500 years of guiding Chinese morality and Chinese history, Confucius is dead.

His was a discriminating love. It was a love of family. The Chinese family historically has been closely knit, highly disciplined, and traditionally loyal. There has been little juvenile delinquency because of family pride and training, and old people have been well cared for by respectful relatives. Cousins, uncles, aunts, and others of the immediate family have been favored over outsiders. This was at once a strength and a weakness in Chinese civilization. The strengths are obvious and beautiful. But the weaknesses led to nepotism, with jobs and favors going to family members rather than to more qualified or deserving people. The weaknesses led to the idea that what was good enough for my fathers is good enough for me and thus to the failure of China to keep pace with a changing world. The weaknesses led, at least in part, to catastrophes for China in the twentieth century.

Actually, the weaknesses were apparent much earlier than the twentieth century. Mo Tzu, who lived only a short time after Confucius and who was considered a leading rival to Confucian thought, believed that discriminating love was narrow-minded. Why discriminate? Why not love all men equally? Only all-encompassing love can bring about harmony in the world. With discriminating love there will always be continuous and bitter conflict.

People being people, individuals being individuals, how can this all-encompassing love be accomplished? Through a ruler who will be an example to the people, said Mo-Tzu; he will persuade and even compel people to love one another. But this compulsion to love, this Mohism, sounds like totalitarianism. It sounds like Karl Marx and Mao Tse-tung—and it is. However, Oriental peoples have never really been oriented to the idea of individualism as it appears in Western civilization—in ancient Greece, in Renaissance Europe, or in modern America—loss of individualism in a totalitarian system doesn't hold the same terrors for them as for us. Chiang Kai-shek once said that China could never operate with the degree of individualism found in the West. There are just too many people for a high degree of individualism to exist. Mao-think virtually compels respect and love for the poor peasant population of China today. Mao is a modern Mo-Tzu, but he has not been successful either. China under Mao has had a riot of conflict.

Ideas and institutions change, but for all the change in time and place, there has remained a central unity in spite of the diversity in world religions. This unity is love. The Christian faith has encompassed such diverse elements as the ascetic pillar saints, rich Calvinists, pacifist Quakers, infallible popes, Christ-like figures such as St. Francis, Italian Communists, and medieval knights marching as to war, fighting and slaughtering one another, each side carrying the Cross and images of the Virgin Mary. The Buddhist faith has encompassed such diverse elements as the sacred Dalai Lama in Tibet, the monastery saints in Cambodia, the warlike and highly nationalistic *bushido* knights in Japan, mean monks in Zen schools, and the faithful marching as to war in China. The manyfold ways in which man behaves is fantastic.

Then, what about love? Should it be self, filial, or all-encompassing? Freud said that man is so much in love with himself that he will destroy himself along with others. Confucius opted for filial love. Mohists, Hindus, Buddhists, and Christians emphasize universal love. Edwin Aldrin said that during the flag ceremony on the moon he and Neil Armstrong sensed "an almost mystical unification of all the people in the world at that moment."[11] Devout Hindus and Buddhists have this feeling all the time.

Then why all the bitterness and conflict these many centuries? What is the real hangup? We can learn to love others. We do learn to love others. But not all others. Unless we land on the moon.

Notes

1 Swami Prabhavananda and Frederick Manchester, translators, *The Upanishads, Breath of the Eternal* (New York: New American Library, 1957), p. 42. By permission of the copyright holder, the Vedanta Society of Southern California.

2 *Ibid.*, p. 88.

3 *Ibid.*, p. 87.

4 Christmas Humphries, *Buddhism* (London: Penguin, 1951), p. 121.

5 *Ibid.*, p. 124.

6 *Ibid.*, p. 79.

7 R. B. Blakney, translator, *The Way of Life, Lao Tzu* (New York: New American Library, 1955, p. 54.

8 Alan W. Watts, *The Way of Zen* (New York: Vintage, 1957), p. 116. By permission of Pantheon Books, a division of Random House, Inc.

9 *Ibid.*, p. 126.

10 *Ibid.*, p. 175.

11 *Life*, August 22, 1969.

Zen Buddhism reaches into aesthetics in many ways, inspiring a high
appreciation for the beautiful in China and Japan; it has had a significant
part in the development of the tea ceremony, painting, gardening, poetry,
and calligraphy. The emphasis in Zen art is on the overall harmony of
life. In the following selection one sees conflict and contrast as part of a unity.

Zen in the Arts

Alan W. Watts

Happily, it is possible for us not only to hear about Zen but also
to see it. Since "one showing is worth a hundred sayings," the expression of Zen in the arts gives us one of the most direct ways of understanding it. This is the more so because the art forms which Zen has
created are not symbolic in the same way as other types of Buddhist
art, or as is "religious" art as a whole. The favorite subjects of Zen
artists, whether painters or poets, are what we should call natural,
concrete, and secular things. Even when they turn to the Buddha, or
to the Patriarchs and masters of Zen, they depict them in a peculiarly
down-to-earth and human way. Furthermore, the arts of Zen are not
merely or primarily representational. Even in painting, the work of
art is considered not only as representing nature but as being itself a
work of nature. For the very technique involves the art of artlessness,
or what Sabro Hasegawa has called the "controlled accident," so that
paintings are formed as naturally as the rocks and grasses which they
depict.

This does not mean that the art forms of Zen are left to mere
chance, as if one were to dip a snake in ink and let it wiggle around
on a sheet of paper. The point is rather that for Zen there is no
duality, no conflict between the natural element of chance and the
human element of control. The constructive powers of the human
mind are no more artificial than the formative actions of plants or
bees, so that from the standpoint of Zen it is no contradiction to say
that artistic technique is discipline in spontaneity and spontaneity in
discipline.

The art forms of the Western world arise from spiritual and philosophical traditions in which spirit is divided from nature, and comes
down from heaven to work upon it as an intelligent energy upon an

inert and recalcitrant stuff. Thus Malraux speaks always of the artist "conquering" his medium as our explorers and scientists also speak of conquering mountains or conquering space. To Chinese and Japanese ears these are grotesque expressions. For when you climb it is the mountain as much as your own legs which lifts you upwards, and when you paint it is the brush, ink, and paper which determine the result as much as your own hand.

Taoism, Confucianism, and Zen are expressions of a mentality which feels completely at home in this universe, and which sees man as an integral part of his environment. Human intelligence is not an imprisoned spirit from afar but an aspect of the whole intricately balanced organism of the natural world, whose principles were first explored in the *Book of Changes*. Heaven and earth are alike members of this organism, and nature is as much our father as our mother, since the Tao by which it works is originally manifested in the *yang* and the *yin*—the male and female, positive and negative principles which, in dynamic balance, maintain the order of the world. The insight which lies at the root of Far Eastern culture is that opposites are relational and so fundamentally harmonious. Conflict is always comparatively superficial, for there can be no ultimate conflict when the pairs of opposites are mutually interdependent. Thus our stark divisions of spirit and nature, subject and object, good and evil, artist and medium are quite foreign to this culture.

In a universe whose fundamental principle is relativity rather than warfare there is no purpose because there is no victory to be won, no end to be attained. For every end, as the word itself shows, is an extreme, an opposite, and exists only in relation to its other end. Because the world is not going anywhere there is no hurry. One may as well "take it easy" like nature itself, and in the Chinese language the "changes" of nature and "ease" are the same word, *i*. This is a first principle in the study of Zen and of any Far Eastern art: hurry, and all that it involves, is fatal. For there is no goal to be attained. The moment a goal is conceived it becomes impossible to practice the discipline of the art, to master the very rigor of its technique. Under the watchful and critical eye of a master one may practice the writing of Chinese characters for days and days, months and months. But he watches as a gardener watches the growth of a tree, and wants his student to have the attitude of the tree—the attitude of purposeless growth in which there are no short cuts because every stage of the way is both beginning and end. Thus the most accomplished master no more congratulates himself upon "arriving" than the most fumbling beginner.

Paradoxical as it may seem, the purposeful life has no content, no point. It hurries on and on, and misses everything. Not hurrying, the purposeless life misses nothing, for it is only when there is no goal and no rush that the human senses are fully open to receive the world. Absence of hurry also involves a certain lack of interference with the natural course of events, especially when it is felt that the natural course follows principles which are not foreign to human intelligence. For, as we have seen, the Taoist mentality makes, or forces, nothing but "grows" everything. When human reason is seen to be an expression of the same spontaneous balance of *yang* and *yin* as the natural universe, man's action upon his environment is not felt as a conflict, an action from outside. Thus the difference between forcing and growing cannot be expressed in terms of specific directions as to what should or should not be done, for the difference lies primarily in the quality and feeling of the action. The difficulty of describing these things for Western ears is that people in a hurry cannot feel. . . .

In his introduction to the great Hindu classic the "Bhagavad-Gita," Aldous Huxley links the great religions of the world to a common ground in what he calls The Perennial Philosophy. Though the religions are far flung across the earth, and though there are great differences from one to another, it is remarkable how they are agreed on fundamental beliefs about God and man. Why is it that man has established universal values and standards? Is he naturally good, as the Confucianist Mencius suggested, or is he fundamentally evil, as some other philosophers believed? Confucius said he did not know, and the Zen Buddhists say that good and evil are complementary. What do you think?

The Perennial Philosophy

Aldous Huxley

More than twenty-five centuries have passed since that which has been called the Perennial Philosophy was first committed to writing; and in the course of those centuries it has found expression, now partial, now complete, now in this form, now in that, again and again. In Vedanta and Hebrew prophecy, in the Tao Teh King and the Platonic dialogues, in the Gospel according to St. John and Mahayana theology, in Plotinus and the Areopagite, among the Persian Sufis and the Christian mystics of the Middle Ages and the Renaissance—the Perennial Philosophy has spoken almost all the languages of Asia and Europe and has made use of the terminology and traditions of every one of the higher religions. But under all this confusion of tongues and myths, of local histories and particularist doctrines, there remains a Highest Common Factor, which is the Perennial Philosophy in what may be called its chemically pure state. This final purity can never, of course, be expressed by any verbal statement of the philosophy, however undogmatic that statement may be, however deliberately syncretistic. The very fact that it is set down at a certain time by a certain writer, using this or that language, automatically imposes a certain sociological and personal bias on the doctrines so formulated. It is only in the act of contemplation, when words and even personality are transcended, that the pure state of the Perennial Philosophy can actually be known. The records left by those who have known it in this way make it abundantly clear that all of them, whether Hindu,

"The Perennial Philosophy" by Aldous Huxley, from Swami Prabhavananda and Christopher Isherwood, translators, *The Song of God, Bhagavad-Gita* (New York: New American Library, 1951), pp. 11–22. By permission of the Vedanta Society of Southern California.

Buddhist, Hebrew, Taoist, Christian or Mohammedan, were attempting to describe the same essentially indescribable Fact.

The original scriptures of most religions are poetical and unsystematic. Theology, which generally takes the form of a reasoned commentary on the parables and aphorisms of the scriptures, tends to make its appearance at a later stage of religious history. The Bhagavad —Gita occupies an intermediate position between scripture and theology; for it combines the poetical qualities of the first with the clear cut methodicalness of the second. The book may be described, writes Ananda K. Coomaraswamy in his admirable *Hinduism and Buddhism,* "as a compendium of the whole Vedic doctrine to be found in the earlier Vedas, Brahmanas and Upanishads, and being therefore the basis of all the later developments, it can be regarded as the focus of all Indian religion." But this "focus of Indian religion" is also one of the clearest and most comprehensive summaries of the Perennial Philosophy ever to have been made. Hence its enduring value, not only for Indians, but for all mankind.

At the core of the Perennial Philosophy we find four fundamental doctrines.

First: the phenomenal world of matter and of individualized consciousness—the world of things and animals and men and even gods —is the manifestation of a Divine Ground within which all partial realities have their being, and apart from which they would be nonexistent.

Second: human beings are capable not merely of knowing *about* the Divine Ground by inference; they can also realize its existence by a direct intuition, superior to discursive reasoning. This immediate knowledge unites the knower with that which is known.

Third: man possesses a double nature, a phenomenal ego and an eternal Self, which is the inner man, the spirit, the spark of divinity within the soul. It is possible for a man, if he so desires, to identify himself with the spirit and therefore with the Divine Ground, which is of the same or like nature with the spirit.

Fourth: man's life on earth has only one end and purpose: to identify himself with his eternal Self and so to come to unitive knowledge of the Divine Ground.

In Hinduism the first of these four doctrines is stated in the most categorical terms. The Divine Ground is Brahman, whose creative, sustaining and transforming aspects are manifested in the Hindu trinity. A hierarchy of manifestations connects inanimate matter with man, gods, High Gods and the undifferentiated Godhead beyond.

In Mahayana Buddhism the Divine Ground is called Mind or the

Pure Light of the Void, the place of the High Gods is taken by the Dhyani-Buddhas.

Similar conceptions are perfectly compatible with Christianity and have in fact been entertained, explicitly or implicitly, by many Catholic and Protestant mystics, when formulating a philosophy to fit facts observed by super-rational intuition. Thus, for Eckhart and Ruysbroeck, there is an Abyss of Godhead underlying the Trinity, just as Brahman underlies Brahma, Vishnu and Shiva. Suso has even left a diagrammatic picture of the relations subsisting between Godhead, triune God and creatures. In this very curious and interesting drawing a chain of manifestation connects the mysterious symbol of the Divine Ground with the three Persons of the Trinity, and the Trinity in turn is connected in a descending scale with angels and human beings. These last, as the drawing vividly shows, may make one of two choices. They can either lead the life of the outer man, the life of separative selfhood in which case they are lost (for, in the words of the Theologia Germanica, "nothing burns in hell but the self"). Or else they can identify themselves with the inner man, in which case it becomes possible for them, as Suso shows, to ascend again, through unitive knowledge, to the Trinity and even, beyond the Trinity, to the ultimate Unity of the Divine Ground.

Within the Mohammedan tradition such a rationalization of the immediate mystical experience would have been dangerously unorthodox. Nevertheless, one has the impression, while reading certain Sufi texts, that their authors did in fact conceive of *al haqq,* the Real, as being the Divine Ground or Unity of Allah, underlying the active and personal aspects of the Godhead.

The second doctrine of the Perennial Philosophy—that it is possible to know the Divine Ground by a direct intuition higher than discursive reasoning—is to be found in all the great religions of the world. A philosopher who is content merely to know about the ultimate Reality—theoretically and by hearsay—is compared by Buddha to a herdsman of other men's cows. Mohammed uses an even homelier barnyard metaphor. For him the philosopher who has not realized his metaphysics is just an ass bearing a load of books. Christian, Hindu and Taoist teachers wrote no less emphatically about the absurd pretensions of mere learning and analytical reasoning. In the words of the Anglican Prayer Book, our eternal life, now and hereafter, "stands in the knowledge of God"; and this knowledge is not discursive but "of the heart," a super-rational intuition, direct, synthetic and timeless.

The third doctrine of the Perennial Philosophy, that which affirms the double nature of man, is fundamental in all the higher religions. The unitive knowledge of the Divine Ground has, as its necessary condition, self-abnegation and charity. Only by means of self-abnegation and charity can we clear away the evil, folly and ignorance which constitute the thing we call our personality and prevent us from becoming aware of the sparks of divinity illuminating the inner man. But the spark within is akin to the Divine Ground. By identifying ourselves with the first we can come to unitive knowledge of the second. These empirical facts of the spiritual life have been variously rationalized in terms of the theologies of the various religions. The Hindus categorically affirm that thou art That—that the indwelling Atman is the same as Brahman. For orthodox Christianity there is not an identity between the spark and God. Union of the human spirit with God takes place—union so complete that the word "deification" is applied to it; but it is not the union of identical substances. According to Christian theology, the saint is "deified," not because Atman *is* Brahman, but because God has assimilated the purified human spirit into the divine substance by an act of grace. Islamic theology seems to make a similar distinction. The Sufi, Mansur, was executed for giving to the words "union" and "deification" the literal meaning which they bear in the Hindu tradition. For our present purposes, however, the significant fact is that these words are actually used by Christians and Mohammedans to describe the empirical facts of metaphysical realization by means of direct, super-rational intuition.

In regard to man's final end, all the higher religions are in complete agreement. The purpose of human life is the discovery of Truth, the unitive knowledge of the Godhead. The degree to which this unitive knowledge is achieved here on earth determines the degree to which it will be enjoyed in the posthumous state. Contemplation of truth is the end, action the means. In India, in China, in ancient Greece, in Christian Europe, this was regarded as the most obvious and axiomatic piece of orthodoxy. The invention of the steam engine produced a revolution, not merely in industrial techniques, but also and much more significantly in philosophy. Because machines could be made progressively more and more efficient, western man came to believe that men and societies would automatically register a corresponding moral and spiritual improvement. Attention and allegiance came to be paid, not to eternity, but to the Utopian future. External circumstances came to be regarded as more important than states of mind about external circumstances, and the end of human life was held to be action, with contemplation as a means to that end. These false and, historically, aberrant and heretical doctrines are now systematically taught in our schools and repeated, day in, day out, by those anonymous writers of advertising copy who, more than any other teachers, provide European and American adults with their current philosophy of life. And so effective has been the propaganda that even professing Christians accept the heresy unquestioningly and are quite unconscious of its complete incompatibility with their own or anybody else's religion.

These four doctrines constitute the Perennial Philosophy in its minimal and basic form. A man who can practice what the Indians call Jnana yoga (the metaphysical discipline of discrimination between the Real and the apparent) asks for nothing more. This simple working hypothesis is enough for his purposes. But such discrimination is exceedingly difficult and can hardly be practiced, at any rate in the preliminary stages of the spiritual life, except by persons endowed with a particular kind of mental constitution. That is why most statements of the Perennial Philosophy have included another doctrine, affirming the existence of one or more human Incarnations of the Divine Ground, by whose mediation and grace the worshipper is helped to achieve his goal—that unitive knowledge of the Godhead, which is man's eternal life and beatitude. The Bhagavad-Gita is one such statement. Here, Krishna is an Incarnation of the Divine Ground in human form. Similarly, in Christian and Buddhist theology, Jesus and Gotama are Incarnations of divinity. But whereas in Hinduism and Buddhism more than one Incarnation of the Godhead is possible (and is regarded as having in fact taken place), for Christians there has been and can be only one.

An Incarnation of the Godhead and, to a lesser degree, any theocentric saint, sage or prophet is a human being who knows Who he is and can therefore effectively remind other human beings of what they have allowed themselves to forget: namely, that if they choose to become what potentially they already are, they too can be eternally united with the Divine Ground.

Worship of the Incarnation and contemplation of his attributes are for most men and women the best prepartion for unitive knowledge of the Godhead. But whether the actual knowledge itself can be achieved by this means is another question. Many Catholic mystics have affirmed that, at a certain stage of that contemplative prayer in which, according to the most authoritative theologians, the life of Christian perfection ultimately consists, it is necessary to put aside all thoughts of the Incarnation as distracting from the higher knowledge of that which has been incarnated. From this fact have arisen misunderstandings in plenty and a number of intellectual difficulties. Here, for example, is what Abbot John Chapman writes in one of his admirable Spiritual Letters: "The problem of *reconciling* (not merely uniting) mysticism with Christianity is more difficult. The Abbot (Abbot Marmion) says that St. John of the Cross is like a sponge full of Christianity. You can squeeze it all out, and the full mystical theory remains. Consequently, for fifteen years or so, I hated St. John of the Cross and called him a Buddhist. I loved St. Teresa, and read her over and over again. She is first a Christian, only secondarily a mystic. Then I found that I had wasted fifteen years, so far as prayer was concerned." And yet, he concludes, in spite of its "Buddhistic" character, the practice of mysticism (or, to put it in other terms, the realization of the Perennial Philosophy) makes good Christians. He might have added that it also makes good Hindus, good Buddhists, good Taoists, good Moslems and good Jews.

The solution to Abbot Chapman's problem must be sought in the domain, not of philosophy, but of psychology. Human beings are not born identical. There are many different temperaments and constitutions; and within each psycho-physical class one can find people at very different stages of spiritual development. Forms of worship and spiritual discipline which may be valuable for one individual may be useless or even positively harmful for another belonging to a different class and standing, within that class, at a lower or higher level of development. All this is clearly set forth in the Gita, where the psychological facts are linked up with general cosmology by means of the postulate of the *gunas*. Krishna, who is here the mouthpiece of Hinduism in all its manifestations, finds it perfectly natural that different men should have different methods and even apparently different objects of worship. All roads lead to Rome—provided, of course, that it is Rome and not some other city which the traveller really wishes to reach. A similar attitude of charitable inclusiveness, somewhat surprising in a Moslem, is beautifully expressed in the parable of Moses and the Shepherd, told by Jalaluddin Rumi in the second book of the Masnavi. And within the more exclusive Christian tradition these problems of temperament and degree of development have been searchingly discussed in their relation to the way of Mary and the way of Martha in general, and a clear conception of what in Buddha's Eightfold Path is called "right livelihood." Thus, for the Buddhist, right livelihood was incompatible with the making of deadly weapons and of intoxicants; for the medieval Christian, with the taking of interest and with various monopolistic practices which have since come to be regarded as legitimate good business. John Woolman, the American Quaker, provides a most enlightening example of the way in which a man may live in the world, while practicing perfect non-attachment and remaining acutely sensitive to the claims of right livelihood. Thus, while it would have been profitable and perfectly lawful for him to sell West Indian sugar and rum to the customers who came to his shop, Woolman refrained from doing so because these things were the products of slave labour. Similarly, when he was in England, it would have been both lawful and convenient for him to travel by stage coach. Nevertheless, he preferred to make his journeys on foot. Why? Because the comforts of rapid travel could only be bought at the expense of great cruelty to the horses and the most atrocious working conditions for the post-boys. In Woolman's eyes, such a system of transportation was intrinsically undesirable, and no amount of personal non-attachment could make it anything but undesirable. So he shouldered his knapsack and walked.

In the preceding pages I have tried to show that the Perennial Philosophy and its ethical corollaries constitute a Highest Common Factor, present in all the major religions of the world. To affirm this truth has never been more imperatively necessary than at the present time. There will never be enduring peace unless and until human beings come to accept a philosophy of life more adequate to the cosmic and psychological facts than the insane idolatries of in particular to the vocation and private devotion of individuals.

We now have to consider the ethical corollaries of the Perennial Philosophy. "Truth," says St. Thomas Aquinas, "is the last end for the entire universe, and the contemplation of truth is the chief occupation of wisdom." The moral virtues, he says in another place, belong to contemplation, not indeed essentially, but as a necessary predisposition. Virtue, in other words, is not the end, but the indispensable means to the knowledge of divine reality. Shankara, the greatest of the Indian commentators on the Gita, holds the same doctrine. Right action is the way to knowledge; for it purifies the mind, and it is only to a mind purified from egotism that the intuition of the Divine Ground can come.

Self-abnegation, according to the Gita, can be achieved by the practice of two all-inclusive virtues—love and non-attachment. The latter is the same thing as that "holy indifference," on which St. François de Sales is never tired of insisting. "He who refers every action to God," writes Camus, summarizing his master's teaching, "and has no aims save His Glory, will find rest everywhere, even amidst the most violent commotions." So long as we practice this holy indifference to the fruits of action, "no lawful occupation will separate us from God; on the contrary, it can be made a means of closer union." Here the word "lawful" supplies a necessary qualification to a teaching which, without it, is incomplete and even potentially dangerous. Some actions are intrinsically evil or inexpedient; and no good intentions, no conscious offering of them to God, no renunciation of the fruits can alter their essential character. Holy indifference requires to be taught in the conjunction not merely with a set of commandments prohibiting crimes, but also with nationalism and the advertising man's apocalyptic faith in Progress towards a mechanized New Jerusalem. All the elements of this philosophy are present, as we have seen, in the traditional religions. But in existing circumstances there is not the slightest chance that any of the traditional religions will obtain universal acceptance. Europeans and Americans will see no reason for being converted to Hinduism, say, or Buddhism. And the people of Asia can hardly be expected to renounce their own traditions for the Christianity professed, often sincerely, by the imperialists who, for four hundred years and more, have been systematically attacking, exploiting and oppressing, and are now trying to finish off the work of destruction by "educating" them. But happily there is the Highest Common Factor of all religions, the Perennial Philosophy which has always and everywhere been the metaphysical system of the prophets, saints and sages. It is perfectly possible for people to remain good Christians, Hindus, Buddhists or Moslems and yet to be united in full agreement on the basic doctrines of the Perennial Philosophy.

The Bhagavad-Gita is perhaps the most systematic scriptural statement of the Perennial Philosophy. To a world at war, a world that, because it lacks the intellectual and spiritual prerequisites to peace, can only hope to patch up some kind of precarious armed truce, it stands pointing, clearly and unmistakably, to the only road of escape from the self-imposed necessity of self-destruction. For this reason we should be grateful to Swami Prabhavananda and Mr. Isherwood for having given us this new version of the book—a version which can be read, not merely without that dull aesthetic pain inflicted by all too many English translations from the Sanskrit, but positively with enjoyment.

And then Gandhi came. He was like a powerful current of fresh air that made us stretch ourselves and take deep breaths, like a beam of light that pierced the darkness and removed the scales from our eyes, like a whirlwind that upset many things but most of all the working of people's minds. He did not descend from the top; he seemed to emerge from the millions of India, speaking their language and incessantly drawing attention to them and their appalling condition. Get off the backs of these peasants and workers, he told us, all you who live by their exploitation; get rid of the system that produces this poverty and misery.
                    —Jawaharlal Nehru, "The Discovery of India"

Mahatma Gandhi

Horace Alexander

India today, . . . the India that is neither a return to the Vedas nor a pale reflection of the West, is essentially the creation of Gandhi.

Gandhi called himself a Hindu to the day of his death. He never changed his religious loyalty. When he was in South Africa, as a young man, he was intimate with evangelically-minded Christians, who for a time influenced him so much that he seriously considered "conversion". . . . But, on full consideration, the young Gandhi decided that there was no reason to cut himself away from his Hindu roots. If Christianity had something to teach Hinduism, then he, as a Hindu, must try to purify Hinduism—for example, by fighting the curse of Untouchability. . . .

Gandhi is the central figure in the new Indian culture; and one essential thing about him is that, while remaining a Hindu all his life, he welcomed and tried to make his own the best in every religious tradition. A century before Gandhi, Ram Mohan Roy, the first inspirer of Indian social reform, gave himself to the study of Persian and of the Koran in his early manhood. It might fairly be argued that Ram Mohan Roy did more to Islamize the Hinduism of Bengal in the early nineteenth century than to Christianize it. At any rate, as far as he could, he did both. But when we come to Gandhi a still more potent Muslim influence suggests itself. Gandhi, in the last phase of his life, began to use a word *sarvodaya* to express his social philosophy. This word, as far as I know, was coined by him to translate the idea conveyed in the title of John Ruskin's essay, "Unto

Consider India: An Essay in Values by Horace Alexander (Bombay: Asia Publishing House, 1961), pp. 39–42, 45, 59–61, 67–70, 73–73. By permission of Asia Publishing House, Inc., New York, 1961.

this Last." At least it means the same thing: the good of all, as opposed to ideas of the greatest good of the greatest number: not the majority, says Gandhi, not even a ninety-nine per cent majority, but *all* must be the concern of the true welfare State. Where did Gandhi get this idea? He may have found it in many places—Ruskin, Rousseau, the New Testament, the Gita, and so on; but surely in part, perhaps even principally, it stems from the Islamic conception of human brotherhood, in which every man is equal in the sight of God. This conception, so alien to the Hindu caste structure; can hardly have come to India from western Christianity, though it is easy enough to find it in the Gospels. Politically, India no doubt has derived the idea of equality largely from the influence of the French and American Revolutions; but in the more fundamental human and religious sense, it has come through Gandhi, and it would seem that he derived it primarily from Islam.

Here are Gandhi's own words about Islam: "Islam's distinctive contribution to India's national culture," he wrote in *Young India* in 1929, "is its unadulterated belief in the oneness of God and a practical application of the truth of the brotherhood of man for those who are nominally within its fold. I call these two distinctive contributions. For in Hinduism the spirit of brotherhood has become too much philosophized. Similarly, though philosophical Hinduism has no other god but God, it cannot be denied that practical Hinduism is not so emphatically uncompromising as Islam. . . ."

Let it never be thought that for Gandhi religion was chiefly a matter of "religions" or of speculation on the nature of the absolute, however profound and truly philosophical. Reginald Reynolds has recently written that Gandhi "emphasized work as worship, community as religion, right action as true idealism." The religious man, in Gandhi's estimation, was not the man who either preached stirring sermons or listened to them, or who faithfully carried out so-called religious practices. Rather, he was the man who lost himself in devotion to the service of humanity.

. . . .

Although this is not primarily a study of politics, Gandhi's part in the liberation of India from British rule is so important that it seems appropriate to draw attention here to the real significance of what happened. Some Britishers are inclined to argue that Gandhi, far from helping forward the process of self-government, actually retarded it. The British government, it is pointed out, had always declared that self-government was the end at which they aimed. India was being prepared for this by successive stages; first municipal self-government, then provincial self-government, and finally the transfer of power at the center was bound to follow. If only Indians would work the new representative institutions with energy and goodwill, the transfer would come speedily.

During the Round Table Conference on the future of Indian government, held in London in the autumn of 1931, Gandhi spent a weekend in the Master's Lodge, at Balliol College, Oxford, meeting informally several leading British public men, official and unofficial, in an endeavour to break the deadlock between the British government and the Indian National Congress. Professor Coupland opened the session by expounding the theory that, in the development of the British Commonwealth of free nations, freedom had broadened down from precedent to precedent in an orderly manner, stage by stage, until in turn Canada, Australia, New Zealand, South Africa and Ireland had all achieved full freedom; and that the more orderly and constitutional the movement in each domain had been, the more rapid had been the development. In a sentence, the British people responded to constitutional appeals, especially when they were backed by efficient discharge of local self-government, whereas they only had their backs put up, and were liable to take a stiff and uncompromising line of resistance, if any kind of pressure through direct action were attempted.

Gandhi listened respectfully, but he proceeded to assure Professor Coupland that he considered him wrong in both history and psychology. He pointed out that the Canadian Rebellion [of 1837] was the shock that led the British people to recognize the need for self-government in Canada. The history of both Ireland and South Africa demonstrated the same thesis. In both cases, after much talk of self-government, it only finally arrived after bloody conflict, when the British people had seen that it could no longer be denied. Even in New Zealand, there had been a Maori Rebellion. Australia alone had come to full self-government in the manner the Professor had suggested was typical. Gandhi went on to say that he did not suggest that the British people meanly surrendered to armed force. On the contrary, they might begin by suppressing the rebellion. But they learnt to respect a nation, when they saw that it was so determined to have its freedom that it was willing to fight and die in the attempt to achieve it. He was convinced that the same would prove true in the case of India. The only way India could achieve real freedom was not by having it handed to them from Britain bit by bit, but by fighting for it, and earning the respect of the British in the process. Only, they meant their fight, unlike the Canadian, Irish and South African fightings, to be nonviolent, so that the Indians would suffer most, and the English as little as possible.

.   .   .   .

[Gandhi's] immense belief in the dignity and strength of a fearless man governed his thought in the economic field no less than the political. He perceived that it is the peasant, the cultivator of the soil, who silently keeps the world alive through times of war and conquest and pestilence. From time to time a whole countryside may be devastated by the scourge of famine or disease or by the sword of a conqueror; but unless the land becomes infertile and reverts to desert, as soon as the pestilence of disease or conquest passes, men return to the land and begin to plough it and sow it and reap crops again. So is the world maintained. It was therefore the dumb millions of food-producing peasants who were Gandhi's chief concern and on whose backs he built his hopes.

In India he found a peasantry whose independence was largely undermined. The British had taught them not to think for themselves, and not to be self-dependent for their clothes and their tools. "We command, you obey," said the British, "for we know what is good for you; we will supply you with better clothes and tools than you can make, and you can buy them at world-market prices." "But you need not obey," said Gandhi, "you can be wholly independent. Moreover, if you make your own clothes and your own tools, you will be beginning the fight against your abject poverty. You can do it for yourselves." So he evolved a "constructive program," which ignored the alien ruler and laid the foundations of political independence on the firm base of economic independence. Let each village first learn to live as an independent unit, feeding itself, making its own clothes from its own cotton, providing its own housing and its own essential tools; then, when it has an upright backbone of its own, it can go on to an honest exchange of goods and services with neighbouring villages, with far away cities, even with the ends of the earth.

It should be noted here that Gandhi was not, as Western people commonly suppose, opposed to all machinery and to all industrialization. The spinning wheel itself, which he asked every Indian to ply, was, as he freely admitted, a machine. He was an enthusiast for the sewing machine, which he regarded as a true labor-saving device. . . . Gandhi's objection was to the craze for machinery—a craze comparable to the addict's constant yearning for more cigarettes or more alcohol or more opium. The test of every new invention should be: Is it really the servant of man—not just to make a few men richer while others become slaves to the machine or are thrown out of work. Far better that thousands of men should carry heavy loads on their heads up steep banks to build a great dam rather than that the work should all be done by great cranes while the men and their families sit idle and starve in their villages. And today in India those are the only alternatives. In twenty years' time the economy may have been so transformed that more labor-saving machinery will be good for India. Gandhi utterly repudiated the argument that the cheapest way of producing goods was necessarily the most economic from the point of view of general human well-being; and it is human well-being, not cheapness, that must be the final test.

His constructive program did, indeed, look to a transformation of Indian life, by fostering village industries and the better use of the land and the breeding of better and fewer cattle. These, Gandhi held, are among the reforms necessary before large-scale industrialization can be usefully introduced into a country like India, whose capital consists largely of manpower and sunpower. Let man become healthy; let nature be harnessed to the service of man; and then industrial development is due. Even so, it is likely that India will be well advised to avoid the industrial concentration that has disfigured the West. In all this, Gandhi has something to say that all Asia and Africa, perhaps some parts of Europe and America too, may well ponder. . . .

The constructive program of Gandhi involved the destruction of ancient abuses such as Untouchability. The rich must shed their riches and become trustees or elder brothers to their poor neighbours. Work that involves men in filth and unpleasantness, the work of the *bhangi,* or sweeper, for instance, which has been despised as the most menial, should rather be treated as the most honorable of all professions. Gandhi's economic and social revolution involved, first and foremost, a change of mind, a wholly new attitude towards manual labor, and especially towards the so-called menial tasks. . . .

Perhaps Gandhi is the first important political leader in the world who has consistently kept the needs of the poorest, and above all the voiceless poor of the villages, who are often beyond the sight and the thought of modern social reformers, in the forefront of his mind and heart. To the day of his death, he had them constantly in his mind. He was always at home when he was among them, and he felt imprisoned when he had to dwell in cities. As far as was possible for a man who had to live the life he was called to, and who had travelled about the earth and been educated in London, he identified himself in his every day life with the poorest and the lowliest and the lost. He must abandon everything that he did not strictly need, not because of the spiritual efficacy of asceticism; in the proper sense, Gandhi was not an ascetic. But, so long as one man remained in abject poverty, he held that possession of anything he did not need was a form of theft. Many of his close friends he considered thieves. He tried not to be one himself.

Questions

1　Is variation, and therefore duality, as necessary for man as for the thermostat?

2　If you believe the answer to the first question is "yes," does this mean that conflict will always be inevitable between individuals, groups, and nations? Consider your answer in light of man's power today to wipe out all life on earth.

3　Is Confucius really dead? If he is, how has Mao replaced him?

4　What famous humans of the twentieth century have demonstrated through their lives a love of all mankind? Explain.

5　What do words and other symbols have to do with our behavior?

6　Can man establish standards of behavior that will permit him to live at peace with his neighbors without a police state or a reliance on a code sanctioned by a deity (whether God or a universal spirit)?

7　If Asia has been the home of so many humanistic religions and philosophies stressing harmony and love, why has its history been so drenched in blood and strife?

8　Is it true that Orientals have a low regard for life? What about our Western regard for life?

lived after them to change the world. The modern age is more sophisticated and in many ways more tolerant than that of seven hundred years ago, but there are nevertheless huge numbers of people, especially among senior citizens, who seem to be rabidly intolerant of new styles of dress, hair, beards, religion, politics, sideburns, and so on. The Kennedys and Martin Luther King, not loved by most traditional types, are only some of the modern martyrs who have inspired their followers to bring about great social and economic changes in a world that is still strongly attached to the old ways. Like Antigone, they spoke out against what they considered to be the tyranny of the majority in compelling conformity to unjust laws. They were not cowed.

The Christian Church was the dominant institution in the Middle Ages, but the conformity it sought was constantly challenged by kings, princes, and poor souls who did not believe in everything the Church stood for. These people spoke out vociferously and put conscience—and often times self-interest—above loyalties to what they considered to be a man-made institution. The Church fathers put up a strong fight against heresies by using such weapons as sermons, excommunications, inquisitions, interdicts, and even war to perpetuate conformity in a world that was pulling in other directions with new ideas, new cities, new nations, and new money enterprises. Power and wealth corrupted individuals within the Church, and this made it easier for heretics to attract followers—just as Christianity had attracted followers from a corrupt Roman Empire a thousand years before.

The man and woman who are now the patron saints of San Francisco and of France refused to submit to those who would force them to conform to traditional ways of behaving. One would today still be a heretic because of his eccentric ways, while the other would be accepted, except, possibly, her bizarre appearance, because she helped change the direction of men's thoughts from Church to nation. John Wycliffe and John Hus were two other heretics whose influence is felt in many places today, particularly in divided Ireland and in nationalist Czechoslovakia. There is a changing face of heresy, and there is also an unchanging face of tradition, from the Middle Ages to modern times.

Both Protestants and Catholics pay homage to the beautiful Christ-like figure of St. Francis, with his love for all mankind and all creation. Though the older generation told him he never had it so good, he gave up a rich family inheritance to devote his life to the poor. He kicked off his fine clothes, took to sackcloth or any other covering he could beg, and began a great movement of purity and poverty that had particular appeal to the youth of the time. His example inspired thousands to reject traditional society for a life devoted to helping others instead of just helping themselves. But a Christ-like figure in any age is considered to be crazy by those whose lives are dedicated to getting ahead.

"Everybody knew, of course, that Franciscans were communists; but this was not so much being a communist as being an anarchist," writes G. K. Chesterton in his biography *St. Francis of Assisi*.[1] Although St. Francis, because of his nonconformity, narrowly escaped being officially declared a heretic, many of his followers received the official seal. Chesterton says:

> If the Franciscan movement had turned into a new religion, it would after all have been a narrow religion. In so far as it did turn here and there into a heresy, it was a narrow heresy. . . . And St. Francis, however wild and romantic his gyrations might appear to many, always hung on to reason by one invisible and indestructible hair.[2]

St. Francis was married to Lady Poverty. Members of his order, called mendicant, begged for food, clothing, and shelter, not to save their own souls so much as to save others'. As someone like St. Dominic was needed to convert the heathen to Christianity, says Chesterton, someone like St. Francis was needed to convert the Christians to Christianity. He lived with lepers, he lived in caves, and he replied to the curses of his father by saying that his Father in Heaven blessed his poverty. Though Franciscans did not conform as so many friends and relatives expected, they themselves demanded conformity in realizing a life of purity. In 1322, nearly one hundred years after the death of Francis, Pope John XXII, from his rich palace at Avignon, condemned as heresy the doctrine of the poverty of Christ. Franciscan extremists, the Spirituals, were branded as heretics, and many were burned at the stake. Both Christ and Francis were heretics because they denied Establishment values of material success and traditional ways.[3]

St. Francis of Assisi was an Italian, an imitator of Christ, dedicated to Poverty. St. Joan of Arc was a Frenchwoman, a teenager extraordinary, dedicated to Frenchmen. She was patriot, nationalist, Protestant, Catholic, individualist, heretic, and saint. She cut her hair short, wore men's clothing, defied Church authority, and thereby irritated to distraction those who were offended by such nonconformist actions. Especially were her critics concerned with her short hair and men's clothing. An old archdeacon said that her dress was scandalous, indecent, and against all custom; she was ridiculed about it throughout her trial for heresy. But she had a mind of her own. As a soldier for France directing men and armies, a leader must not appear to be too feminine. As a young woman of nineteen on trial for her life, she was still not going to let others tell her how she should appear. Joan was Joan and that was that.

She was one of the first apostles of nationalism, says Bernard Shaw, and as such she fell afoul the power of the Church. She placed ultimate faith in her God instead of in her Church and thereby became a Protestant one hundred years before Martin Luther. She was a woman at war with foreigners in her country. George Bernard Shaw, Dublin Protestant, but sympathetic biographer of St. Joan, describes the trial and the indictment against her. Warwick, an English nobleman during the Hundred Years' War, and Cauchon, the Bishop of Beauvais, who had brought Joan to trial with the help of the English, are speaking:

> WARWICK [*playing the pink of courtesy*]   I think you are not entirely void of sympathy with The Maid's secular heresy, my lord. I leave you to find a name for it.

> CAUCHON   You mistake me, my lord. I have no sympathy with her political presumptions. But as a priest I have gained a knowledge of the minds of the common people; and there you will find yet another most dangerous idea. I can express it only by such phrases as France for the French, England for the English, Italy for the Italians, Spain for the Spanish, and so forth. It is sometimes so narrow and bitter in country folk that it surprises me that this country girl can rise above the idea of her village for its villagers. But she can. She does. When she threatens to drive the English from the soil of France she is undoubtedly thinking of the whole extent of country in which French is spoken. To her the French-speaking people are what the Holy Scriptures describe as a nation. Call this side of her heresy Nationalism if you will: I can find you no better name for it. I can only tell you that it is essentially anti-Catholic and anti-Christian; for the Catholic Church knows only one realm, and that is the realm of Christ's kingdom. Divide that kingdom into nations, and you dethrone Christ. Dethrone Christ, and who will stand between our throats and the sword? The world will perish in a welter of war.

> WARWICK   Well, if you will burn the Protestant, I will burn the Nationalist, though perhaps I shall not carry Messire John with me there. England for the English will appeal to him.[4]

Scene IV of the play concludes with a statement by the chaplain that England for the English is natural but that Joan's wearing men's clothing and fighting is not; she has rebelled against the Church, against God, and against England. "Let her perish. Let her burn." In 1431, at the age of nineteen, she was burned at the stake. In 1920, nearly five hundred years later, she was canonized as a saint. Which of today's heretics will be tomorrow's heroes?

The nationalism kindled at this time burns fiercely today in the hearts of men around the world, although the highly romantic kind of nationalism Joan may have held in her heart did not take immediately since monarchy was at that time the only political vehicle available to bring about national unity. It remained for the American and French revolutions and Napoleon to germinate a new peoples' nationalism, which took root in the nineteenth century and blossomed with great vigor in the twentieth with Hitler, de Gaulle, Ho Chi-minh, and everywhere flags, flags, flags. Joan was a warrior saint. She, together with the royal imperative toward territorial conquest, projected a new and unique institution in human history. She could neither read nor write but she was a patriot, and that is what counts under the king or under the national flag.

As the Middle Ages moved toward the Renaissance, the idea of a nation began to eat away at the idea of a universal Church. The Great Schism, 1378–1417, divided loyalties along national lines, with some new nations loyal to a pope at Rome and some to another at Avignon. At one time there were three popes claiming the chair. The great Schism gave the Englishman John Wycliffe more reason to continue his attack on the established Church and on the papacy, which he saw as a tyranny over the minds of men. He agreed with the radical element of the Franciscans who believed the holding of property by the clergy was against the teachings of Christ, and he agreed with other Franciscans, such as Roger Bacon, Duns Scotus, and William of Ockham, who contested some of the beliefs of Thomas Aquinas of the rival Dominican order. Heresy was in the air at this time—a time of challenge to the old guard. Even Aquinas was considered a heretic by some for bringing Aristotle and other pagan philosophers into Christian dogma. Roger Bacon and other Oxford University Franciscans encouraged scientific experimentation and questioned papal authority. Although Bacon was imprisoned at one time for the novelties of his teaching, he escaped the official tag of heretic.

Wycliffe exhibited something of the rising national feeling by objecting to English moneys being sent to the Roman pontiff, and then he went on to demonstrate Protestant beliefs some one hundred and fifty years before Martin Luther nailed the ninety-five Theses to the church door at Wittenberg: like Luther, he objected to the sale of indulgences used as pardons for sins, he rejected six of the seven sacraments, and he said that the worship of saints and veneration of their relics was false because these and other practices of the Church were man-made. He declared that all necessary religious truth can be learned from the Bible, which he and other Oxford scholars, contrary to Church authority, translated into English. Of course, he was tried as a heretic, but the trial in London was broken up by mob violence. Six years later, in 1383, he was called to Rome for another trial, but he refused to go and thus escaped the official tag of heretic while he lived. However, the Council of Constance declared him a heretic long after he was dead and ordered his remains dug up to be scattered on unhallowed ground.

Wycliffe's ideas caught on among the Czechs in Bohemia, where John Hus and students of the new University of Prague took up the cry of independence from Rome and independence from the German influence that was quite strong in that land. As rector of the University, he wrote and preached that many of the Church doctrines were simply human invention, and especially he protested the idea of indulgences. He was excommunicated by the pope but secured from the Emperor Sigismund a guarantee of safe passage to and from the Council of Constance to present his case.

Hus refused to recant, and in July of 1415 he was burned at the stake. Instead of purifying the air by burning out heresy, the martyrdom of Hus made heresy catch on. A holy crusade had to be organized against the rebellious Husites in Bohemia. The bloodletting lasted about twenty years, the crusade failed, and the heresy persisted on to the time of the Reformation.

The Age of Intolerance, with its Inquisition, its religious persecution, and its religious wars, was to last until the time of the English civil wars and the Thirty Years' War (1618–1648), when Cardinal Richelieu of France aligned his Catholic country with some Protestant countries to kill other Catholics and Protestants of enemy countries; the war that started as a religious war ended as a national war. The process that had begun in the late Middle Ages was now complete— nationalism had replaced Catholicism in demanding the ultimate loyalties of men. What had begun as heresy had ended in conformity.

European man has successively extended his identity, starting with family, then clan, then from clan to tribe, from tribe to feudal principality, and, aside from religious loyalty to the Church universal, from feudal principality to nation. Of the heretics we have discussed, only one was not wrapped up in the national institution. He extended his identity as far as all mankind.

But all mankind is too large a thought for many, who are tied up in the smaller dimensions of identifying with nation, state, tribe, clan, family, and self. It would be heresy today to extend one's identity by flying the United Nations flag over the national flag. One would surely be persecuted by conformists, just as the Romans persecuted the Christian minorities and the Christians later persecuted the heretics. Some would even consider flying the United Nations flag a Communist conspiracy.

Actually, it is a Christian conspiracy. And it is a Buddhist, Jewish, Bahai, and Muslim conspiracy that someday might actually succeed. That is, if one is an optimist about man's behavior and his potentialities and thinks man will succeed as Christ and Francis hoped he would. On the other hand, if one is a pessimist about man's behavior and his limitations, and points to the Berlin Wall separating communists and capitalists and the more recent Belfast Wall separating Catholics and Protestants, then man will not succeed in creating One World. One World is impossible, just as over 200 million people of diverse natures living peacefully in the United States is impossible . . . It is a heresy.

Notes

1 G. K. Chesterton, *St. Francis of Assisi* (London: Hodder and Stoughton, 1964), p. 178.

2 *Ibid.*, pp. 184–185.

3 A cartoon in the *Wall Street Journal* pictured a Christ-like figure with robe, long hair, beard, and bare feet walking the streets of Manhattan carrying a sign: YOU WOULDN'T BELIEVE ME IF I TOLD YOU.

4 Bernard Shaw, *Saint Joan* (Baltimore, Md.: Penguin, 1952), p. 99.

Hippies and yippies, beatniks and bohemians, have disgusted many members of the current Establishment. Each is a bit different from the other, but there are similarities in their rejection of traditional society— their unusual appearance, their communal living, their heretical ideas. Traditional types of any age would make life difficult for the bizarre young man discussed in this article.

A Bizarre Young Man

Jeffery and Elizabeth Smith

This is the true story of a young man who grew up with all the advantages of a well-to-do family, a devoted mother, and a stern but just father, a prominent businessman respected throughout the community.

As a teen-ager he seemed a normal young man, gifted and promising, with a successful career before him in the family business. Though quite a party goer, and not adverse to a little hard drinking, he was active in church work, and served a brief hitch as an officer in the army.

On a "Trip"

Then suddenly a change came over him. Within a year he had broken with his family, and, without visible means of support, was drifting from one leaky pad to another, bearded, barefoot, dirty, and in rags. The change came about in a strange way.

Though his case history shows no sign of drug addition, he began to act, much of the time, as though he were on a "trip," withdrawn and experiencing visions and hallucinations. These triggered a series of violent and criminal acts, directed, significantly, against his own family.

He was caught robbing his father's warehouse, selling the goods at a fraction of their value, and squandering the money on strange whims. His father in desperation took him to court.

This led to a terrible scene. Judicial proceedings had just got under way, when suddenly the youth became very violent, stripped off all his expensive clothes, threw them at his father's feet, and stormed naked into the street.

From "A Bizarre Young Man" by Jeffrey and Elizabeth Smith, *This World* magazine, *San Francisco Chronicle,* May 28, 1967.

Total Integration

From this time on his actions and way of life became increasingly bizarre. He insisted nothing mattered but the practice of "love" and "brotherhood." He took up with peace, and advocated integration, not just racial but a kind of total integration.

He turned against education and urged the runaways and dropouts who flocked to share his pads to stay away from books. Often he would block traffic by dancing wildly in the streets. He and his friends spent their days looking for handouts and standing on street corners shouting their "love" and "brotherhood" harangues at passing crowds.

Teen-age girls, many of them beautiful, talented and of good family, left home under his influence. They cut their hair as short as possible, dressed in odd clothes, and refused to have anything to do with marriage. Instead they engaged in all sorts of pacifistic acts and extreme do-gooderism.

"Live Like Jesus"

The young man claimed he was trying to "live like Jesus," all the while growing dirtier and more ragged, begging, mumbling to sticks and stones, "communicating" with anything that happened along. He dragged more and more fine young people away from their homes, schools, careers, into this squalid and appalling way of life, all of them, like him, hipped on "Love, Love, Love."

Although his address was not Haight-Ashbury, but Assisi, he belongs, in a way, to San Francisco. It was named for him.

The Middle Ages was a time of extreme religious fervor, with inquisitions,
official and unofficial, to ferret out religious heresy and new ideas.
Our contemporary world is experiencing a time of extreme "political"
fervor, with similar inquisitions to root out political heresy and new ideas.
Some people are afraid of ideas, and political prisoners, both communist
and capitalist, are found on both sides of the Iron Curtain. Pope Innocent III
ordered a crusade against the heretical Albigensians of southern France,
who were crushed after great violence and bloodshed. About the same time,
the Dominican order was formed to try to convert the Albigensians and
eventually to assist the Office of the Holy Inquisition to fight heresy.
Bernard Gui (1261–1331) was an ardent Dominican from Spain who
presided over hundreds of trials for heresy. The Waldenses, of whom
he speaks, were victims of another bloody crusade.

The Manual of the Inquisitor

Bernard Gui

Of the Sect of the Waldenses and First of Its Origins and Beginnings

The sect or heresy of the Waldenses or the Poor of Lyon came into
being about the year of our Lord 1170. The man responsible for
its creation was an inhabitant of Lyon, Waldes or Waldo, whence the
name of its devotees. He was wealthy, but, after giving up all his
property, determined to practice poverty and evangelic perfection in
the manner of the apostles. He had had the Gospels and several other
books of the Bible translated into vulgar tongue for his use, as well
as several maxims of Saints Augustine, Jerome, Ambrose and Gregory, grouped under titles, which he and his followers called sentences.
They read them very often, although they hardly understood them;
nevertheless, infatuated with themselves, although they had little
learning, they usurped the role of the apostles and dared to preach
the Gospel in the streets and public squares. The said Waldes or
Waldo drew into this presumption numerous accomplices of both
sexes whom he sent out preaching as disciples.

These people, although stupid and unlearned, traveled through
the villages, men and women, and entered homes, and, preaching in
the squares and even in the churches, the men especially, spread about
them a mass of errors.

Summoned by the Archbishop of Lyon, the lord Jean aux Blanches-

Mains, who forbade them such a presumption, they refused obedience, declaring, in order to excuse their madness, that one should obey God rather than man. God ordered the apostles to preach the Gospel to all beings, they said, applying to themselves that which had been said of the apostles, whose followers and successors they boldly declared themselves to be, by a false profession of poverty and by masquerading under an appearance of holiness. Indeed they despised the prelates and clergy because, they said, they owned great wealth and lived in pleasures.

Owing to this arrogant usurpation of the function of preaching, they became teachers of error. Summoned to renounce preaching, they disobeyed and were declared in contempt, and consequently excommunicated and banished from their town and country. Finally, as they persisted, a council held at Rome before the Lateran Council [reference is to fourth Lateran Council, 1215] declared them schismatic and condemned them as heretics. Thus multiplied upon the earth they scattered through the provinces, into neighboring regions and unto the borders of Lombardy. Separated and cut off from the Church, and joining, on the other hand, with other heretics and drinking in their errors, they blended with their own concoctions the errors and heresies of earlier heretics.

The Errors of the Present Waldenses (They Previously Held Several Others)

Disdain for ecclesiastical authority was and still is the prime heresy of the Waldenses. Excommunicated for this reason and delivered over to Satan, they have fallen into innumerable errors, and have blended the errors of earlier heretics with their own concoctions.

The misled believers and sacrilegious masters of this sect hold and teach that they are in no way subject to the lord Pope or Roman Pontiff, or to the other prelates of the Roman Church, and that the latter persecute and condemn them unjustly and improperly. Moreover, they declare that they cannot be excommunicated by this Roman Pontiff and these prelates, and that obedience is owed to none of them when they order and summon the followers and masters of the said sect to abandon or abjure this sect, although this sect be condemned as heretical by the Roman Church.

Miss Lela Kahl wrote this take-home essay, while a freshman student at San Diego Mesa College, in response to the Ismene quotation from Sophocles' "Antigone" below. The paper was written during the week in October 1969 that Vice-President Spiro Agnew (drawing cheers from his partisan audience) called the Vietnam-war protest organizers "merchants of hate" and "parasites of passion" and said the nation can "afford to separate them from our society—with no more regret than we should feel over discarding rotten apples from a barrel." Mr. Agnew and Miss Kahl may be in disagreement over what is positive rebellion and creative protest. Were Antigone and St. Francis "rotten apples"?

Let Us Defend Authority?

Lela Kahl

ISMENE   And, now, we two are left.
Think how much worse our end will be than all
The rest, if we defy our sovereign's edict
And his power. Remind ourselves that we
Are women, and as such are not made to fight
With men. For might unfortunately is right
And makes us bow to things like this and worse.
Therefore shall I beg the saints below
To judge me leniently as one who kneeled
To force. I bend before authority.
It does not do to meddle.

Conformity to society and to the laws of the land has been inherent in every civilization since the dawn of culture on this earth. Since the emergence of the primitive societies consisting of the family unit, the clan, the tribe and eventually the villages and towns, conformity and adaptation have been essential. Most people in the past were forced to adjust. The powers which ruled them tolerated only one way of life—that of mandatory conformity. The process of social indoctrination, the platicizing of the individual (adaptation), begins at birth. Even in the most primitive tribal society, the child was molded and trained to the job he would perform in the future. The young male was taught fighting, self-defense, courage, hunting techniques and leadership ability. He was prepared by a series of rigorous tests until he was fully initiated as a grown male member of the tribe. Likewise,

From "Let Us Defend Authority?" by Lela Kahl. By permission of Lela Kahl and Eric and Eva Kahl.

the female child was prepared throughout her life for maternal duties which included cooking, cleaning, childcare and subservience to her husband. Children were considered outcasts of society if they displayed "abnormal" characteristics such as rebellious individuality or excessive questioning of traditional social myths. This is true even today (the "angry young man" in Britain, the beatnik, hippie, etc.).

Adaptation has been the theme of every church, club, fraternity and party. Conformity has been the requirement of all associations, especially religious, for it is vital for the individual to be accepted by the group and by himself. Primitive man revered the spirits of the animals he hunted for food, in order to be assured of a good hunt and harvest. This led to totemism and the worship of the fertility goddess. In order to be assured of a happy afterlife, primitive man revered his own spirit as well as his ancestors' and made sacrifices to the gods, as well as placing food and implements alongside his carefully buried dead. Religion's seductive promises of eternal paradise strengthened the "virtue" of acceptance.

Adaptation has been the code of every written and understood law. In primitive societies, the chief, the council of elders and the jury of adult males were the lawgivers and enforcers. In the civilizations of Mesopotamia, the "lugals," kings and priests dictated the law and they were obeyed (Hammurabi's code). In Egypt, the pharoahs were the lawmakers. The archons in Greece prescribed the law and, for the most part, it was followed. Pericles describes this in his Funeral Oration (by Thucydides):

> . . . in our public acts we are prevented by doing wrong by fear; we respect the authorities and the laws, especially those which are ordained for the protection of the injured as well as those unwritten laws which bring upon the transgressor admitted dishonor.

Laws have been at work as long as man has been here. All laws have been recognized, observed and broken, but traditionally, it has been the "good" man who has acted according to the law (such as Ismene). But what about those people who break the law (Antigone) or stray away from the norms in areas such as religion, politics and society in general? Do they have any effect on history—are they important? The answer is an emphatic "yes!", for it is these individuals who prove a basic truth in human behavior—we cannot conform. There seems to be a pattern in man's behavior such that he can submit only up to a certain point and then he must rebel. Because of man's instinct of rebellion, he has never been satisfied with the limits of his body. Even in primordial times, he investigated the world about him and harnessed energy to help do his work. The discovery of fire, the wheel, the domestication of animals, methods of scientific agriculture—all these are basic examples of rebellion against nature.

From ancient Egypt comes an example of nonconformity in terms of religion. During the reign of Amenhotep IV (1375–1358 B.C.) the traditional God Amon-Re was rejected. Amenhotep adopted as his religion (and his peoples') the worship of Aton in the place of Amon-Re. The pharoah changed his name to Akhentaton ("He who is devoted to Aton"), left Amon-Re's city to found a new capital (Akhetaton) and passed the rest of his life in worshipping Aton and in composing hymns and prayers. After his death, his weak successor, Tutankhamen, returned to the ancient capital of Thebes and the worship of Amon-Re.

In the field of politics and social dissension, Thucydides (460–400 B.C.) was certainly a pace-setter. In his account of the Peloponnesian Wars, he fixes the blame on his home city-state of Athens. He declares that it was due to Athens' imperialistic attitude and "territorial imperative" that she fought Sparta and eventually caused her own decadence and decline. Even in the free thinking and open society which Athens enjoyed, Thucydides' direct attack on his homeland (in the form of a written account) was unheard-of and certainly a display of a rebellious, nonconforming attitude.

In the play *Antigone,* Sophocles gives a prime example of conformity and rebellion in the area of law and order. A perfect excerpt from the play:

> CREON   And art thou not ashamed to act apart from the rest of them . . .?
>
> ANTIGONE   No; there is nothing shameful in piety to a brother.

In the same sense, there is nothing shameful in following one's own principles when one is willing to accept the consequences, even death.

These examples from ancient history all have one thing in common—they are constructive rebellions, not minor ones concerning dress, manners and tastes (in today's society these are expressed by long hair, hippie movements, etc.). But most important is the fact that there are so few of them, a major concept in understanding the theories of this paper. Constructive rebellion is the productive way toward nonconformity, involving positive criticism in the fields of basic human values, such as religion, politics and morality. In American history, examples of constructive rebellion can be found in the Declaration of Independence, the Bill of Rights, the abolition movement, women's suffrage, labor strikes and, recently, the October 1969

Moratorium Day protests against our involvement in the war in Vietnam.

Constructive rebellion, protest, and revolt are *vital* to every society, for without them the society becomes stagnant and most assuredly deteriorates. Perhaps because there was not enough constructive rebellion in the ancient civilizations (probably because the masses were not given the opportunity to protest), those societies did not have the chance to change and better themselves. The examples which I *have* cited are so prominent in history because they are the rarities of their societies. If the United States today attempts to learn anything from past history to insure the continuence of its progressive culture, it must recognize the mistakes past civilizations made in quenching forms of constructive protest. Positive revolt is natural to man and beneficial to society, and by using it to better his world, the man of today can be assured of an improved environment tomorrow.

Ismene, the beautiful character in Sophocles' "Antigone," conformed and gave good reasons why one should conform. But Antigone is a beautiful character, too. She was a heretic. Is it possible to see timeless beauty in both characters, one demonstrating the necessity for conformity and the other demanding the freedom to object to conformity? Miss America of 1970 is a different character. Compare her to Ismene, or to Miss France of 1430, Saint Joan. Do you find here the reasoned conformity of Ismene?

No Generation Gap at Beauty Pageant

Judith Martin

"Anybody here over 35?" shouted Bert Parks.

"Yaaay" came back the answer from the crowd gathered in Atlantic City's Convention Hall last weekend to watch the Miss America Pageant.

They had come to cheer their idea of what youth should be like and 50 girls had tried all week to personify that idea. Miss America girls do not smoke, drink, date, discuss controversial topics or go around unchaperoned during the pageant—the winner agrees to behave that way for a year—and they are very polite to their elders.

They support their government, condemn dissent, and set their goals on spending a year or two in traditional female occupations—modeling or elementary school teaching—until the right man comes along.

Miss America of 1970, Pamela Anne Eldred of Detroit, gave a press conference in which she said she was a spokesman for her generation and she made a statement about the Establishment:

"I feel that the people who were voted into office must have the intelligence to know what to do and that everybody should have faith in them."

She Didn't Object to Pageant Aides' Gag Rule

She said she did not object when pageant officials refused to let her speak on certain subjects. "I feel that they are older and wiser than I am and I can always learn something especially from someone who is older. If I am told I can't do something, I am told for a reason and I don't challenge it."

From "No Generation Gap at Beauty Pageant" by Judith Martin, *Washington Post*. Reprinted in *Los Angeles Times*, September 14, 1969.

"God love you," said a state pageant official from Michigan.

Other pageant officials, the audience and the judges all talked about how comforting it was to see this girl and the others like her. They called them "true representatives of American youth."

For a few magic days the drug scene, the sexual revolution, and the civil rights, antiwar, female liberation and student protest movements seemed to them to have been just bad dreams populated by "a tiny minority of kooks."

Miss America told her admirers that the war was right because otherwise the government never would have gotten into it. Miss Minnesota, Judith Claire Mendenhall, a runner-up to the title, told them that women shouldn't try to run things "because they are more emotional and men can overcome their emotions with logic."

Miss Virginia, Sydney Lee Lewis, won a talent award for a speech in which she condemned student reform movements but lauded her generation for things like "conceiving the Rally for Decency."

The theme of this year's pageant was "the sound of youth." There was much talk in it about the new sound and then one talent winner sang "Get Happy" and another played "Bumble Boogie" on the piano.

"Each generation has its own translation of young, and this generation's is a search for the golden rainbow of peace and understanding" said Parks to introduce Miss America 1969, Judi Ford, who wore a Ginger Rogers white pleated chiffon dress and danced the kind of number which used to be the finale of motion picture musical-comedies of the '40s.

The pastel chiffon dresses with sequined tops, which the girls wore with 18-button length white cotton gloves in the evening dress competition, had to be specially made. So did the one-piece, solid-color, no-cutouts bathing suits, which are no longer stocked commercially. Spiked-heeled, pointed-toed shoes dyed to match were worn with the bathing suits.

Evening culottes were permitted during the talent competition but most girls favored the sequined, drum majorette type of costume. Several chose mid-knee cocktail dresses just a shade longer than the new habits of a group of nuns who attended the preliminary competition one night.

Make-up was used in the shows to create the kewpie doll look of decades ago—bright red lipstick, blue eye shadow and hair teased into bee-hives with wiglets of curls added.

Off-stage, however, the girls were more contemporary with shoulder length hairstyles and little wool dresses which gave them the look of 50 Tricia Nixons.

The judges said they were gratified at what they saw and had a hard time picking a winner.

"It renews my faith in youth," said Hollywood make-up man Bud Westmore, a judge, whose wife was Miss California of 1952.

"We have a complete misconception of what is going on when we see the New York hippies who don't wash," said Leon Leonidoff, another judge, who has been staging Radio City Music Hall spectaculars since 1932. "This country is wholesome and healthy." His wife is a former Miss New Jersey and he had been going around all week offering contracts to his favorite contestants.

"We really haven't got a thing to worry about," said judge Jane Pickens Langley, who describes herself as "singer, artist and philanthropist."

There's Never a Breath of Scandal About Them

"These aren't the girls you hear about because there is never any scandal attached to them," said judge Zelma George, executive director of the Cleveland Job Corps Center for Women. "Someone should do a master's thesis on them."

"You don't hear about them later because basically they are not ambitious," said writer Joan Crosby, a judge. "They want to be good wives and mothers."

No one seemed to know, however, why most of the past Miss Americas have been divorced at least once.

The pageant officials expressed their delight with the way Miss America 1970 handled reporters' questions.

Topics on which she smiled and said, "I really couldn't voice an opinion—I don't know enough about that" included drugs, nudity in the theater, unisex fashions, student unrest, what the priorities of America should be, and whether 18-year-olds should have the vote. She also said that she was happy about the moon shot "which proves that the United States is a great country" and that her goal in life is "to be a nice person."

Her mother, Mrs. William B. Eldred, who broke in once just after the crowning to tell Miss America, "You are no expert," said that she and her daughter feel alike on all topics. "There is no generation gap," said Mrs. Eldred.

Miss America's one moment of confusion was when she was asked where her father works. He is an employee of Chrysler and loyalty to the pageant's sponsors, one of which is Oldsmobile, is an important quality of Miss America.

Miss America 1969 said that, during her year, love of Toni hair products, Pepsi Cola and Oldsmobile became a spontaneous part of her.

The past and present Miss Americas looked very much alike— both with blond bouffant hairdos, green eyes, pale skin and wide smiles. They are both, said Bert Parks, "composites of positive wonders. All Miss Americas are," he said.

Questions

1 Mothers, fathers, children, cousins, and so forth, are alone and often lost in a great, wide world. They want to identify with something. Why?

2 Why are so many people intolerant of nonconformists?

3 In the United States it is a crime, punishable by fine and imprisonment, to burn or deface the flag. Why? Would the same penalty apply to the burning of the cross? What flag and what cross and under what conditions?

4 How different are the hippies and yippies from the "cult of poverty" movement of St. Francis' time? Can you easily generalize about the youth movement today?

5 Explain the tyranny of convention, giving examples.

8 Medieval Universities Then and Now

Resemblances between certain aspects of university life in the Middle Ages and the present are remarkable. Then, as now, administrators grappled with the challenges of university governance and finance, faculties sought protection for prerogatives such as academic freedom, and students sought release from the pent-up pressures of pedagogical routines. The striking similarities, and some of the differences, are shown in the essay below.

Campus Capers From Manuscript to Microfilm

Melvin Steinfield

From ornate Carolingian manuscripts to soaring Gothic cathedrals, from stirring poetry to speculative philosophy, from beautiful tapestries to haunting melodies, from art to science, the contributions of medieval civilization to the Western heritage are rich and colorful. Many of these achievements have become a vital part of modern life.

Yet the generalization we stubbornly cling to, in the face of considerable evidence to the contrary, is that the Middle Ages deserves to be characterized as the "Dark Ages." Both the "Dark Ages" label and the picture of the Middle Ages as a thousand-year period of mostly wasted time is an indictment that was handed to us by a biased little group of Renaissance historians who were so proud of their way of life that they could not acknowledge objectively their debts to their medieval forerunners.

Nor could they recognize the worth of the medieval values that their own age was rejecting with vehement denunciations. Limited by the perspective of their own historical period, the Renaissance historians created a distorted image which disparaged and minimized the actual accomplishments of the Middle Ages. Like other writers before and after, they could not seem to break out of the narrow box of their own time and place.

Recently, historians began to take a fresh look at some of the neglected aspects of the medieval past. They started their probing research without the Renaissance hangups that have encouraged most people to frown upon the Middle Ages. This contemporary re-evaluation has produced a more favorable verdict on the nature of the medieval achievements and shortcomings. It has certainly shed new light on perhaps the most significant legacy of the Middle Ages: the University. It has not been adequately stressed that the university is a creation of the Middle Ages. And that it was surprisingly modern in many ways.

"The university is a medieval contribution to civilization, and more specifically, a contribution of the twelfth century,"[1] writes one authority, Charles Homer Haskins. Another author notes the connection between the modern university and the medieval university:

> The first debt which the modern university owes to its medieval predecessor is one of existence. Great as were the other civilizations of the past, none of them produced universities as we understand the term today. There is nothing like the continuity of preserving, teaching and finding knowledge that is the glorious history of the medieval universities. Their primary contribution is themselves. Although we have changed some of the methods, added new studies, and multiplied buildings, resources, and faculties, basically the essential idea of the medieval university as a place where an apprentice to learning could become a master of it has remained the same. Our modern universities are perhaps our most medieval organizations.[2]

Thus one must be cautious when confronted with condemnations of the "medieval" elements in the modern university.

The university then, as now, provided the "degree." This degree was the "union card" or ticket to Establishment success; with it one's credentials were sound. Then, as now, the chief motivation for many students was not learning for its own sake, nor the pursuit of truth unto its innermost parts; then, as now, the chief motivation for many students appears to have been the practical one of securing a better job. Another incentive was that students who attended medieval universities were generally exempted from military service.

The facts attest that whether we are talking about superficial matters such as academic dress, or more substantive matters such as approach and organization, the modern university resembles its medieval counterpart quite closely in many ways. The concepts of bachelor's, master's, and doctor's degrees, faculty organizations, lecture methods, and examinations originated in the medieval university. Students wrestled with financial problems and administrators wrestled with the problems of unruly students.

Student recreational activities were well-developed arts and included, but were not limited to, drinking, gambling, loving, and rioting. They were as energetic in the pursuit of fun as today's students. Perhaps even more so:

> The students of the medieval universities were, on the whole, rowdier and more exuberant than students of American universities today, more imaginative in their pranks, and more hostile toward the surrounding towns. Thus the history of medieval

universities is punctuated by frequent town-gown riots. New students were hazed unmercifully; unpopular professors were hissed, shouted down, and even pelted with stones.[3]

Girl-watching was a favorite form of eye-exercise for students who felt they had been hitting the books too much. There were students who ". . . affect rooms overlooking the street to see the girls across the way or those who pass by, or who often appear in church principally on this account, that you may see the ladies!"[4] (At first the universities did not own any buildings; they rented facilities from the townspeople. Students had to arrange their own dormitory deals. Presumably the prices for rooms with a "view" were higher.)

In surveying the varieties of student life on the university campus in the Middle Ages, one soon discovers that girl-watching was often merely a mild prelude to other forms of student affairs:

> Jacob Butrigarius and Baldus write that it is enough to prove a woman a prostitute if students visit her by day and night, without proving the commission of any sexual act, since, when a student talks with such a one, it is not to be presumed that he is repeating the Lord's prayer. And the same Baldus says that the leaser of a house to a student cannot evict him because he has brought prostitutes there and therefore injured the property, since this should have been presumed as a common occurrence.[5]

Another diversion was scribbling sexual epithets on the walls. Heidelberg University still has graffiti from the Middle Ages.

If there was lots of sex on campus, there was also lots of liquor, especially during exam periods. In the medieval university, beer gushed into steins and students poured into town. When both occurred simultaneously townspeople questioned the value of living near a university. Groups of restless students with beer on their breaths roamed the streets in search of excitement. More than once they found it. The rival gangs of students threw rocks, made noise, and in general carried on. Student rampages developed into a major problem:

> Various forms of practical joking of the more violent order enjoyed a high degree of popularity. Among the archives of the University of Leipzig is a "libellus formularis" or collection of forms for rectorial proclamations against the various kinds of disorder which were wont to break out periodically in a medieval university like the recurrent epidemics of pea-shooting, catapulting, and the like at a modern school. Among these is a form of proclamation against destroying trees and crops in the ad-

joining country, against "wandering with arms after the town-hall bell," against throwing water out of the window upon passers-by, against wandering at night and beating the watch . . . against interfering with the hangman . . . in the performance of his duty . . .[6]

It seems that nearly everywhere in medieval European universities students were involved in vigorous releases of surplus calories. When students at Leipzig made throwing stones at professors a regular activity, it became necessary for the administration to devise a scale of ascending punishments for "hitting without wounding" and "wounding without mutilation."

"Oxford students went through the streets with swords and bows and arrows shortly before the hour of curfew and assaulted all who passed by." Students at Rome went "wandering armed from tavern to tavern and other unhonest places. . . ." "The student is much more familiar," says Robert de Sorbon [a founder of the University of Paris], "with the text of the dice, which he recognizes at once, no matter how rapidly they are thrown, than with the text of the old logic." Students at Paris even had to be warned to stop playing dice on the altar of Notre Dame after one of their festival processions.[7]

Thus it can be seen that Medieval students were no less rambunctious than modern students.

Besides the similarity of student recreational activities, there are other ways in which the medieval university was remarkably modern. Competition among universities to attract students is not limited to the twentieth century Big Ten and Ivy League. Charles of Anjou informed the teachers and students of the University of Paris in 1272 that the University of Naples ". . . has just been opened with modern improvements, with assurance of suitable protection, and appropriate favors to help its development." He continued in a modern vein when he cited the attractions of the setting of the university: "This very city . . . is praised for the purity of its air, its comparable and healthful location, its richness in all products of the soil, its convenience for communication by sea with other parts of Italy." His conclusion was a perfect Madison Avenue punchline: "Wherefore [to all beginners and graduates] let them come, in so far as they are able, to this University, as to a great feast which is adorned by the presence of illustrious guests and which overflows with an abundance and variety of refreshing food."[8]

The concept of learning by osmosis was not confined to the modern university student: "And the spoken word of the professor has some occult virtue that penetrates deeper into the mind of the hearer and makes a greater impression upon the memory than private reading. . . ."⁹

The notion of group instruction was unknown in antiquity—it was a contribution of the medieval university. Another concept that originated in the Middle Ages was the formal teaching license. The idea of a general liberal arts curriculum also originated at this time.

In addition to the many similarities between medieval and modern universities, there were several instances in which the medieval university actually outshone the modern one. For example, academic freedom was protected in the thirteenth century more than it has been at times in the twentieth. In the thirteenth century, the Papacy failed on several occasions to prevent the study of Aristotelian philosophy at Paris. It met with less success in thwarting the study of a radical doctrine then than Senator Joseph McCarthy did in the early 1950's. (However, Peter Abelard was driven out of Paris by St. Bernard.)

On the other hand, professors were in a poorer position with respect to their students than has thus far been the case in twentieth-century America. Some student guilds were so powerful that the authority of the faculty looked quite small by contrast. The students at Bologna directly paid and controlled their professors' salaries. According to the 1317 statutes of the University of Bologna, a professor desiring a leave of absence even for a single day had to obtain permission from his own students. That did not leave much time for honeymoon or bereavement unless the students approved.

Whenever faculty, students, and administration acted in unison, they were a formidable force. The mere threat of moving to another town would invariably gain concessions or price reductions from the town merchants who catered to the university food, clothing, and lodging trade. As universities acquired their own buildings, this threat lost its effectiveness. Thus, ironically, greater wealth brought a partial reduction of university power in the community, because the more it gained in material resources, the more intertwined it became in the power structure of the town and the less likely it would be to move to another town.

There were, of course, significant differences between medieval and modern universities. Students and professors could not enjoy the advantages of large modern libraries since, for all practical purposes, they simply did not exist. Emphasis in courses was on learning to master specific authoritative texts. Course selection was much more limited than today. College-sponsored extracurricular events were unheard of. Lectures could not be varied with electronic audio-visual aids, and the general physical comforts of modern technological society were not available in the cold, damp lecture halls. Taken together, these differences meant that the medieval student would have to overcome more severe obstacles to learning than the modern student. But happiness and contentment are relative states of mind. Students through the ages tend to adjust to the conditions of learning.

On the whole, then, the modern university is not as different from the medieval university as is sometimes supposed. "Medieval," therefore, need not be a pejorative term. For it must be remembered that the university as we know it today was essentially a medieval creation. While witch trials were being conducted in Salem, Massachusetts, in the late seventeenth century, the University of Bologna in Italy and the University of Paris in France could point to a history that at that time was already more than five centuries long. And when Harvard College was founded in Cambridge, Massachusetts, in the seventeenth century, it could draw from the rich record of experiences that had been accumulating at Oxford University in England and at Valencia in Spain since the early 1200's.

From the panty raids of the 1950's to the more politically motivated sit-ins and demonstrations of the 1960's, American students (whose oldest university goes back a mere three hundred and fifty years) have been behaving in a manner little different from their counterparts in the Middle Ages—where it all began.

Notes

1 Charles Homer Haskins, *The Renaissance of the Twelfth Century* (Cambridge, Mass.: Harvard University Press, 1927). Quoted in Brisson D. Gooch, *Interpreting Western Civilization*, Vol. I (Homewood, Ill.: Dorsey, 1969), p. 167.

2 L. J. Daly, *The Medieval University* (New York: Sheed & Ward, 1961), p. 213.

3 C. Warren Hollister, *Medieval Europe—A Short History,* second edition (New York: Wiley, 1968), p. 261-262.

4 Gerald M. Straka, *The Medieval World and Its Transformations,* Vol. II of *Western Society: Institutions and Ideals* (New York: McGraw-Hill, 1967), p. 255.

5 *Ibid.*

6 Hastings Rashdall, *The Universities in the Middle Ages,* F. M. Powicke and A. B. Emden, eds. (London: Oxford University Press, 1958), Vol. 3, p. 426. Quoted in Norman F. Cantor and Michael S. Werthman, *The History of Popular Culture to 1815* (New York: Macmillan, 1968), p. 170.

7 James Westfall Thompson and Edgar Nathaniel Johnson, *An Introduction to Medieval Europe* (New York: Norton, 1937), pp. 735–736. These were quotes by much earlier sources which Thompson and Johnson were reprinting. The last sentence is Thompson and Johnson's own words.

8 *Ibid.*

9 Straka, *op. cit.*, p. 256.

Peter Abelard (1079–1142) was the bold thinker whom students flocked to hear in the formative days of the University of Paris. The introduction to his famous book "Sic et Non" outlines an approach to authority that is distinctively modern in its outlook.

The Modern Outlook

Peter Abelard

There are many seeming contradictions and even obscurities in the innumerable writings of the church fathers. Our respect for their authority should not stand in the way of an effort on our part to come at the truth. The obscurity and contradictions in ancient writings may be explained upon many grounds, and may be discussed without impugning the good faith and insight of the fathers. A writer may use different terms to mean the same thing, in order to avoid a monotonous repetition of the same word. Common, vague words may be employed in order that the common people may understand; and sometimes a writer sacrifices perfect accuracy in the interest of a clear general statement. Poetical, figurative language is often obscure and vague.

Not infrequently, apocryphal works are attributed to the saints. Then, even the best authors often introduce the erroneous views of others and leave the reader to distinguish between the true and the false. Sometimes, as Augustine confesses in his own case, the fathers ventured to rely upon the opinions of others.

Doubtless the fathers might err; even Peter, the prince of the apostles, fell into error; what wonder that the saints do not always show themselves inspired? The fathers did not themselves believe that they, or their companions, were always right. Augustine found himself mistaken in some cases and did not hesitate to retract his errors. He warns his admirers not to look upon his letters as they would upon the Scriptures, but to accept only those things which, upon examination, they find to be true.

All writings belonging to this class are to be read with full freedom to criticize, and with no obligation to accept unquestioningly; otherwise the way would be blocked to all discussion, and posterity be deprived of the excellent intellectual exercise of debating difficult questions of language and presentation. But an explicit exception must be

From *Sic et Non* by Peter Abelard, from James Harvey Robinson, *Readings in European History,* Vol. I (Boston: Ginn, 1904), pp. 450–451.

made in the case of the Old and New Testaments. In the Scriptures, when anything strikes us as absurd, we may not say that the writer erred, but that the scribe made a blunder in copying the manuscripts, or that there is an error in interpretation, or that the passage is not understood. The fathers make a very careful distinction between the Scriptures and later works. They advocate a discriminating, not to say suspicious, use of the writings of their own contemporaries.

In view of these considerations, I have ventured to bring together various dicta of the holy fathers, as they came to mind, and to formulate certain questions which were suggested by the seeming contradictions in the statements. These questions ought to serve to excite tender readers to a zealous inquiry into truth and so sharpen their wits. The master key of knowledge is, indeed, a persistent and frequent questioning. Aristotle, the most clear-sighted of all the philosophers, was desirious above all things else to arouse this questioning spirit, for in his *Categories* he exhorts a student as follows: "It may well be difficult to reach a positive conclusion in these matters unless they be frequently discussed. It is by no means fruitless to be doubtful on particular points." By doubting we come to examine, and by examining we reach the truth.

"The history of Paris," writes Paul Lacroix, "teems with episodes, some curious, and only too many tragic, which denote the turbulent and seditious tendencies of the University students." In Lacroix's selection below he makes some mention of student militancy but also refers to milder forms of amusement. The games and rampages at the University of Paris were typical of activities engaged in by medieval students at other universities.

Student Anarchy

Paul Lacroix

But if the books of study used in the ancient schools are now out of date and long since forgotten, such is not the case with the different kinds of recreation in which boys and young men used to indulge as a relaxation from a course of study often abstract and always severe. The *Gargantua* of Rabelais, and the familiar dialogues of Mathurin Cordier, enable us to frame a list of games which are still played, though in some cases under slightly different names; as, for instance, the ball, prisoner's-base, leap-frog, quoits, *clicquette* (pieces of wood, or shords, which were beaten one against another to make them ring), ninepins, bat and trap, spinning-tops and whipping-tops, the *fossette,* or pitch-farthing (which was formerly played with nuts), odd or even, cards, draughts, tennis, heads or tails, tip-cat, etc.

These were the peaceable games of children and scholars, but they were too tame for the turbulent tastes of the older students, whose bad reputation is still proverbial. From all time, grave magistrates, illustrious writers, famous citizens, and even saintly personages have prefaced their career of labor, study, and virtue by a more or less prolonged sowing of wild oats. At all times, moreover, Paris offered only too many temptations to vice and dissipation. It is easy, therefore, to understand what must have been the condition, in the twelfth and thirteenth centuries, when the police as an institution, were hardly known, and when public morality still felt the effects of long years of decadence, of a population of students penned up in a territory which they looked upon as a freehold, consisting, as they did, of youths on the verge of manhood and of full-grown men, belonging to various nationalities, and left to their own passions. When it is further remembered that a degree of arts could not be obtained before the age of one-and-twenty, and one of theology till the age of thirty-five

From *Science and Literature in the Middle Ages and the Renaissance* by Paul Lacroix (New York: Frederick Ungar, 1964), pp. 30–33.

(after eight years' study in the latter case), no wonder that this turbulent quarter was a nuisance, and even a danger for the honest and peaceful inhabitants of Paris.

The whole city was more than once disturbed, and public safety endangered, by the aggressive and disorderly habits of the students. Not a day passed without quarrels and fights, arising out of the most futile causes. The insulting epithets which the students applied to each other show, moreover, the antipathies which prevailed amongst them, and the coarseness which was common to them all. The English had the reputation of being cowards and drunkards; the French were proud and effeminate; the Germans dirty, gluttonous, and ill-tempered; the Normans boastful and deceitful; the Burgundians brutal and stupid; the Flemish bloodthirsty, vagabond, and house-burners; and so forth for the rest.

With all this, the person of a *clerk* (a title appertaining to every student who had obtained his license) was, according to the canons of the Church, inviolable; to lay hands upon a student was to commit a crime which entailed excommunication, and which the Pope alone could absolve. This will explain the audacity and arrogance of the students, and it is no wonder that the civil authorities were, for all the most minute precautions, continually at a loss how to repress the excesses of these riotous youths, who, going about day and night in armed bands, indulged in every kind of disorder, and did not stop at any crime.

The establishment of the colleges led to a decided change for the better. Previously to this happy innovation the students took advantage of the most trifling religious or literary occurrence to increase the number of festivals, which were celebrated with no lack of dancing, masquerades, banquets, etc. All these scholastic rejoicings were afterwards reduced to two *refreshments* (days intended for a carousal), one at the beginning, the other at the end of the public examinations, a period at which the candidates elected a captain from amongst themselves, and to a fête in honor of the patron saint of each nation. This was exclusive of the great festivals celebrated in honor of such and such a *patron* of the University corporation.

College life in the Middle Ages was, of course, not just a series of riotous incidents and wild fun. There were classes to attend, assignments to perform, and schedules to follow. From the selection below, it would appear that the medieval student was expected to adhere to a more demanding regimen than his modern counterpart—at least, in theory.

A Typical Schedule

L. J. Daly

The medieval student seems to have been a hardier individual than his modern successor when it comes to certain aspects of his ordinary class schedule. At least he started classes a bit earlier than is our wont today. Generally, the first lecture of the daily grind seems to have begun about six in the morning or, at the latest, about seven. There is a daily class schedule which has come down to us from the University of Leipzig, unfortunately a bit later than one would like (1519), but undoubtedly mirroring conditions which were customary. According to this timetable the student began classes at 6 A.M. with a lecture on metaphysics! At Bologna the student attended a lecture in the morning which had to be finished by tierce (9 A.M.), and then two lectures in the afternoon, from 2 to 4 P.M. and from 4 to 5:30 P.M. during the summer. Robert Goulet in his account of the University of Paris (1517) presents his ideal schedule for a student:

> Rise at 4 A.M.
> Arts lecture at 5
> Mass at 6, breakfast
> The regents go to their classes 8–10 (or 9–11 during Lent)
> Formal debates before the noon meal
> Repetitions
> Lectures 3–5
> Disputations 5–6
> Repetitions after evening meal
> Off to bed at 9 P.M.

The average lecture often lasted for two hours. For example, the city regulations of the commune of Bologna (1475) with regard to the professors whose salary was paid by the city declared that those professors were required to lecture for one or two hours, according to

From *The Medieval University* by L. J. Daly, S. J., pp. 108–112. © Sheed & Ward Inc., 1961.

the statutes of the university. At Padua, the doctor or professor was directed by statute to lecture for two hours, and students were forbidden, likewise by statute, to beat upon desks or benches to bring him to an earlier stop!

There were, as we have already noted, two chief types of lectures, one called the "ordinary" lecture and the other called the "extraordinary" at Bologna or the "cursory" at Paris. The difference between these two kinds of instruction has been a disputed point, but it now seems safe to say that they are distinguished by several characteristics. Usually, the "ordinary" lectures were the most important and formed the basis of the curriculum; they were generally given during the morning hours and by the salaried professors. The "extraordinary" lectures were delivered later on in the day, and frequently, especially at Paris, they covered the matter in a more "cursory" way. Sometimes they were given by the bachelors and were presented sketchily by way of review. Thus it might happen that a book was taken in the "ordinary" way one year, and in the following year studied in a briefer —more of a survey—presentation. The student might hear it in this way either for the first time or by way of review.

Besides these formal lectures there were other intellectual exercises from which learning might be gained. First, there were various kinds of disputations. *A disputation basically is the presentation, explanation, and proof of some statement or theory and the answering of objections against it put by an opponent.* Sometimes the defender would be a student in a private class, where for the sake of practice this sort of review might be demanded weekly; at other times the apprentice teacher, the "bachelor" was the defendant and answered objections put to him by another; or again, the defendant might be the professor himself, who held the field against all comers. Young students present at these various kinds of intellectual tournaments naturally learned from others' experiences.

Another type of scholastic exercise was a kind of catechetical repetition of the materials covered in class during which the scholars were quizzed about the lecture either by the lecturer himself or someone else. It is thus described in an ordinance for Louvain in 1476:

> . . . After lunch, each one having brought to the table his books, all the scholars of the Faculty together, in the presence of a tutor, shall review that regular lecture; and in the review the tutor shall follow a method which will enable him by discreet questioning of every man to find out if each of them listened well to the lecture and remembered it and which will also recall the

whole lecture by having its parts recited by individuals. And if watchful care is used in this, one hour will suffice.[1]

There were numerous holidays during the scholastic year. In fact at Bologna, if there was no holiday during the week, Thursday was taken as the day off for that week. On these feast days the ordinary and extraordinary lectures were not given, but on other subjects lectures were allowed; for example, in the Rules for the University of Paris as given in 1215 by the cardinal legate Robert de Courçon, it is stipulated that "they shall not lecture on feast days except on philosophers and rhetoric and the *quadrivium* and *Barbarismus* (*Ars Maior* of Donatus, Book III), and ethics if it please them, and the fourth book of the *Topics*." Thus on holidays students could pick up additional knowledge, oftentimes on various subjects of the *trivium* or *quadrivium*.

The history of the student vacations in the Middle Ages is one of expansion! In 1231 Gregory XI, in his reformatory bull "the Magna Carta of Paris University," lays down that "henceforward the summer vacation shall not exceed one month," and he allowed the bachelors to continue their lectures if they wished. At the end of the fourteenth century, however, the long vacation began on the vigil of the feast day of Sts. Peter and Paul (June 28) and lasted until the feast of St. Louis for the faculty of arts (August 25) or until the day after the Exaltation of the Holy Cross (September 16) for the faculties of theology and canon law. At these dates, lectures could be begun, but actually it seems that the feast of St. Remigius (October 1) was the formal opening of the school term. There were two major divisions in the school year; the "great ordinary," from October 1 to Easter, and the "little ordinary," from Easter until the end of June. There were a few days off at Christmas and Easter, and even during the "long vacation" "cursory" lectures could still be given.

The place of lectures is one of the great differences between the medieval university and its modern counterpart. In the beginning the professor used his own room or rooms, and when the classes became too large he would have to hire a hall. Later on at Paris, for example, the nations had their own schools for the "ordinary" lectures. For the "extraordinary" type, the teacher had to fend for himself. At Bologna for the large student assemblies, or for doctoral inceptions, they used a nearby church or the cathedral. The master, or professor, paid his own rent to some individual owner of the building. Later on, by 1400, when the various nations at Paris owned their own buildings, the master rented from them instead. If the master did not have a benefice or salary, he was dependent on the fees of his students, chiefly those levied at the "determination" of his bachelors. The college system brought about an advantage to the master because the college furnished him a place to teach and relieved him of any rent problems.

Note

1 Quoted from A. Norton, *Readings in the History of Education* (Cambridge, 1909), p. 132.

This selection points out the problems of university students as shown in their own letters to people at home. Apparently, college life could become difficult in those days, too. The letters and sermons that are discussed reflect the concerns of students who are trying to make the grade when the going gets rough.

The Inside View

L. J. Daly

Because letter-writing was not within the scope of everyone's ability, there were in the Middle Ages "professors of correspondence," who practiced and taught the art of official letter-writing and even private correspondence. These *dictatores,* as they were called, taught in the schools or chanceries or took to the road with their knowledge of letter-writing, an art "often and exceeding necessary for the clergy, for monks suitable, and for laymen honorable." They advocated a very formalized type of letter, generally in five parts: the salutation (each medieval class had its own special greeting); the *exordium,* which was to render the reader benevolent; the statement, or narration, of the letter; the petition, which generally took the form of a conclusion from the *exordium* as a major, and narration as a minor, premise in the epistolary syllogism; and finally, the proper phrases of the conclusion.[1]

The complicated construction of the medieval letter demanded more than ordinary skill, and the result was the wholesale copying of letters, as well as the editing of hundreds of "model" letters of various types, put out in correspondence copybooks. Real or fictitious letters might thus be drawn upon. For the historian of diplomatics, such models, since they are offered as examples, are open to serious question. But for the historian of customs and medieval society, they can be a true source of information, particularly if the conditions they describe are found so generalized that it is evident that they were commonplaces. Such is the case in the various collections of letters from students to their parents. These mention the various universities of Bologna, Naples, Vienna, Prague, Oxford, Orleans, and Paris. Some are written in a popular Latin, others are quite stiff and formalized; but all of them picture to us the student problems of the Middle Ages.

From *The Medieval University* by L. J. Daly, S. J., pp. 174–181. © Sheed & Ward Inc., 1961. Letters from "The Life of Medieval Students as Illustrated by Their Letters," *Studies in Medieval Culture* by C. H. Haskins (Oxford, 1929), pp. 1–36, by permission of the Clarendon Press, Oxford.

Often, were the letter in English, or some other modern language, and the date-line contemporary, it might be mistaken for that of a present-day student.

The preponderant item in the letters from students to their parents or relatives is not news but *cash*. One father says in a model letter that the student's first song is a demand for money.[2] How to sugar-coat this ever-present pill was the most difficult task facing the letter-writer. Generally the student describes his situation at some center of learning, himself as well and happy, but in great need of money for books and other necessary expenses, as in this example supposedly written from Oxford:

> B. to his venerable master A., greeting. This is to inform you that I am studying at Oxford with the greatest diligence, but the matter of money stands greatly in the way of my promotion, as it is now two months since I spent the last of what you sent me. The city is expensive and makes many demands; I have to rent lodgings, buy necessaries, and provide for many other things which I cannot now specify. Wherefore I respectfully beg your paternity by the promptings of divine pity you may assist me, so that I may be able to complete what I have well begun. For you must know that without Ceres and Bacchus, Apollo grows cold. . . .[3]

Sometimes the student asked for the things he needed directly from home rather than for money to purchase them, as in a twelfth-century letter from Chartres in which two brothers ask their mother for "some thick lambskin for winter clothes, parchment for a psalter, some good chalk, and finally, for Papa's great boots." At times the students attributed their plight to the higher cost of living due to a bad winter, a threatened siege, or a crop failure; or sometimes they laid the blame on a previous messenger who had run away with the money. One letter purports to come from some scholars writing from the dungeon of a prison where they were living on hard and mouldy bread, drinking water bitter with their own tears, and surrounded with a darkness so dense they could feel it. In another, a lad writes to his sister (because he is afraid to write home to his parents) that he is without a blanket to cover him, without shoes or shirt—will she send him clothes and money? The good sister, horrified at his plight, sends him money and some cloth, but cautions him not to tell her husband, because if he hears of it she's "as good as dead."

Not all the answering letters contained only money; many inclosed advice on how *not* to spend it; the student is advised to recall how his Uncle John got along well enough on much less *per diem*;

he must remember the needs of the others in the family; or he is told that he should be at home helping his parents make money, and not extorting it from them by letter. Sometimes the father or guardian had apparently received a quite different report about the student from that contained in the student's own letter, and the response would be somewhat like the following:

> To his son G. residing at Orleans, P. of Besançon sends greeting with paternal zeal. It is written, "he also that is slothful in his work is brother to him that is a great waster." I have recently discovered that you live dissolutely and slothfully, preferring license to restraint and play to work and strumming a guitar while the others are at their studies, whence it happens that you have read but one volume of law while your more industrious companions have read several. Wherefore I have decided to exhort you herewith to repent utterly of your dissolute and careless ways, that you may no longer be called a waster and that your shame may be turned to good repute.[4]

Sometimes the student did include some bits of news, or at least some description of his student life, as the following letter shows:

> To their very dear and respected parents M. Martre, knight and his wife, M. and S. their sons send greetings and filial obedience. This is to inform you that, by divine mercy, we are living in good health in the city of Orleans and are devoting ourselves wholly to study, mindful of the words of Cato, "to know anything is praiseworthy, etc." We occupy a good and comely dwelling, next door but one to the schools and marketplace, so that we can go to school every day without wetting our feet. We have also good companions in the house with us, well advanced in their studies and of excellent habits—an advantage which we well appreciate, for as the Psalmist says, "With an upright man thou wilt show thyself upright." Wherefore lest production cease from lack of material, we beg your paternity to send us by the bearer B., money for buying parchment, ink, a desk, and the other things which we need, in sufficient amount that we may suffer no want on your account (God forbid!) but finish our studies and return home with honor. The bearer will also take charge of the shoes and stockings which you have to send us, and any news at all.[5]

From the various letters it would seem that the journey to the university was not always a happy one, despite the privileges accorded to the traveling student by emperor, king, or pope. Evidently the medieval highwaymen did not respect the student's love of knowledge any more than they did the merchant's love of gain. One letter tells of a student who in crossing the Alps on his way to Bologna was robbed of his clothes, horses, books, and money, and forced to take refuge in a nearby monastery to await further subsidization. Another on his way to Paris joined a group of four fellow travelers only to find that they were robbers who had disguised themselves as clerics.

Once the student arrived at his chosen place of study, according to these letters, he was loth to quit the student life. There are letters of petition for an extension of time for study, no matter what the reason for return home might be; despite the death of loved ones, the difficulties of dividing the inheritance, the danger of war, the student always pleads for permission to remain a little longer at his books. One student of Siena received word that he should return home to marry and that the selected spouse was a good match; he replied that one can always get a wife, but that science once forsaken cannot be re-gained. There was the ever-present problem of securing books, which cost so much more than modern ones. There was not only the question of the text itself, but the glosses which had to be copied in a large and readable hand. A student of Orleans wrote home that he had become a famous dialectician, and that he would like to study theology. His father, however, wrote back that, although he praised his ambition he could not afford the cost of a Bible, and his son should turn his thoughts to a more lucrative profession.

Many of the letters describe the expense of taking a degree, with special emphasis on the inception banquet. A student of Paris wrote to a friend asking him to explain to his father how it was that after he had studied so much, now nothing was lacking but the money for the graduation ceremonies, "for the simple lay mind does not grasp such things"! There were also the letters written home to describe the successful graduation ceremonies, as this model letter of Buoncompagno, a professor of Bologna and author of several rhetorical works, testifies:

> Sing unto the Lord a new song, praise him with stringed in-struments and organs, rejoice upon the high-sounding cymbals, for your son has held a glorious disputation, which was attended by a great number of teachers and scholars. He answered all questions without a mistake. Moreover, he celebrated a famous banquet, at which both rich and poor were honored as never before, and he has duly begun to give lectures which are already so popular that others' classrooms are deserted and his own are filled.[6]

According to the picture painted in the average letter, the student of the medieval university was diligent and studious, went usually to three lectures a day and strove to excel even the professors in his grasp of knowledge. Buoncompagno has a letter for the student who studies too much—who rises in the morning before the bell, comes to school before his fellow students and leaves after all others have departed; at other times stays in his room to study; meditates his lectures at meal time, and even argues in his sleep. But the author also adds that the same form letter could be sent as irony to one who does not take his university work very seriously!

Another source of information on the daily life of the medieval student is the medieval sermon. This type of information, however, must be used with great caution, for the purpose of the preacher was not to write history but to convert a soul. The various sermons of preachers in or near universities with the examples which they use to illustrate their doctrine and keep their hearers awake frequently give us a glimpse into the evil side of student activities. There is the instance of the conceited and proud master whose vain boasts about his prowess in explication of difficult texts caused him to be struck dumb on the very morning of his lecture, and it was with the greatest difficulty that he relearned the seven penitential psalms. The gambling students who do not hesitate to gamble even in church, the wine-bibbers and drunkards, the frequenters of taverns and houses of ill-fame, the violent students ever ready for a street fight and armed only with a knife and without helmet, rushing into a fray that even an armed knight would have sense enough to avoid—these are all described.

Various student attitudes are portrayed for us in these sermons. In one example three Flemish students discuss their future; one plans to become a Cistercian monk, another desires a master's chair at Paris, the third decides for the career of a jongleur [minstrel]. There is the poor student whose only friend is St. Nicholas, and who copies for himself or for others those glosses and texts so necessary for study; but, though he copies correctly, others copy more rapidly and in a better hand. Then there are the rich students who have beautiful books which they never even open.

The masters also come in for their share of castigation. Some teach before they know enough. Copying their lectures from books of others and not drawing on personal knowledge, *they* have to pay the students to come to their classes. Others there are whose sole desire is a crowded classroom, and to obtain it they do not scruple to teach unusual and strange doctrines, and on Sunday or holy days. There are the indulgent masters who allow their students to sleep late and amuse themselves in going about the city, and sometimes they connive at their charges' worst vices. There is also mention of the master who desires not to instruct others but to be thought learned, and who speaks in an obscure manner in order to be thought profound!

Notes

1 Cf. C. H. Haskins, *Studies in Medieval Culture* (Oxford, 1929), pp. 1–36, on which the following pages largely depend.

2 Haskins, *op. cit.,* p. 7.

3 Haskins, *op. cit.,* p. 10.

4 Haskins, *op. cit.,* p. 15.

5 Haskins, *op. cit.,* p. 17.

6 Haskins, *op. cit.,* p. 28.

After reading about the pranks of medieval students, one might wonder whether they left any room for creative innovations. The following survey of contemporary revelry shows that today's college students are also quite imaginative.

Modern Ingenuity

Jerrold Footlick

. . . Fun on the American campus takes many forms. Some of it is well organized, perhaps over-organized. Almost every college has its spring carnival, its homecoming weekend, its student union with organized activities.

Some pranks turn into destruction or tragedy. Riots may begin as simply a way to let off steam, but sometimes people are hurt and property is damaged.

Occasionally, a fraternity pledge has been seriously injured, or has died, in initiation rites or hazing permitted to get out of control. That aspect of college life seems to be diminishing. The National Inter-Fraternity Conference contends that dangerous hazing has disappeared from fraternity life.

Some college fun is spontaneous, inventive, hilarious. Some is aimed at puncturing hallowed traditions, or spoofing the college administration. And some fun has no point to it at all.

Consider the annual Bladderball Day at Yale University. On a Saturday morning in autumn, hundreds of students show up to see, and be swept into, a wild scuffle in the middle of New Haven, Conn.

The contestants ostensibly are six teams: from two Yale literary magazines, a parody magazine, a scientific magazine, the Yale Daily News, and Yale radio station WYBC. For a week ahead of time, these six hurl insults and outrageous challenges at one another belittling all opponents and threatening their annihilation.

About 10 A.M. on the day of the contest, the teams mass on the great grass court known as Old Campus. Each team comes cloaked in its own battle dress, which may mean a football helmet or a nightgown. By 10:30 the crowd has increased to several hundred, and the chant begins: "We want the ball!" By 11 o'clock a stately procession of campus police appears, pushing the Bladderball before them.

A Bladderball is a canvas-covered balloon about 20 feet in circumference and taller than a man. As the police roll it into the crowd, the

From *College Scene Now* by Jerrold Footlick (1967), pp. 38–41, 42–44, 45–47. By permission of *The National Observer*.

shouting dies down momentarily. The teams fall back about 15 feet from the ball, the police retreat, and with a yell, the mass closes in on the ball.

The point is that there is no point. The ball is tossed into the air and bounces over the heads of students who stampede after it around a courtyard. Many trip and fall in a crush of flailing arms and tangled legs, and emerge with a shirt ripped off or a shoe missing.

After about 30 minutes of this, WYBC reports that "victory is ours," and the Yale Daily News distributes a special edition headlining its own victory. The Bladderball by this time has been pushed toward one of the spiked iron fences that line the Old Campus. The remaining contenders make their final lunge, and the ball bounds over the fence into the arms of the campus police, who roll it away and deflate it for another year.

Autumn is also the time of college fun revolving around football and homecoming.

At the University of Oregon, a huge St. Bernard dog named "Horse" was elected homecoming queen one year by a large margin over five coeds. "Horse," the mascot of Phi Kappa Psi fraternity, was not permitted to wear her crown, but she did accompany the homecoming court as official chaperon.

Down the Pacific coast at Stanford University, the first homecoming queen contest in the school's 75-year history was held in 1966. It also was probably the last.

As the contest votes were counted, it became clear that a dreamy blond, Wendy G. Wonka, would finish high among the contestants. Winsome Wendy really was a dream—it soon turned out that she didn't exist. She was entered in the contest as a joke. The Stanford students promptly held a referendum and abolished the contest.

Stanford's big football game each year is against nearby University of California at Berkeley. The night before the game there is a huge bonfire rally in the bottom of Stanford's Lake Lagunita (dry in the fall). And for three nights, the Big Game Gaities—a musical spoof of Berkeley—is performed.

For the 1967 Big Game, Stanford engineering students designed a home-made cannon to launch a water-filled balloon from the Stanford rooting section across the field to drench the Cal fans.

At Cornell University in Ithaca, N.Y., the student newspaper has become well known for its pranks and bogus editions.

In 1954, the staff of The Cornell Daily Sun went to Syracuse University, overpowered the printers of The Syracuse Daily Orange (reportedly without injuries), and distributed an edition of its own on the morning of the Cornell-Syracuse football game. The "Daily Orange" edition reported on a "grid scandal" at Syracuse.

In 1965, just before the Cornell-Princeton basketball game, a bogus edition of The Daily Princetonian was published and distributed on the Princeton campus by Cornell students. The edition reported the loss of All-America Bill Bradley to the Princeton team, but Bradley turned up very healthy at the game and led Princeton to a 107-84 rout of Cornell.

During freshman orientation time at Rice University in Houston, a freshman beanie is placed atop a 24-foot, greased pole. The pole itself is in the middle of a pit about 10 yards in diameter and three feet deep; the pit is filled with mud obtained from oil-well drilling.

Rice freshmen (volunteers) are given a one-minute head start to go after the beanie. After the minute, the sophomores come after them and try to keep them from the goal.

For several years the beanie was unattainable, but in 1963 an enterprising group of freshmen hired a helicopter. Exactly on signal, the copter flew in and hovered over the pole while a freshman leaned out and grabbed the beanie above the heads of muddy and infuriated sophomores.

"Placard cheering" is a football-game tradition at Syracuse University and some other schools. Syracuse freshmen are given three cards of different colors and herded—boy, girl, boy, girl—into a special card section at the games. Various numbers are called off, corresponding to colors, and the cards are held up. When everything works right, the result is a huge picture for those across the field or for the television cameras. West Coast colleges pioneered card sections.

Fence painting also was big at Syracuse while there was a fence around the construction of the new physics building. A fence-painting contest highlighted one homecoming weekend, and painters came up with such slogans as, "Tomorrow has been cancelled . . . God." With the end of the construction job, artists were looking for new fences.

At Indiana University, painting of sidewalk stencils has become popular. Using large, home-made stencils, students have painted such sidewalk slogans as "Beware the Bushawg" or "Who is the Green Rabbit?"

Painting is part of homecoming at Kent State University in Ohio. On the front campus there are large stone letters—K E N T—and the night before the homecoming game, fraternity men and independents face each other, paint brushes in hand.

The Greeks try to paint the stone letters, and the independents try to stop them. By the time it's over, there is more paint on the students than on the letters.

Springtime at Kent State brings heavy rain, turning the campus commons into mud. On the first warm evening, male students are likely to jump into the gooey mess and start throwing it around. A passing coed may be tossed into the mud, and her laughter (or screaming) brings girls running from their dormitories, dressed in their grubbiest clothes.

Then the mud slinging really begins, "with the basic pursuit of getting filthy," as one Kent student said. When the mud fight is over, the participants are covered with mud and their clothing is ready for the incinerator.

Spring brings the spring riot to many campuses. After a long winter of study, the students are ready to let loose.

At Syracuse, for instance, 1966 was the year of the water riot. It began as a small fight between a fraternity and a sorority, but by the time it ended there were an estimated 3,000 students roaming the streets, filling pails and trash cans at faucets and hydrants, and dousing everyone in sight.

When they marched on the campus business area of Marshall Street, things got a bit too destructive and the police were called. They were doused, too, as were university officials who tried to stop the riot.

Hundreds of students applauded when the Dingleman (a traveling snack bar) was drenched. Several small restaurants were ankle deep in water.

"That year," said a Syracuse student somewhat proudly, "our spring riot made *The New York Times.*"

At the University of Illinois, students for years greeted spring with a water fight that was more of a frolic than a riot. But in 1961 it got out of hand and turned into a real riot with injuries and destruction.

Thousands of students turned on fire hydrants and milled through the campus and streets in mobs, daring police to break them up. Women's dormitories were raided and panties were obtained. Street lights were put out, and a local policeman was handcuffed to his own, overturned car.

When a newspaper photographer was blinded in one eye by the swarming mob, university officials vowed it would never happen again. Some students were expelled, and more were suspended or placed on probation. Stiffer rules were enacted, and riot-control techniques were developed.

. . . When all other efforts at spontaneity fail at Illinois, there are always the 13 beer pubs on the Urbana campus.

Alcoholic beverages are a noticeable part of many campuses, but are strictly prohibited on others. The college man sometimes consumes great quantities of beer, and usually regrets it the next day. The weekend "beer bust" is a regular event for some collegians.

In Madison, Wis., home of the University of Wisconsin Badgers, some bars sell beer in half-gallon bottles, while many sell it by the pitcher. A pitcher of beer and a bratwurst has been a popular meal at the university for years.

One verse of a well-known Madison song goes like this:

Did you ever see a Badger who would pass up a saloon,
By the bright, shining light, by the light of the moon.

At Notre Dame University, alcoholic beverages have been prohibited in the residence halls, but the rule reportedly has not been strictly enforced recently. Some private colleges seem to be relaxing rules against alcohol in the dormitories, with the idea that a student should be given more responsibility over his own behavior.

Beer is combined with bicycle racing at Rice University and several other schools. The Rice race involves four teams, each consisting of ten "drinkers" and ten "riders."

The relay race begins with a drinker from each team "chugging" down a can of warm, flat beer—Rice students contend the beer goes down faster in that form. As each drinker finishes, the first rider on the team catapults out of the starting lane to race around an .88 mile quadrangle on campus. Each rider completes the circuit at full speed, and is stopped by "catchers" on his team. Then the next drinker goes into action.

The riders, who have practiced for months, sometimes complete the circuit in less than two minutes. The drinkers, who also practice industriously, ordinarily guzzle a can of beer in five to eight seconds, although the record is less than four seconds.

For Rice coeds, there is the tea-trike race, with a shorter course, five drinkers and five riders on each side, and the ladylike substitute for the beverage.

Good fellowship and camaraderie are often part of college fun. After midnight on George Washington's Birthday in Sewanee, Tenn., the tuxedo-clad members of the Red Ribbon Society march a little unsteadily across the campus of the University of the South. The student society's annual march follows a long evening of revelry.

A competing student group, the Green Ribbon Society, holds its annual revelry on St. Patrick's Day. The Green Ribbons have been known to stop a bus on the main street of Sewanee (population 1,464), and plaster it with St. Patrick's Day stickers. Then they head for the university dormitories to fight the dorm students with paint and firecrackers.

A third society was formed by students to offset the other two. It is the Black Ribbon Society, and it does absolutely nothing. Its motto, loosely translated and sanitized, is "I don't care."

The location of a college, the geography of it, often is important in the kind of fun on the campus. Lakes, deserts, rivers, mountains, big cities, small towns—they all tend to shape the fun.

Stanford's Lake Lagunita is full of water in spring, and also is full of sailboats, canoes, and swimmers. Next to Lake Lag is the Stanford golf course, rated as one of the best in California. San Francisco's entertainment is 45 minutes away, as is the Pacific Ocean.

The second weekend after New Year's Day is set aside for Stanford's winter carnival. The Stanford Ski Club rents most of Olympic Village at Squaw Valley—six hours to the east in the Sierra Nevada mountains—and more than 1,000 students move in for the weekend. Dances are held each evening in the main lodge.

The University of New Mexico is at Albuquerque in rodeo country, and so the university's spring fiesta features rodeo events. The men compete in bulldogging, calf-roping, bullriding, bareback riding, and a wild steer race. The student with the most impressive beard wins a prize.

The coeds compete in some unusual events: goat-tying, dogie-diapering, and barrel-racing.

There is a Western clothing day, and anyone not suitably garbed must spend the day in jail. At the university's Tingley Coliseum on a Friday night, several hundred students throw eggs, chase greased pigs, and dance to Western music.

The University of Wisconsin is on the shore of Lake Mendota, and there are many other lakes nearby. Students go swimming and boating in the summer, and skating, ice-boating, and ice-fishing in the winter.

At both Cornell and Syracuse, in heavy snow country, students smuggle trays out of dining halls and use them as sleds. At Cornell they zip down ice-slicked Library Slope at high speeds. At Syracuse, the steep hill from Crouse College is the favorite sledding spot.

When spring finally arrives in Syracuse, it is greeted with delight. Some students were so joyful in spring, 1967, that they formed the Sunbathers Society. After adopting an attention-getting slogan of "expose yourself," the society sponsored a successful sunbathing session on the quad.

A Syracuse student says that although the society conducted itself in good taste, it has since dissolved because of a general misconception of its objectives.

The University of Oregon Ducks have a webfoot tradition associated with the Millrace, a channel of water which crosses the campus and is described by a student as "slow-moving, muddy, but adequate." During the springtime Millrace Olympics, students engage in tugs of war by throwing a rope across the stream and having people pull at both ends. The losers are pulled into the muddy Millrace.

The university infirmary furnishes tetanus shots, crutches, and bandages for those who need them.

Some college fun comes from a specific individual or event in the past. At Indiana University there once was an instructor named Ed Kitch. When he graded his students' papers, he would often write in the margin, "Ok, Ed Kitch." That phrase caught the students' imagination and became a catch-all remark for anything good and desirable.

During one Indiana commencement ceremony at the stadium in Bloomington, a small plane flew over dragging a streamer that read, "Ok Ed Kitch."

One of the more recent traditions at venerable Harvard is the semi-annual Humphrey Bogart festival. Many Harvard students take their dates to the Brattle Theatre to see "Casablanca," "Key Largo," "To Have and Have Not," "The Maltese Falcon," and others. They have seen the movies so often they can quote whole stretches of dialogue, and often do.

Once, during the scene in "Casablanca" when Paul Henreid leads the people in Bogie's cafe in a rendition of *La Marseillaise,* a group in the audience stood and began singing too, until the entire theater was on its feet defying the frowns of "Nazi" Conrad Veidt.

Bogart buttons are handed out, and below the theater are the Club Casablanca and the Blue Parrot Coffee House. They are decorated with posters of Bogie and Lauren Bacall, and the juke box in the Club Casablanca has a recording of Miss Bacall's laugh.

At the Brattle and another nearby movie theater, the audiences are typically rowdy. They hiss villains and egregiously bad lines; they cheer heroes and good lines. They shout out wisecracks—but they had better be good or the hissing starts.

. . . Few alumni of the College of William and Mary in Virginia are inclined to forget the peculiar jurisprudence practiced at the Freshman Tribunal. Those freshmen who during their first weeks at college in some way annoy the sophomores, are placed on trial and immediately punished. One alumnus, who as a freshman wrote a letter to the campus newspaper complaining about the stupidity of sophomores, remembers receiving a colorful punishment. He was dunked in a vat of purple vegetable dye.

At the same trial, a coed who was disrespectful to sophomores was directed to dress up in a red union suit, place a huge dummy-bottle of whisky on her shoulder, and sing "Show Me the Way to Go Home."

At Harvard, a plan to re-enact William the Conqueror's crossing of the English Channel was cancelled by the university after it was learned that the Harvard Lampoon, the humor magazine, planned to march real elephants across the Charles River bridges.

At the University of the South, an Episcopal-related school, students came back from a showing of "Exodus" at the town's one movie theater and placed a giant Star of David on top of the university chapel.

At many a campus, students stuff a room with wads of paper, or run a bicycle up a flagpole, or carry a car into a lake, or engage in a shaving-cream fight. At one campus, fraternity members painted a giant auto-race "rallye stripe" across a sorority house, thus suggesting that the sorority girls were "fast."

At Cornell, a freshman who was president of his dormitory was shocked to find on his bed what appeared to be a small packet of marijuana. A neatly lettered note next to the packet asked the president to hide it for the two freshmen who signed the note.

The flustered freshman president ran to the proctor's office and nervously handed over the packet. The proctor's assistant broke it open and found tea leaves.

At North Carolina, in a prank typical of those elsewhere, a student came back to his room at 2 A.M. and found a note urging him to call "Carl" immediately at such-and-such a number. Fortunately, the student waited until the next day to call "Carl," who turned out to be University Chancellor J. Carlyle Sitterson.

Without a doubt, the American college student will continue to have his fun, despite increasing study loads, war and tension, and the trend toward organized activities. And the fun of today is not too different from that of years past, although the subject matter may be different.

An example of this is at Cornell, where Hugh Troy pulled a "rhinoceros invasion" stunt in the 1930s. He borrowed a wastebasket, shaped like a rhinoceros foot, from the campus naturalist. One snowy night, Mr. Troy and his friends tramped all over the campus, making rhinoceros tracks.

The next day a zoology professor solemnly validated the tracks as those of a rhinoceros, and traced them to the source of the university's water supply. Most students stopped drinking water.

Also at Cornell in the early 1930s, a banquet was held for Hugo N. Frye, who was billed as a founder of the Republican Party in New York. The banquet was in honor of the sesquicentennial of his birth, and invitations were sent to prominent Republicans.

The vice-president of the United States, Republican Charles Curtis, was said to have sent a telegram saying he regretted being unable to attend, and congratulating Cornell for "paying this respect to the memory of Hugo N. Frye."

Frye, of course, had never existed.

Thirty years later, Cornell students were still at the pranks. On November 5, 1965, The Cornell Daily Sun printed a banner headline: "Draft System Ends Student Deferment."

The Sun explained: "The student II-S deferment classification will be abolished immediately, University Registrar Herbert H. Williams was notified last night by telegram from the Selective Service System in Washington.

"Lt. Gen. Lewis B. Hershey, director of Selective Service, advised Williams and thousands of other college officials throughout the nation of the major change in draft policy."

The Sun explained further that the new draft classification for college students would be I-AI, meaning that the students "may get shipped out any time after one month."

There was one loophole, reported The Sun. Students could escape immediate service in the Army by joining the ROTC (Reserve Officers Training Corps) immediately.

Scores of freshmen—who weren't aware of The Sun's semi-annual prank editions—ran to the ROTC headquarters on campus before breakfast, ready to sign up. They soon found out the newspaper story was a joke, and waited for next year when a new crop of freshmen would be fooled by a new story.

Questions

1   How much has the medieval university improved during the past seven centuries?

2   Has the function of the university changed in the twentieth century?

3   Do discussions of student pranks tend to create distorted images of college life?

4   What pressures did the medieval student have to face?

5   Do you think of your college or university as "medieval" or "modern"?

9 Individualism in Renaissance Italy

In this essay we return to a theme discussed in Chapter 4. Unlike the ancient Greeks, Renaissance Italians were not conditioned by hubris or polis hangups. As a consequence, the call to unrestrained, exuberant individualism was very strong. However, the Italians did have their own hangup, "braggadocio." It led to some strange behavior—by our standards.

Men Can Do All Things If They Will

Melvin Steinfield

Behavior that is frowned upon by one society may be encouraged by another. By studying behavior patterns of other societies we gain perspective from which to understand our own. A study of individualism in the Italian Renaissance may help expose some of our own hangups.

When former world heavyweight boxing champion Joe Louis used to knock out an opponent in the early rounds of a title match, he did no boasting. The champion would invariably mumble something about how well the other fellow fought, and that it was a great fight. But he never took any credit for his own fantastically fast and powerful punches or his boxing skill. Joe Louis was the epitome of the modest and unassuming American athlete that American sports fans have come to admire. He knew the ropes of the ring and the rules of the game. As a result, he remains one of America's all-time favorite sport figures.

Muhammad Ali (also known as Cassius Clay) was different. Before scheduled defenses of his world heavyweight boxing title, Ali would generally boast about his skills and predict the round in which he expected to knock out his challenger. Frequently he would compose rhymes that ridiculed his opponent, and the press would make the most of it. Ali was remarkably accurate in predicting the details of his ring victories. Like Joe Louis, he was undefeated as heavyweight champion. Muhammad Ali, however, never enjoyed the popularity of Louis, partly because of his political activities, but mostly because he violated a fundamental ethic of American sports: he was not humble. Many Americans tended to resent Ali's boastful behavior.

By accident of birth, Joe Louis fit well into the mold of American society; Muhammad Ali did not. With different timing, these two men might have experienced quite different receptions for their style of behavior. If Muhammad Ali had lived during the Italian Renaissance, he would have found a favorable reception for his proud claims of ring success; Joe Louis would have been lost in the shuffle.

One of the traits exhibited by Renaissance men was *braggadocio*, or bragging about one's achievements. Instead of being frowned upon, this trait was encouraged. And that's not all. Braggadocio was merely one particular manifestation of the Renaissance ideal of individualism, which helped shape so much of the behavior of Renaissance Man. The Renaissance Man was supposed to develop his talents in as many ways as he could. There were none of the restrictions that were imposed by Greek society.

The Renaissance did, of course, revive some elements of classical antiquity, but it did not restore precisely the same conditions. Lacking a strong sense of polis, Renaissance men were not disturbed by exile as much as the ancient Greeks had been. Lacking a hubris-nemesis doctrine, Renaissance men felt fewer restraints upon individual self-fulfillment than did the hubris-conscious Greeks. Thus while the Renaissance was to a degree a revival of antiquity, it was not a complete duplication of it.

During the Renaissance glory was actively sought. Successes were proudly announced—loudly and often. These behavior traits were part of the accepted quest for attaining that state of well-roundedness known as "uomo universale." The "universal man" must not hide his talents. Rather, he should feel free to boast of them proudly. That was a vital element in the spirit of the Renaissance.

The Autobiography of Benvenuto Cellini is replete with statements in praise of the author. They are in keeping with the unabashed and sometimes exaggerated pride felt by Renaissance men who accomplished varied feats. Cellini certainly achieved a lot—and he does not refrain from telling us about it. The opening line of the autobiography leaves no doubt about the absence of Joe Louis-type thoughts in Cellini: "It is a duty incumbent on upright and credible men of all ranks, who have performed any thing noble or praiseworthy, to record, in their own writing, the events of their lives. . . ."[1]

Besides the many statements of his own that praised his works, Cellini frequently reported the praise that others uttered in his behalf. For example, when Cellini had completed work on a silver basin and cup, the author tells us that the French King said: "It is my real opinion that the ancients were never capable of working in so exquisite a taste. I have seen all the masterpieces of the greatest artists of Italy, but never before beheld anything that gave me such high satisfaction."[2]

There were other famous Italians of the Renaissance who shared the self-confidence of Cellini. The great poet Dante had been exiled from the city of Florence for his political activities. After several years, he was offered an opportunity to return, but the terms were not entirely to his liking. Since Renaissance men did not share the deep sense of polis that the ancient Greeks had felt, Dante could afford to take an independent stand without violating any basic Renaissance values. He did just that, as the following excerpt from his reply indicates: "Can I not everywhere behold the light of the sun and the stars; everywhere meditate on the noblest truths, without appearing ingloriously and shamefully before the city and the people? My bread will not fail me."[3]

In classical Greece, that type of behavior would have been considered arrogant and highly intemperate, just as Muhammad Ali's remarks were considered intemperate in his time. But Dante was lucky—he lived in Italy during the Renaissance.

Other trends of the Italian Renaissance can be understood against the backdrop of the all-important concept of individualism. For instance, the sonnet, developed by Petrarch, shows earthy and personal elements that are missing in the poetry of the Middle Ages. The sonnets went much deeper into the love between man and woman than did the lyrics of the Minnesingers when they were celebrating the cult of the Virgin in the late Middle Ages. The sonnet was a long way from the stylized court poetry of the medieval troubadours.

Petrarch and Boccaccio, author of the *Decameron,* demonstrate the new secularism just as the rise of the scientific spirit and the beginnings of the exploration phase do. The early explorers, freed of the medieval spiritual orientation, now moved to discover more about their physical surroundings as well as to express their individual interests in worldly things.

At the core of these related Renaissance trends is the exuberant braggadocio which often took interesting forms. A dramatic visual example is provided in the work of the sculptor, Lorenzo Ghiberti. His famous bronze doors for the baptistery of San Giovanni in Florence contain biblical scenes which are engraved in less than two-inch relief. Embellishing the borders of the doors are busts of prophets, including one of Ghiberti himself, protruding three inches. The scenes are of significant Biblical events, such as Abraham about to slay Isaac, yet Ghiberti allowed his self-portrait to be one of the most prominent features of the doors. What better symbol of unrestrained individualism could one find than that smiling Ghiberti bust positioned in a strategic corner of his greatest work of art? Ghiberti outdid John Hancock. One is tempted to wonder, how would bold signatures like that be received in American society today? Imagine the Apollo 11 moon plaque with the artist's face embellishing the astronauts names! Ghiberti also inscribed the following at the top of the door: "made by the amazing skill of Lorenzo di Ghiberti."

The beautiful and memorable artistic creations of Cellini and Ghiberti earned them the right to practice braggadocio. Their individual achievements more than made up for their overbearing manner. For during the Italian Renaissance the worth of an individual was not undermined by extraneous factors—not even those such as illegitimate birth or illegitimate accession to political power. Jacob Burckhardt's classic study of the Renaissance describes the prevailing attitude toward illegitimate birth and its relationship to the worth of an individual:

> Closely connected with the political illegitimacy of the dynasties of the fifteenth century was the public indifference to legitimate birth, which to foreigners—for example, to Comines —appeared so remarkable. The two things went naturally together. . . . In Italy . . . there no longer existed a princely house where, even in the direct line of descent, bastards were not patiently tolerated. The Aragonese monarchs of Naples belonged to the illegitimate line, Aragon itself falling to the lot of the brother of Alfonso I. The great Federigo of Urbino was, perhaps, no Montefeltro at all. When Pius II was on his way to the Congress of Mantua (1459), eight bastards of the house of Este rode to meet him at Ferrara, among them the reigning duke Borso himself and two illegitimate sons of his illegitimate brother and predecessor Lionello. The latter had also had a lawful wife, herself an illegitimate daughter of Alfonso I of Naples by an African woman. The bastards were often admitted to the succession where the lawful children were minors and the dangers of the situation were pressing; and a rule of seniority became recognized, which took no account of pure or impure birth. The fitness of the individual, his worth and capacity, were of more weight than all the laws and usages which prevailed elsewhere in the West. It was the age, indeed, in which the sons of the Popes were founding dynasties.[4]

A person of illegitimate birth does not have much chance in American politics; a pervasive Puritanism hovers righteously over the heads of would-be Presidents. Nelson Rockefeller's divorce unquestionably ruined his bid for the Republican presidential nomination in 1964. Adlai Stevenson's divorced status contrasted sharply with Republican campaign literature, which featured Ike-and-Mamie photos in both campaigns of the 1950's.

Renaissance politics were rough, but at least the politicians' marital status was not a hangup. Of course, Renaissance politicians had to watch their step, too. But the great political realist Machiavelli was not troubled by fears of religious or moral restrictions. His secular attitude was practical and concentrated on what was necessary for the individual in power to survive. As Machiavelli states in *The Prince,* "Therefore it is necessary for a prince, who wishes to maintain himself, to learn how not to be good, and to use this knowledge and not use it, according to the necessity of the case."[5]

The Prince, in other words, was another manifestation of the individualism of the Renaissance. The individual Prince, according to Machiavelli, was entitled to engage in all sorts of dishonorable behavior. Indeed, he had to engage in dishonorable behavior in order to survive, to preserve his power. For the furtherance of his own ambitions, he was entitled to step on other people. "Thus it is well to seem merciful, faithful, humane, sincere, religious, and also to be so; but you must have the mind so disposed that when it is needful to be otherwise you may be able to change to the opposite qualities."[6] Often *The Prince* is capsulized by the slogan, "The end justifies the means."

This same self-interest is also revealed in Rabelais' *Gargantua and Pantagruel,* where the rule of the Abbey was DO AS THOU WOULDST. How unlike the somber warnings to the ancient Greek that he not forsake his family or community. How different from the admonishment not to get carried away with one's own importance, or one's own power.

As a matter of fact, Renaissance individualism actively sought to inspire men to the highest pursuits. Thus Leon Battista Alberti wrote: "Men can do all things if they will." There was no limit to the ambition of Renaissance Man. Not polis, not hubris, not humility. Humility was a medieval virtue. It was a Renaissance vice.

Another medieval virtue but Renaissance vice was the idea of this life being merely a preliminary to a more important heavenly life. In the Renaissance the emphasis was on the now. Pico della Mirandola's "Oration on the Dignity of Man" emphasizes the importance of man and his right to seek happiness in this life through varied attainments:

> At last the Best of Artisans ordained that that creature to whom he had been able to give nothing proper to himself should have joint possession of whatever had been the peculiar characteristics of the different creatures. He therefore accorded to Man the function of a form not set apart, and a place in the middle of the world, and addressed him thus: "I have given

thee neither a fixed abode nor a form that is thine alone nor any function peculiar to thyself, Adam, to the end that, according to thy longing and according to thy judgment, thou mayest have and possess that abode, that form, and those functions which thou thyself shalt desire. The nature of all other things is limited and constrained within the bounds of laws prescribed by me: thou, coerced by no necessity, shalt ordain for thyself the limits of thy nature in accordance with thine own free will, in whose hand I have placed thee. I have set thee at the world's center, that thou mayest from thence more easily observe whatever is in the world. I have made thee neither of heaven nor of earth, neither mortal nor immortal, so that thou mayest with greater freedom of choice and with more honor, as though the maker and moulder of thyself, fashion thyself in whatever shape thou shalt prefer."[7]

Man is the moulder of his own destiny, and it can be a glorious destiny if he aims high enough, says Pico. Elsewhere Pico encourages man to "let a certain holy ambition invade our souls, so that, not content with the mediocre, we shall pant after the highest. . . . "

It is not by accident that there were many individuals who achieved remarkable virtuosity during the Renaissance. Nor is it coincidental that perhaps the greatest of all well-rounded universal geniuses lived then. Leonardo da Vinci was an unusual person even for Renaissance Italy. His achievements are too well known to cite here. At the age of 30, Leonardo engaged in a bit of braggadocio when he applied for a job. His letter to the Duke of Milan reveals no reluctance to list his talents, among which were: "When a place is besieged I know how to cut off water from the trenches, and how to construct an infinite number of bridges, mantlets, scaling ladders, and other instruments which have to do with the same enterprise."[8] Observe that Leonardo could construct "an infinite" number, not just a whole bunch.

Besides war-making talents, Leonardo possessed peacetime skills, according to his letter, the complete text of which appears in the readings at the end of this chapter. Leonardo's letter ends with:

In time of peace I believe I can give you as complete satisfaction as anyone else in architecture in the construction of buildings both public and private, and in conducting water from one place to another. Also, I can execute sculpture in marble, bronze, or clay, and also painting, in which my work will stand comparison with that of anyone else, whoever he may be.[9]

Leonardo's letter reached the Duke of Milan. He was hired. Braggadocio paid off again. If not for Muhammad Ali, at least for Leonardo.

This bold and Promethean individualism was reflected in another trend in art: portrait painting and sculptured busts. In contrast with medieval paintings, which tended to subdue the role of the individual as well as to pay little attention to the physical qualities of people and things, Renaissance art highlighted the individual. Very close attention was paid to human anatomy and to other naturalistic features. Because individuals were now being thought of as important in their own right, portrait painting flourished, and people were appearing as the exclusive or main interest in paintings. This contrasts not only with medieval style but also with the more generalized treatment given faces and bodies in the Hellenic Period. And how the medieval artists must have been rolling over in their heavenly berths when they saw those nude statues.

A favorite nude theme for Renaissance sculptors was David, the giant slayer. What greater heights of individual achievement could one hope to attain than killing a giant? Michaelangelo's "David" is one of the most widely acclaimed sculptures in the history of Western Man. It portrays David as the model of self-confident, powerful, dignified individualism. Ah, yes, Alberti said it, and Michaelangelo sculpted it, and Leonardo lived it. *Men can do all things if they will.*

Notes

1 *The Autobiography of Benvenuto Cellini* (Reading, Pa.: Spencer Press, 1963), p. 1.

2 *Ibid.,* p. 249.

3 Jacob Burckhardt, *The Civilization of the Renaissance in Italy* (London: Phaidon Press, 1955), p. 83.

4 *Ibid.,* p. 12.

5 Niccolo Machiavelli, *The Prince* (New York: New American Library, 1954), p. 92.

6 *Ibid.,* p. 102.

7 Pico della Mirandola, *"Oration on the Dignity of Man,"* Elizabeth L. Forbes, trans. From *Journal of the History of Ideas,* Vol. III (1942), p. 348. Reprinted with permission from the *Journal of the History of Ideas.*

8 *The Literary Works of Leonardo da Vinci,* Irma A. Richter, ed. (New York: Oxford University Press, 1939).

9 *Ibid.*

When Jacob Burckhardt's "The Civilization of the Renaissance in Italy"
was published in 1860, it did not attract much attention at first, nor
did it sell very well; but gradually his book became the best known
and most authoritative study of the Renaissance until well into the
twentieth century. Recently, however, scholars have begun to question
his work. The following selection discusses some of the problems connected
with Burckhardt's book and helps illuminate the difficulties of interpreting
a historical period.

Burckhardt Challenged

Anthony E. Neville

Dictionaries define "renaissance" as "a new birth or revival." History books apply the term to a period of Western history. Is the label a deserved one? Was the Renaissance a distinct break from the period that preceded it? When did it begin? What were its characteristics? To what extent were those characteristics the beginning of our modern culture? And finally, some ask: Since the label itself accounts for some of these difficult questions, should we discard the term "Renaissance"?

High-school texts and coffee-table art books aren't bothered by these questions, but serious historians are. Especially in the last half-century, the "Renaissance controversy" has been one of the central debates of the discipline. The questions have been useful ones: They have led historians to a more careful evaluation, not only of the period commonly called the Renaissance, but of its precursory developments in medieval Europe.

The popular conception of the Renaissance—as a distinct break from the darkness of the Middle Ages and a rebirth of a secular high culture—stems from two sources. The first is a characterization the Renaissance humanists themselves applied to their age. Petrarch, in the fourteenth century, was the first to formulate the idea of "an age of darkness" from which a new era had dawned, but Boccaccio credited the earlier Dante as the "first to open the way for the return of the Muses, banished from Italy." Rabelais, a figure of the later Northern Renaissance, wrote: "Out of the thick Gothic night our eyes are opened to the glorious torch of the sun."

The other source of the popular conception of the Renaissance is

From "The Renaissance? *What* Renaissance?" by Anthony E. Neville, *The Johns Hopkins Magazine,* Spring 1967, pp. 1–6.

the writings of several nineteenth-century scholars, chiefly Jules Michelet and Jacob Burckhardt. It was Michelet who, in 1855, characterized the Renaissance in the now-famous phrase, "the discovery of the world and of man." Burckhardt's *Civilization of the Renaissance in Italy,* published five years later, assessed the Renaissance with similar enthusiasm. Burckhardt was a calmer writer and a better historian than Michelet, and his book, an ambitious synthesis of many aspects of Renaissance culture, had a far more pervasive influence on scholarship than Michelet's.

If the test of a great book is the furor it produces, Burckhardt had a long time to await satisfaction. Eighteen months after the book was published, the Basel professor wrote to a friend: "We have not sold two hundred copies." But the academic study of history as we know it today was just beginning, and expert appraisals were slow in coming. Burckhardt's analysis was read, often uncritically, and amended; historians wrote books which extended his thesis into cultural areas Burckhardt had neglected. Burckhardt's view of the Renaissance—as an abrupt departure from the Middle Ages and the beginning of all that is modern—held sway.

Gradually, notes Karl H. Dannenfeldt, "others began to feel that his harmonious picture of the Italian Renaissance was just too perfect and static. As specialized studies contributed to the knowledge of other periods, especially that of the Middle Ages, questions began to arise in the minds of historians."

To "tune in" on the middle of the Renaissance debate which Burckhardt generated, one need only turn back a quarter of a century from the present. By then, scholars had more basic information, objectively assessed, than Burckhardt's contemporaries could have had. By then, the discipline of history, particularly of intellectual history, had matured greatly under the tutelage of great scholars like Hopkins' Arthur O. Lovejoy.

In the *Journal of the History of Ideas,* which Lovejoy had helped to found in 1940, the "Renaissance controversy" became a major theme. The first 74 pages of the volume for 1943 were devoted exclusively to the matter.

The opening shot was fired by Dana B. Durand, an historian of science from Mt. Holyoke College, who examined the question of how much fifteenth-century Italy had contributed to the progress of science. "The instance is crucial," said Durand, "since by general consent science is fundamental to the modern world, and yet Burckhardt in his *Culture of the Renaissance in Italy* ignored it almost completely."

With fifteenth-century Italy (called "Quattrocento" in the historians' shorthand) as his target, Durand was aiming at the time and place where, by traditional assessment, the Renaissance had achieved its first full bloom. He was not impressed with what he saw there, especially in comparison with the preceding century. The scholastic method of medieval science, "so frequently dismissed as sterile," Durand argued, "was in fact peculiarly apt to produce . . . innovation." Since scholastic writings always began with arguments *against* the orthodox proposition to be proved, they were "bound in certain minds to provoke an interest in the arguments *for* the radical or heterodox position." This method had flourished at Paris and Oxford a century earlier, and Quattrocento science was simply a "critical elaboration of scholastic tradition."

Examining particular sciences—cosmology, mathematics, and physics—Durand found a strong persistence of tradition and few innovations of significance. In the case of cartography, the strides that were made in fifteenth-century Italy could be attributed to German and Scandinavian geographers working for Cardinal Nicholas of Cusa in Rome. Concluded Durand: "The balance of tradition and innovation in fifteenth-century Italy was not so decisively favorable as to distinguish that century radically from those that preceded it, nor to constitute the Quattrocento a unique and unrivaled moment in the history of Western thought."

Hans Baron, standing at the Burckhardt barricades, fired back. It is perfectly true, Baron acknowledged, that the Quattrocentro humanists had ignored natural science. But what needs to be considered, he wrote in his *Journal* article, is the possibility that "the Quattrocento may have produced such philosophic views and intellectual habits as on the one hand could foreshadow characteristics of the later 'scientific mind' and on the other in due time react on science itself." In man-centered humanistic thought, Baron suggested, may have been the true beginnings of modern science.

He considered the case of Nicholas of Cusa. Not much of a scientist, Nicholas nevertheless had developed the notion that the earth was not low and vile, as medieval cosmologists had insisted, but was itself a "noble star." "He rejoiced over this vindication of the earth in words that were well known to, and almost literally repeated by, the founders of the heliocentric theory in the sixteenth century." Baron reminded his audience that it was the lingering insistence that the earth is vile (and thus at the center and bottom of the universe) that accounted for resistance to the Copernican theory even in the seventeenth century.

Modern science, Baron argued, could not be born until the medieval belief in the universe as an immovable, God-given order had been overcome. This transformation of intellectual habits did not begin in science. But by the end of the Quattrocento a dynamic, decentralized view had emerged in history and political science, and the extension of this view to notions about nature made great scientific achievements possible in succeeding centuries. "When the historical outlook and the ideas of human nature had been remade, the change in perspective, in a second phase, would react on natural science."

Baron had a further argument. The unimpressive strides in mathematics in Italian universities were of little consequence in the development of science; the great sixteenth-century scientists like Tartaglia and Galileo learned their mathematics, not from university scholars, but from artists, architects, and engineers. Thus the infusion of mathematics into science, a crucial step in its progress, depended on the "emergence of groups educated and engaged in technological pursuits." The first such group were the Quattrocento artists and architects, and their most shining example was, of course, Leonardo da Vinci. Not only did Leonardo insist on mathematical methods in the investigation of nature, but his dynamic view of nature showed a "substantial affinity" to the modern scientific outlook.

"Experimental observation, mathematical method, and the dynamic view of a decentralized nature" were the most important elements in the modern science that began with Galileo. "All these basic avenues of later science," Baron concluded, "Quattrocento thought had entered a century before, and in no half-hearted fashion."

Burckhardt was vindicated. His "analysis of the Renaissance as a new phase of psychological and intellectual development," said Baron, "still holds its own. . . . At the basis of the fifteenth-century Renaissance there was a fundamental change in man's outlook on life and the world—the coming of the 'first-born among the sons of modern Europe.' "

The Durand-Baron exchange was a repeat of their joint performance before the Renissance section of the American Historical Association's annual meeting a year earlier. The editors of the *Journal of the History of Ideas* now produced five distinguished scholars to comment on their papers.

The first of these, Ernst Cassirer, tended to side with Baron. "Mathematics had been an *element* in culture long before the Renaissance," Cassirer argued, "but in the Renaissance, with thinkers like Leonardo or Galileo, it became a new culture *force*. It is the intensity with which this new force fills the whole intellectual life and transforms it from within that we should regard as what is significantly new."

But Cassirer had warnings to his fellow scholars about how terms like "Middle Ages" and "Renaissance" should be employed. They are ideas of historical "style," he argued; "they can be used to *characterize* and *interpret* intellectual movements, but they express no actual historical *facts* that ever existed at any given time." It is useless, Cassirer felt, to argue about exactly when the Middle Ages "stopped" and the Renaissance "began."

All one can safely say, according to Cassirer, is that from the beginning of the fifteenth century onward, the *balance* among particular forces (society, state, church, science, etc.) begins to shift slowly. When making comparisons between the Middle Ages and the Renaissance, Cassirer maintained, it is never enough to single out a particular idea; what the historian must study is the importance that idea possessed and the strength with which it acted in the whole structure.

The historian of ideas is like a scientist studying a river. The water in the river changes its composition very slowly; ideas appear again and again and are maintained for centuries. What is of interest is not the composition of a drop of water but the width and depth of the river and the force and velocity of the current. "What he is studying—or should be studying—is less the *content* of ideas than their *dynamics*." And that, concluded Cassirer, is why the Renaissance cannot be denied: "The dynamics of ideas has changed."

In the next succeeding paper, Francis R. Johnson chastised Baron for his "hazardous" assertion that Quattrocentro artists and craftsmen had a profound influence on scientific thought. Our knowledge of *medieval* technology, Johnson maintained, is too slim for historians to assert that the influence of architects and builders of medieval cathedrals was any less important.

In his assessment of fifteenth-century Italy, Johnson took the middle ground. The Quattrocento, he said, "stands forth neither as a period of spectacular achievement in scientific discovery nor as one in which science was stagnant and neglected." Traditional material was reexamined and elaborated, scientists and artists began to work cooperatively, and changing social conditions left their impress on scientific thought.

Johnson likened the Quattrocento to the phase of a military campaign following a great advance in the field, when the advance is consolidated, old units are regrouped and new forces are brought up, and the ground is prepared for the next forward lunge. "The military strategist will usually rate this second, less spectacular, phase of a campaign as the more important, demanding greater skill. Unless it is successfully executed, seeming victory is transformed into stalemate or defeat."

The Quattrocentro, therefore, "should be assigned a significance of its own in the complete history of science." It is unjust, Johnson felt, to compare it adversely with the century that preceded it or the age that followed.

The "problem of the Renaissance," began the next paper, "is largely a pseudo-problem." It is impossible, said Paul Oskar Kristeller, to interpret a complex historical period "in terms of a brief definition which would at the same time distinguish it from all other periods of history. Such definitions are apt to be too narrow or too broad."

Surely, said Kristeller, the Renaissance had a "distinctive physiognomy," and there is no reason to doubt its very existence just because there is no satisfactory definition of it. "The best procedure would be rather to start with a tentative conception of the Renaissance, and to take this idea as a guiding principle when investigating the actual facts and sources of the period under consideration."

Kristeller agreed with Durand that fifteenth-century Italy contributed no basic change in the methods and results of natural science, but disagreed with the implications for the Renaissance he seemed to draw from this conclusion. As Baron suggested, we must look beyond the scientific community itself to find intellectual currents that may affect science. The one intellectual current that was characteristic, indeed pervasive, in this period was humanism. Indifferent as the humanists were to science, said Kristeller, they did popularize "the entire body of ancient Greek learning and literature and thus made available new source material of which the professional scientists and philosophers could not fail to take advantage."

But that is a tentative conclusion, said Kristeller, returning to historiographical questions, "and subject to further revision." The only thing that really counts in Renaissance studies, he said, "is the actual investigation of the extensive source materials which have not yet been included in any extant synthesis." All scholars should cooperate in such an investigation, whatever their point of view.

"Such an evaluation will not depend wholly on the influence, direct or distant, which each phenomenon has exercised on later developments, but will also acknowledge the inherent, 'absolute' significance of many ideas and achievements which for some reason or other failed to have any visible influence. It is this significance, rather than any incidental sequence of changes or influences, which in my opinion should be the ultimate purpose of the history of ideas, if not of all history."

Kristeller's suggestion that there is flotsam on the river of history worth study in its own right does not apply to the history of science. Or so it would seem in the estimation of Dean P. Lockwood, whose paper followed.

Noting that the Renaissance contributed almost nothing to modern medicine (likewise the Middle Ages; likewise the Greeks), Lockwood remarked: "Therein lies just the difference between the attitude of the scientist and that of the humanist toward the Renaissance—or toward the whole past, for that matter!" In the humanities, he argued, we can go back to the Renaissance for inspiration and for guidance in the great problems of human life. "But modern science looks to the past no more. It had its roots in the past, of course; but to trace them is merely to satisfy a curiosity, to pursue an intellectual hobby." *Vale,* the history of science.

By virtue of alphabetical ordering, the last word went to Lynn Thorndike, and he enjoyed the role thoroughly.

Thorndike confessed a strong aversion to the term "Renaissance." "Religion may have its resurrections and revivals, but I have even less faith than Nicodemus in rebirths or restorations of whole periods of human history. . . . Legacies from the past? Yes. Inheritances from previous periods? Yes. Survivals? Yes. Resemblances to our forebears? Yes. Reformations? Perhaps. Reactions? Unfortunately. But no rebirths and no restorations!"

A girl of eighteen, Thorndike argued, who dressed up in clothes which her grandmother wore when she was eighteen "may look more like her grandmother as she was then than her grandmother herself does now. But she will not feel or act as her grandmother felt and acted half a century or more ago."

(Erwin Panofsky was led to reply in the *Kenyon Review*: "If this girl decides to adopt the clothes of her grandmother for good and wears them all the time in the serious conviction that they are more appropriate and becoming than those she used to wear before, this very decision not only induces but actually presupposes a change in her whole personality and way of life—a change not sufficient to make her a duplicate of her grandmother [which no one has claimed to be true of the Renaissance period in relation to classical Antiquity], but basic enough to make her 'feel and act' quite differently from the way she did as long as she believed in slacks and polo shirts.")

Thorndike turned to specific issues. Durand, he noted, had criticized medieval translators for neglecting Ptolemy's *Geography*. "If they did—for a previous translation may have escaped our notice—it is to be remembered after all the text in question consists largely of lists of ancient place-names, many of which cannot be identified and located with any assurance." Moreover, Ptolemy had made the Mediterranean Sea too short by one-third; there is at least one medieval map that is more accurate than any other map of the Mediterranean until the eighteenth century. Medieval maps also more accurately portrayed the Far East and the islands of the Atlantic. The translation and subsequent vogue of Ptolemy's *Geography,* Thorndike commented, "were therefore in some ways regrettable."

This did not prevent the translator of the *Geography* from touting it as another of the "resuscitated liberal studies which had grown almost torpid." The resuscitation claim of Renaissance writers and translators extended to all kinds of inappropriate fields: astronomy, anatomy, magic, astrology. "Publishers who printed a text for the first time, even if it was a typical product of medieval scholasticism, represented themselves as snatching it from Gothic filth and dust and mildew and cobwebs and bringing it to the light of fairest impressions with the text . . . freed from barbarisms, when in reality they were very likely using a single inferior manuscript and neglecting a dozen older and superior versions."

What distinguished the Quattrocento from the preceding century, according to the testimony of the humanists themselves, was the revival of Greek, the purification of Latin diction and grammar, and a return from medieval texts to the old classic texts. Upon these differences—not any differences in social and moral values—hung their grand, glorious, complacent feeling about their age.

"As the study and reading of Latin and Greek waned, however—and this was partly because the humanists and classicists had substituted a dead for a living language—fewer and fewer persons could sincerely share in this thrill or impart it to others." Fervor for the concept "Renaissance" was largely confined to the realm of the fine arts, Thorndike argued, where the term had been applied to the post-Gothic period. Then along came Michelet and Burkhardt, to attribute to the Renaissance "the discovery of the world and of man." "The Renaissance," wrote Thorndike, "was no longer regarded as primarily a rebirth of classical learning and culture but rather as a prebirth or precursor of present society and of modern civilization.

"This," he continued, "made a well-calculated appeal to the average reader who is little interested to be told that Erasmus was a great Greek scholar or that Leonardo da Vinci copied from Albert of Saxony, but whose ego is titillated to be told that Leonardo was an individual like himself or that Erasmus's chief claim to fame is that he was the first modern man—the first one like you and me. All this was quite soothing and flattering and did much to compensate for one's inability to read Horace or to quote Euripides."

Hans Baron and other apologists for Burckhardt, Thorndike complained, keep "retreating to new standing ground of plausible hypothesis and ingenious conjecture, when some of Burckhardt's old bulwarks are proved to be untenable by new masses of facts concerning either or both the Middle Ages and the Quattrocento."

Would it not make things clearer, he pleaded, "if they ceased to employ the old name, since the old concept has been abandoned, and, instead of talking of the Renaissance, spoke of the period or movement or whatever it is they have in mind as the *Pre*naissance?" (Italics added—*Ed.*)

Thorndike had few kind words for Burckhardt's book. The section on the revival of antiquity was scholarly enough, he conceded, but in other sections the phenomena which Burkhardt attributes to the Renaissance were "almost equally characteristic of Italy at any time from the twelfth to the eighteenth century inclusive." Burckhardt did, in fact, include some thirteenth-century figures within the Renaissance, and thus "freed the movement from the embarrassment of chronological limits and made any differentiation between it and medieval culture well-nigh impossible.

"In general," Thorndike summed up, "Burckhardt devoted so much of his pages and energy to the attempt to trace intangibles, such as personality, imagination, passion, spirit, the popular mind, the feeling for this and that, such and such a sentiment, that his book hardly touches the domain of intellectual history and seems to possess a will-o'-the-wisp sort of character."

Thorndike had a few more rounds of grapeshot still to be fired. His next target: Burckhardt's contention that in the Renaissance "man became a spiritual individual and recognized himself as such," whereas "in the Middle Ages both sides of human consciousness— that which was turned within as that which was turned without— lay dreaming or half awake beneath a common veil."

Quite apart from the fact "that individualism may be a mark of decline rather than progress," there is no foundation, Thorndike complained, for Burckhardt's argument. With quotations from other scholars to support him, Thorndike maintained that "no period in the history of philosophy has discussed individuality and its problems more often or more subtly than did the medieval schoolmen." In contrast, "the humanists were imitative in their writing, not original. . . . Renaissance architects came to follow authority far more than their creative Gothic predecessors. For the Middle Ages loved variety; the Renaissance, uniformity."

No less objectionable was Burckhardt's contention that "appreciation of natural beauty" was introduced by the Italian Renaissance. "One has only to examine the sculpture of the great thirteenth-century cathedrals to see that the craftsmen of the towns were close observers of the world of nature, and that every artist was a naturalist too."

To the question of whether the Renaissance was truly the seed-bed of the modern spirit Thorndike posed a counter-question: "Are not our political, economic, charitable, educational, and ecclesiastical institutions quite as much an outgrowth from medieval life?"

The term "Renaissance," in short, ought to be discarded. "It is too suggestive of a sensational, miraculous, extraordinary, magical, human and intellectual development, like unto the phoenix rising from its ashes after five hundred years. . . . It has led to a chorus of rhapsodists as to freedom, breadth, soaring ideas, horizons, perspectives, out of fetters and swaddling clothes, and so on."

Worst of all, said Thorndike, "it has kept men in general from recognizing that our life and thought is based more nearly and actually on the Middle Ages than on distant Greece and Rome, from whom our heritage is more indirect, bookish and sentimental, less institutional, social, religious, even less economic and experimental."

Thus ended the Great Debate of 1943 but not the "Renaissance controversy." In succeeding years, the *Journal of the History of Ideas,* among other scholarly publications, gave frequent attention to the subject.

In 1950, for example, Hans Baron reviewed a book by Wallace K. Ferguson, *The Renaissance in Historical Thought: Five Centuries of Interpretation.* It was a friendly review of a very excellent book, but critical of Ferguson's very facile division of post-Burckhardt interpreters into "traditionalists" and "revisionists." "If a major concern of Renaissance scholars for ninety years has really been either to vindicate or refute Burckhardt's picture of the Renaissance, we should have to conclude that Renaissance scholarship has long been in a period of stagnation," Baron wrote.

In the *Journal* of October, 1951, Ferguson, admitting he was "rushing in where not only angels but even fools would fear to tread," offered a definition of the Renaissance which he hoped all factions would accept. The Renaissance, he said, was "the age of transition from medieval to modern civilization, a period characterized primarily by the gradual shift from one fairly well coordinated and clearly defined type of civilization to another, yet, at the same time, possessing in its own right certain distinctive traits and a high degree of cultural vitality." He set the years 1300–1600 as the boundaries of the Renaissance.

Predictably, not everyone was happy with Ferguson's definition. Dayton Phillips replied in the *Journal*: "The facts do not seem to support either such a general European period, or any period characterized peculiarly by a 'Renaissance.' Developments from 1350 to 1500 seem to me to stand in about the same relation to those from 1500 to 1650 as do each of these epochs to those preceding and following them, and I believe that use of the term 'Renaissance' is misleading because of its connotations of unity and novelty." Hans Baron, still at the Burckhardt barricades, was just as displeased. Purge Burckhardt of the seeming "exaggerations" which Ferguson found, and you still do not come up with a Renaissance that is simply a "period of transition," Baron objected.

On through the 1950's Baron and Ferguson, and occasionally others, debated their differences.

An epilogue to this brief survey of the "Renaissance controversy"—though not to the controversy itself, which continues—is supplied by George Boas, professor emeritus of the history of philosophy at Johns Hopkins.

In a book review published in the *Journal of the History of Ideas* three years ago, Boas wrote:

In my opinion, for what it is worth, periods have outlived any usefulness they may once have had. But they are clearly still in fashion and the problem is how to recognize them. We have dates and places pretty well settled for most of the philosophers, scientists, and artists who might be said to form—or be formed by—a time or period or culture or movement. We know who were the well-known men living in the various Italian states from, let us say, 1450 to 1550. Scholars have not only written their biographies but also have described the economic, military, and social structures of that century. And from all this a concept of something called the Renaissance has emerged.

Just what it was has been hotly debated, largely because, one suspects, it was not anything specifiable. It was a period in which men and women lived and thought and worked and squabbled and manifested all the diversities that have been manifested in any other well-documented period of the past. During such a time some people agree and others disagree. If you pick out those who agree, of course you can set up a cultural homogeneity. And if you are convinced that cultural homogeneity is more important as a subject of meditation than cultural hetereogeneity, then you will call the men who do not fit in with your generalization exceptions.

The notion that every period has tensions, conflicts, clashes in opinion which are just as characteristic of it as the agreements, seems to have impressed no one in particular and yet it is precisely these conflicts which raise the problems which occupy the men living in any given time.

The following selection from Jacob Burckhardt's "The Civilization of the Renaissance in Italy" discusses individualism in its many facets. It also includes a short biography of one of the Renaissance giants, Leon Battista Alberti.

The Many-Sided Man

Jacob Burckhardt

Despotism, as we have already seen, fostered in the highest degree the individuality not only of the tyrant or Condottiere himself, but also of the men whom he protected or used as his tools—the secretary, minister, poet, and companion. These people were forced to know all the inward resources of their own nature, passing or permanent; and their enjoyment of life was enhanced and concentrated by the desire to obtain the greatest satisfaction from a possibly very brief period of power and influence.

But even the subjects whom they ruled over were not free from the same impulse. Leaving out of account those who wasted their lives in secret opposition and conspiracies, we speak of the majority who were content with a strictly private station, like most of the urban population of the Byzantine empire and the Mohammedan States. No doubt it was often hard for the subjects of a Visconti to maintain the dignity of their persons and families, and multitudes must have lost in moral character through the servitude they lived under. But this was not the case with regard to individuality; for political impotence does not hinder the different tendencies and manifestations of private life from thriving in the fullest vigor and variety. Wealth and culture, so far as display and rivalry were not forbidden to them, a municipal freedom which did not cease to be considerable, and a Church which, unlike that of the Byzantine or of the Mohammedan world, was not identical with the State—all these conditions undoubtedly favored the growth of individual thought, for which the necessary leisure was furnished by the cessation of party conflicts. The private man, indifferent to politics, and busied partly with serious pursuits, partly with the interests of a *dilettante*, seems to have been first fully formed in these despotisms of the fourteenth century. Documentary evidence cannot, of course, be required on such a point. The novelists, from whom we might expect information, describe to us oddities in plenty, but only from one point of view and in so far as the needs of the story demand. Their scene, too, lies chiefly in the republican cities.

From *The Civilization of the Renaissance in Italy* by Jacob Burckhardt (London: Phaidon Press, 1955), pp. 82–87.

In the latter, circumstances were also, but in another way, favorable to the growth of individual character. The more frequently the governing party was changed, the more the individual was led to make the utmost of the exercise and enjoyment of power. The statesmen and popular leaders, especially in Florentine history, acquired so marked a personal character that we can scarcely find, even exceptionally, a parallel to them in contemporary history, hardly even in Jacob van Arteveldt.

The members of the defeated parties, on the other hand, often came into a position like that of the subjects of the despotic States, with the difference that the freedom or power already enjoyed, and in some cases the hope of recovering them, gave a higher energy to their individuality. Among these men of involuntary leisure we find, for instance, an Agnolo Pandolfini (d. 1446), whose work on domestic economy is the first complete program of a developed private life. His estimate of the duties of the individual as against the dangers and thanklessness of public life is in its way a true monument of the age.

Banishment, too, has this effect above all, that it either wears the exile out or develops whatever is greatest in him. "In all our more populous cities," says Gioviano Pontano, "we see a crowd of people who have left their homes of their own free will; but a man takes his virtues with him wherever he goes." And, in fact, they were by no means only men who had been actually exiled, but thousands left their native place voluntarily, because they found its political or economic condition intolerable. The Florentine emigrants at Ferrara and the Lucchese in Venice formed whole colonies by themselves.

The cosmopolitanism which grew up in the most gifted circles is in itself a high stage of individualism. Dante, as we have already said, finds a new home in the language and culture of Italy, but goes beyond even this in the words, "My country is the whole world." And when his recall to Florence was offered him on unworthy conditions, he wrote back: "Can I not everywhere behold the light of the sun and the stars; everywhere meditate on the noblest truths, without appearing ingloriously and shamefully before the city and the people? Even my bread will not fail me." The artists exult no less defiantly in their freedom from the constraints of fixed residence. "Only he who has learned everything," says Ghiberti,[1] "is nowhere a stranger; robbed of his fortune and without friends, he is yet the citizen of every country, and can fearlessly despise the changes of fortune." In the same strain an exiled humanist writes: "Wherever a learned man fixes his seat, there is home."[2]

An acute and practiced eye might be able to trace, step by step, the increase in the number of complete men during the fifteenth century. Whether they had before them as a conscious object the harmonious development of their spiritual and material existence, is hard to say; but several of them attained it, so far as is consistent with the imperfection of all that is earthly. It may be better to renounce the attempt at an estimate of the share which fortune, character, and talent had in the life of Lorenzo il Magnifico. But look at a personality like that of Ariosto, especially as shown in his satires. In what harmony are there expressed the pride of the man and the poet, the irony with which he treats his own enjoyments, the most delicate satire, and the deepest goodwill!

When this impulse to the highest individual development was combined with a powerful and varied nature, which had mastered all the elements of the culture of the age, then arose the "all-sided man"— "l'uomo universale"—who belonged to Italy alone. Men there were of encyclopedic knowledge in many countries during the Middle Ages, for this knowledge was confined within narrow limits; and even in the twelfth century there were universal artists, but the problems of architecture were comparatively simple and uniform, and in sculpture and painting the matter was of more importance than the form. But in Italy at the time of the Renaissance, we find artists who in every branch created new and perfect works, and who also made the greatest impression as men. Others, outside the arts they practiced, were masters of a vast circle of spiritual interests.

Dante, who, even in his lifetime, was called by some a poet, by others a philosopher, by others a theologian,[3] pours forth in all his writings a stream of personal force by which the reader, apart from the interest of the subject, feels himself carried away. What power of will must the steady, unbroken elaboration of the *Divine Comedy* have required! And if we look at the matter of the poem, we find that in the whole spiritual or physical world there is hardly an important subject which the poet has not fathomed, and on which his utterances —often only a few words—are not the most weighty of his time. For the visual arts he is of the first importance, and this for better reasons than the few references to contemporary artists—he soon became himself the source of inspiration.[4]

The fifteenth century is, above all, that of the many-sided men. There is no biography which does not, besides the chief work of its hero, speak of other pursuits all passing beyond the limits of dilettantism. The Florentine merchant and statesman was often learned in both the classical languages; the most famous humanists read the

Ethics and Politics of Aristotle to him and his sons; even the daughters of the house were highly educated. It is in these circles that private education was first treated seriously. The humanist, on his side, was compelled to the most varied attainments, since his philological learning was not limited, as it is now, to the theoretical knowledge of classical antiquity, but had to serve the practical needs of daily life. While studying Pliny, he made collections of natural history; the geography of the ancients was his guide in treating of modern geography, their history was his pattern in writing contemporary chronicles, even when composed in Italian; he not only translated the comedies of Plautus, but acted as manager when they were put on the stage; every effective form of ancient literature down to the dialogues of Lucian he did his best to imitate; and besides all this, he acted as magistrate, secretary and diplomatist—not always to his own advantage.

But among these many-sided men, some, who may truly be called all-sided, tower above the rest. Before analyzing the general phases of life and culture of this period, we may here, on the threshold of the fifteenth century, consider for a moment the figure of one of these giants—Leon Battista Alberti (b. 1404, d. 1472). His biography, which is only a fragment, speaks of him but little as an artist, and makes no mention at all of his great significance in the history of architecture. We shall now see what he was, apart from these special claims to distinction.

In all by which praise is won, Leon Battista was from his childhood the first. Of his various gymnastic feats and exercises we read with astonishment how, with his feet together, he could spring over a man's head; how, in the cathedral, he threw a coin in the air till it was heard to ring against the distant roof; how the wildest horses trembled under him. In three things he desired to appear faultless to others, in walking, in riding, and in speaking. He learned music without a master, and yet his compositions were admired by professional judges. Under the pressure of poverty, he studied both civil and canonical law for many years, till exhaustion brought on a severe illness. In his twenty-fourth year, finding his memory for words weakened, but his sense of facts unimpaired, he set to work at physics and mathematics. And all the while he acquired every sort of accomplishment and dexterity, cross-examining artists, scholars, and artisans of all descriptions, down to the cobblers, about the secrets and peculiarities of their craft. Painting and modelling he practiced by the way, and especially excelled in admirable likenesses from memory. Great admiration was excited by his mysterious "camera obscura,"[5] in which he showed at one time the stars and the moon rising over rocky hills, at another wide landscapes with mountains and gulfs receding into dim perspective, and with fleets advancing on the waters in shade or sunshine. And that which others created he welcomed joyfully, and held every human achievement which followed the laws of beauty for something almost divine. To all this must be added his literary works, first of all those on art, which are landmarks and authorities of the first order for the Renaissance of Form, especially in architecture; then his Latin prose writings—novels and other works—of which some have been taken for productions of antiquity; his elegies, eclogues, and humorous dinner-speeches. He also wrote an Italian treatise on domestic life in four books; and even a funeral oration on his dog. His serious and witty sayings were thought worth collecting, and specimens of them, many columns long, are quoted in his biography. And all that he had and knew he imparted, as rich natures always do, without the least reserve, giving away his chief discoveries for nothing. But the deepest spring of his nature has yet to be spoken of—the sympathetic intensity with which he entered into the whole life around him. At the sight of noble trees and waving cornfields he shed tears; handsome and dignified, old men he honored as "a delight of nature," and could never look at them enough. Perfectly formed animals won his goodwill as being specially favored by nature; and more than once, when he was ill, the sight of a beautiful landscape cured him. No wonder that those who saw him in this close and mysterious communion with the world ascribed to him the gift of prophecy. He was said to have foretold a bloody catastrophe in the family of Este, the fate of Florence and that of the Popes many years beforehand, and to be able to read in the countenances and the hearts of men. It need not be added that an iron will pervaded and sustained his whole personality; like all the great men of the Renaissance, he said, "Men can do all things if they will."

And Leonardo da Vinci was to Alberti as the finisher to the beginner, as the master to the *dilettante*. Would only that Vasari's work were here supplemented by a description like that of Alberti! The colossal outlines of Leonardo's nature can never be more than dimly and distantly conceived.

Notes

1 In *secondo commentario,* being Ghiberti's autobiography; see the complete translation of it in the Phaidon Edition of *Ghiberti*. The paragraph to which Burckhardt refers is actually a quotation from Vitruvius's *Architecture*, VI, 2.

2 *Codri Urcei Vita,* Bologna, 1502.

3 Boccaccio, *Vita di Dante.* (English translation by Philip H. Wicksteed, in *The King's Classics,* London, 1904.)

4 The angels which he drew on tablets at the anniversary of the death of Beatrice (*Vita Nuova*) may have been more than the work of a dilettante. Leonardo Aretino says he drew "egregiamente" and was a great lover of music.

5 Other inventions, especially an attempt at a flying-machine, had been made about 880 by the Andalusian Abul Abbas Kasim ibn Firnas. (See Guayangos, *History of the Muhammedan Dynasties in Spain,* London, 1840, Vol. I, p. 148 *et seq.* and 425–7.)

If Burckhardt is correct that "Leonardo da Vinci was to Alberti as the finisher to the beginner, as the master to the dilettante," then one can scarcely conceive the dimensions of da Vinci's achievements. As Burckhardt says: "Would only that Vasari's work were here supplemented by a description like that of Alberti! The colossal outlines of Leonardo's nature can never be more than dimly and distantly conceived." Nevertheless, Vasari did attempt to outline da Vinci's achievements, as the following selection indicates. A contemporary of the great sixteenth-century artists and a critic and artist in his own right, Vasari draws a verbal picture of Leonardo well worth consulting in its entirety.

Leonardo da Vinci

Giorgio Vasari

The richest gifts are occasionally seen to be showered, as by celestial influence, on certain human beings, nay, they some times super-naturally and marvellously congregate in one sole person; beauty, grace, and talent being united in such a manner, that to whatever the man thus favored may turn himself, his every action is so divine as to leave all other men far behind him, and manifestly to prove that he has been specially endowed by the hand of God himself, and has not obtained his pre-eminence by human teaching, or the power of man. This was seen and acknowledged by all men in the case of Leonardo da Vinci, in whom, to say nothing of his beauty of person, which yet was such that it has never been sufficiently extolled, there was a grace beyond expression which was rendered manifest without thought or effort in every act and deed, and who had besides so rare a gift of talent and ability, that to whatever subject he turned his attention, however difficult, he presently made himself absolute master of it. Extraordinary power was in his case conjoined with remarkable facility, a mind of regal boldness and magnanimous daring; his gifts were such that the celebrity of his name extended most widely, and he was held in the highest estimation, not in his own time only, but also, and even to a greater extent, after his death, nay, this he has continued, and will continue to be by all succeeding ages.

Truly admirable, indeed, and divinely endowed was Leonardo da Vinci; this artist was the son of Ser Piero da Vinci; he would without doubt have made great progress in learning and knowledge of the sciences, had he not been so versatile and changeful, but the instability

From Giorgio Vasari, Mrs. Jonathan Foster, trans., *Lives of the Most Eminent Painters, Sculptors, and Architects* (London: Henry G. Bohn, 1914), Vol. II, pp. 366–390.

of his character caused him to undertake many things which having commenced he afterwards abandoned. In arithmetic, for example, he made such rapid progress in the short time during which he gave his attention to it, that he often confounded the master who was teaching him, by the perpetual doubts he started, and by the difficulty of the questions he proposed. He also commenced the study of music, and resolved to acquire the art of playing the lute, when, being by nature of an exalted imagination and full of the most graceful vivacity, he sang to that instrument most divinely, improvising at once the verses and the music.

But, though dividing his attention among pursuits so varied, he never abandoned his drawing, and employed himself much in works of relief, that being the occupation which attracted him more than any other. His father, Ser Piero, observing this, and considering the extraordinary character of his son's genius, one day took some of his drawings and showed them to Andrea del Verrocchio, who was a very intimate friend of his, begging him earnestly to tell him whether he thought that Leonardo would be likely to secure success if he devoted himself to the arts of design. Andrea Verrocchio was amazed as he beheld the remarkable commencement made by Leonardo, and advised Ser Piero to see that he attached himself to that calling, whereupon the latter took his measures accordingly, and sent Leonardo to study in the bottega or workshop of Andrea. Thither the boy resorted therefore, with the utmost readiness, and not only gave his attention to one branch of art, but to all the others, of which design made a portion. Endowed with such admirable intelligence, and being also an excellent geometrician, Leonardo not only worked in sculpture (having executed certain heads in terra-cotta, of women smiling, even in his first youth, which are now reproduced in gypsum, and also others of children which might be supposed to have proceeded from the hand of a master); but in architecture likewise he prepared various designs for ground-plans, and the construction of entire buildings: he too it was who, though still but a youth, first suggested the formation of a canal from Pisa to Florence, by means of certain changes to be effected on the river Arno. Leonardo likewise made designs for mills, fulling machines, and other engines, which were to be acted on by means of water; but as he had resolved to make painting his profession, he gave the larger portion of time to drawing from nature. He sometimes formed models of different figures in clay, on which he would arrange fragments of soft drapery dipped in plaster; from these he would then set himself patiently to draw on very fine cambric or linen that had already been used and rendered smooth, these he executed in black and white with the point of the pencil in a most admirable manner, as may be seen by certain specimens from his own hand which I have in my book of drawings. He drew on paper also with so much care and so perfectly, that no one has ever equalled him in this respect: I have a head by him in chiaro-scuro, which is incomparably beautiful. Leonardo was indeed so imbued with power and grace by the hand of God, and was endowed with so marvellous a facility in reproducing his conceptions; his memory also was always so ready and so efficient in the service of his intellect, that in discourse he won all men by his reasonings, and confounded every antagonist, however powerful, by the force of his arguments.

This master was also frequently occupied with the construction of models and the preparation of designs for the removal or the perforation of mountains, to the end that they might thus be easily passed from one plain to another. By means of levers, cranes, and screws, he likewise showed how great weights might be raised or drawn; in what manner ports and havens might be cleansed and kept in order, and how water might be obtained from the lowest deeps. From speculations of this kind he never gave himself rest, and of the results of these labors and meditations there are numberless examples in drawings, etc., dispersed among those who practice our arts: I have myself seen very many of them. Besides all this he wasted not a little time, to the degree of even designing a series of cords, curiously intertwined, but of which any separate strand may be distinguished from one end to the other, the whole forming a complete circle: a very curiously complicated and exceedingly difficult specimen of these coils may be seen engraved; in the midst of it are the following words: —*Leonardus Vinci Academia.* Among these models and drawings there is one, by means of which Leonardo often sought to prove to the different citizens—many of them men of great discernment—who then governed Florence, that the church of San Giovanni in that city could be raised, and steps placed beneath it, without injury to the edifice: he supported his assertions with reasons so persuasive, that while he spoke the undertaking seemed feasible, although every one of his hearers, when he had departed, could see for himself that such a thing was impossible. In conversation Leonardo was indeed so pleasing that he won the hearts of all hearers, and though possessing so small a patrimony only that it might almost be called nothing, while he yet worked very little, he still constantly kept many servants and horses, taking extraordinary delight in the latter: he was indeed fond of all animals, ever treating them with infinite kindness and consideration; as a proof of this it is related, that when he passed places where birds were sold, he would frequently take them from their cages, and having paid the price demanded for them by the sellers, would then let them fly into the air, thus restoring to them the liberty they had lost. Leonardo was in all things so highly favored by nature, that to whatever he turned his thoughts, mind, and spirit, he gave proof in all of such admirable power and perfection, that whatever he did bore an impress of harmony, truthfulness, goodness, sweetness and grace, wherein no other man could ever equal him.

Leonardo, with his profound intelligence of art, commenced various undertakings, many of which he never completed, because it appeared to him that the hand could never give its due perfection to the object or purpose which he had in his thoughts, or beheld in his imagination; seeing that in his mind he frequently formed the idea of some difficult enterprise, so subtle and so wonderful that, by means of hands, however excellent or able, the full reality could never be worthily executed and entirely realized. His conceptions were varied to infinity; philosophizing over natural objects; among others, he set himself to investigate the properties of plant, to make observations on the heavenly bodies, to follow the movements of the planets, the variations of the moon, and the course of the sun.

Having been placed then by Ser Piero in his childhood with Andrea Verrocchio, as we have said, to learn the art of the painter, that master was engaged on a picture the subject of which was San Giovanni baptizing Jesus Christ; in this Leonardo painted an angel holding some vestments; and although he was but a youth, he completed that figure in such a manner, that the angel of Leonardo was much better than the portion executed by his master, which caused the latter never to touch colors more, so much was he displeased to find that a mere child could do more than himself.

Leonardo received a commission to prepare the cartoon for the hangings of a door which was to be woven in silk and gold in Flanders, thence to be despatched to the king of Portugal; the subject was the sin of our first parents in Paradise: here the artist depicted a meadow in chiaro-scuro, the high lights being in white lead, displaying an immense variety of vegetation and numerous animals, respecting which it may be truly said, that for careful execution and fidelity to nature, they are such that there is no genius in the world, however God-like, which could produce similar objects with equal truth. In the fig-tree, for example, the foreshortening of the leaves, and the disposition of the branches are executed with so much care, that one finds it difficult to conceive how any man could have so much patience; there is besides a palm-tree, in which the roundness of the fan-like leaves is exhibited to such admirable perfection and with so much art, that nothing short of the genius and patience of Leonardo could have effected it: but the work for which the cartoon was prepared was never carried into execution, the drawing therefore remained in Florence, and is now in the fortunate house of the illustrious Ottaviano de'Medici, to whom it was presented, no long time since, by the uncle of Leonardo.

It is related that Ser Piero da Vinci, being at his country house, was there visited by one of the peasants on his estate, who, having cut down a fig-tree on his farm, had made a shield from part of it with his own hands, and then brought it to Ser Piero, begging that he would be pleased to cause the same to be painted for him in Florence. This the latter very willingly promised to do, the countryman having great skill in taking birds and in fishing, and being often very serviceable to Ser Piero in such matters. Having taken the shield with him to Florence therefore, without saying any thing to Leonardo as to whom it was for, he desired the latter to paint something upon it. Accordingly, he one day took it in hand, but finding it crooked, coarse, and badly made, he straightened it at the fire, and giving it to a turner, it was brought back to him smooth and delicately rounded, instead of the rude and shapeless form in which he had received it. He then covered it with gypsum, and having prepared it to his liking, he began to consider what he could paint upon it that might best and most effectually terrify whomsoever might approach it, producing the same effect with that formerly attributed to the head of Medusa. For this purpose therefore, Leonardo carried to one of his rooms, into which no one but himself ever entered, a number of lizards, hedgehogs, newts, serpents, dragon-flies, locusts, bats, glow-worms, and every other sort of strange animal of similar kind on which he could lay his hands; from this assemblage, variously adapted and joined together, he formed a hideous and appalling monster, breathing poison and flames, and surrounded by an atmosphere of fire; this he caused to issue from a dark and rifted rock, with poison reeking from the cavernous throat, flames darting from the eyes, and vapors rising from the nostrils in such sort that the result was indeed a most fearful and monstrous creature: at this he labored until the odors arising from all those dead animals filled the room with a mortal fetor, to which the zeal of Leonardo and the love which he bore to art rendered him insensible or indifferent. When this work, which neither the countryman nor Ser Piero any longer inquired for, was completed, Leonardo went to his father and told him that he might send for the shield at his earliest convenience, since so far as he was concerned, the work was finished; Ser Piero went accordingly one morning to the room for the shield, and having knocked at the door, Leonardo opened it to him, telling him nevertheless to wait a little without, and having returned into the room he placed the shield on the easel, and shading the window so that the light falling on the painting was somewhat dimmed, he made Ser Piero step within to look at it. But the latter, not expecting any such thing, drew back, startled at the first glance, not supposing that to be the shield, or believing the monster he beheld to be a painting, he therefore turned to rush out but Leonardo withheld him, saying: —The shield will serve the purpose for which it has been executed, take it therefore and carry it away, for this is the effect it was designed to produce. The work seemed something more than wonderful to Ser Piero, and he highly commended the fanciful idea of Leonardo, but he afterwards silently bought from a merchant another shield, whereon there was painted a heart transfixed with an arrow, and this he gave to the countryman, who considered himself obliged to him for it to the end of his life. Some time after Ser Piero secretly sold the shield painted by Leonardo to certain merchants for one hundred ducats, and it subsequently fell into the hands of the Duke of Milan, sold to him by the same merchants for three hundred ducats.

No long time after Leonardo painted an admirable picture of Our Lady, which was greatly prized by Pope Clement VII.; among the accessories of this work was a bottle filled with water in which some flowers were placed, and not only were these flowers most vividly natural, but there were dewdrops on the leaves, which were so true to nature that they appeared to be the actual reality. . . .

Leonardo also had a fancy to paint the head of a Medusa in oil, to which he gave a circlet of twining serpents by way of head-dress; the most strange and extravagant invention that could possibly be conceived: but as this was a work requiring time, so it happened to the Medusa as to so many other of his works, it was never finished. . . .

Leonardo was so much pleased when he encountered faces of extraordinary character, or heads, beards, or hair of unusual appearance, that he would follow any such, more than commonly attractive, through the whole day, until the figure of the person would become so well impressed on his mind that, having returned home, he would draw him as readily as though he stood before him. Of heads thus obtained there exist many, both masculine and feminine; and I have myself several of them drawn with a pen by his own hand, in the book of drawings so frequently cited. Among these is the head of Amerigo Vespucci, which is a very beautiful one of an old man, done with charcoal, as also that of the Gypsy Captain Scaramuccia, which had been left by Gianbullari to Messer Donato Valdambrini, of Arezzo, Canon of San Lorenzo. A picture representing the Adoration of the Magi was likewise commenced by Leonardo, and is among the best of his works, more especially as regards the heads; it was in the house of Amerigo Benci, opposite the Loggia of the Peruzzi, but like so many of the other works of Leonardo, this also remained unfinished.

On the death of Giovanni Galeazzo, Duke of Milan, in the year 1943, Ludovico Sforza was chosen in the same year to be his successor, when Leonardo was invited with great honor to Milan by the Duke, who delighted greatly in the music of the lute, to the end that the master might play before him; Leonardo therefore took with him a certain instrument which he had himself constructed almost wholly of silver, and in the shape of a horse's head, a new and fanciful form calculated to give more force and sweetness to the sound. Here Leonardo surpassed all the musicians who had assembled to perform before the Duke; he was besides one of the best *improvisatori* in verse existing at that time, and the Duke, enchanted with the admirable conversation of Leonardo, was so charmed by his varied gifts that he delighted beyond measure in his society, and prevailed on him to paint an altar-piece, the subject of which was the Nativity of Christ, which was sent by the Duke as a present to the Emperor. For the Dominican monks of Santa Maria delle Grazie at Milan, he also painted a Last Supper, which is a most beautiful and admirable work; to the heads of the Apostles in this picture the master gave so much beauty and majesty that he was constrained to leave that of Christ unfinished, being convinced that he could not impart to it the divinity which should appertain to and distinguish an image of the Redeemer. But this work, remaining thus in its unfinished state, has been ever held in the highest estimation by the Milanese, and not by them only, but by foreigners also: Leonardo succeeded to perfection in expressing the doubts and anxiety experienced by the Apostles, and the desire felt by them to know by whom their Master is to be betrayed; in the faces of all appear love, terror, anger, or grief and bewilderment, unable as they are to fathom the meaning of their Lord. Nor is the spectator less struck with admiration by the force and truth with which, on the other hand, the master has exhibited the impious determination, hatred, and treachery of Judas. The whole work indeed is executed with inexpressible diligence even in its most minute part, among other things may be mentioned the table-cloth, the texture of which is copied with such exactitude, that the linen-cloth itself could scarcely look more real. . . .

For Francesco del Giocondo, Leonardo undertook to paint the portrait of Mona Lisa, his wife, but, after loitering over it for four years, he finally left it unfinished. This work is now in the possession of the King Francis of France, and is at Fontainebleau. Whoever shall desire to see how far art can imitate nature, may do so to perfection in this head, wherein every peculiarity that could be depicted by the utmost subtlety of the pencil has been faithfully reproduced. The eyes have the lustrous brightness and moisture which is seen in life, and around them are those pale, red, and slightly livid circles, also proper to nature, with the lashes, which can only be copied, as these are, with the greatest difficulty; the eyebrows also are represented with the closest exactitude, where fuller and where more thinly set, with the separate hairs delineated as they issue from the skin, every turn being followed, and all the pores exhibited in a manner that could not be more natural than it is: the nose, with its beautiful and delicately roseate nostrils, might be easily believed to be alive; the mouth, admirable in its outline, has the lips uniting the rose-tints of their color with that of the face, in the utmost perfection, and the carnation of the cheek does not appear to be painted, but truly of flesh and blood: he who looks earnestly at the pit of the throat cannot but believe that he sees the beating of the pulses, and it may be truly said that this work is painted in a manner well calculated to make the boldest master tremble, and astonishes all who behold it, however well accustomed to the marvels of art. Mona Lisa was exceedingly beautiful, and while Leonardo was painting her portrait, he took the precaution of keeping some one constantly near her, to sing or play on instruments, or to jest and otherwise amuse her, to the end that she might continue cheerful, and so that her face might not exhibit the melancholy expression often imparted by painters to the likenesses they take. In this portrait of Leonardo's, on the contrary, there is so pleasing an expression, and a smile so sweet, that while looking at it one thinks it rather divine than human, and it has ever been esteemed a wonderful work, since life itself could exhibit no other appearance. . . .

On the exaltation of Pope Leo X to the chair of St. Peter, Leonardo accompanied the Duke Giuliano de' Medici to Rome: the Pontiff was much inclined to philosophical inquiry, and was more especially addicted to the study of alchemy: Leonardo, therefore, having composed a kind of paste from wax, made of this, while it was still in its half-liquid state, certain figures of animals, entirely hollow and exceedingly slight in texture, which he then filled with air. When he blew into these figures he could make them fly through the air, but when the air within had escaped from them they fell to the earth. One day the vine-dresser of the Belvedere found a very curious lizard, and for this creature Leonardo constructed wings, made from the skins of other lizards, flayed for the purpose; into these wings he put quicksilver, so that when the animal walked, the wings moved also, with a tremulous motion: he then made eyes, horns, and a beard for the creature, which he tamed and kept in a case; he would then show it to the friends who came to visit him, and all who saw it ran away terrified. He more than once, likewise, caused the intestines of a sheep to be cleansed and scraped until they were brought into such a state of tenuity that they could be held within the hollow of the hand, having then placed in a neighboring chamber a pair of black-smith's bellows, to which he had made fast one end of the intestines, he would blow into them until he caused them to fill the whole room, which was a very large one, insomuch that whoever might be therein was compelled to take refuge in a corner: he thus showed them transparent and full of wind, remarking that, whereas they had previously been contained within a small compass, they were now filling all space, and this, he would say, was a fit emblem of talent or genius. He made numbers of these follies in various kinds, occupied himself much with mirrors and optical instruments, and made the most singular experiments in seeking oils for painting, and varnishes to preserve the work when executed. About this time he painted a small picture for Messer Baldassare Turini, of Pescia, who was Datary to Pope Leo: the subject of his work was Our Lady, with the Child in her arms, and it was executed by Leonardo with infinite care and art, but whether from the carelessness of those who prepared the ground, or because of his peculiar and fanciful mixtures for colors, varnishes, etc., it is now much deteriorated. In another small picture he painted a little Child, which is graceful and beautiful to a miracle. These paintings are both in Pescia, in the possession of Messer Giulio Turini. It is related that Leonardo, having received a commission for a certain picture from Pope Leo, immediately began to distil oils and herbs for the varnish, whereupon the pontiff remarked, "Alas! the while, this man will assuredly do nothing at all, since he is thinking of the end before he has made a beginning to his work." There was perpetual discord between Michelagnolo Buonarroti and Leonardo, and the competition between them caused Michelagnolo to leave Florence, the Duke Giuliano framing an excuse for him, the pretext for his departure being that he was summoned to Rome by the Pope for the Facade of San Lorenzo. When Leonardo heard of this, he also departed and went to France, where the king, already possessing several of his works, was most kindly disposed towards him, and wished him to paint the cartoon of Sant' Anna, but Leonardo, according to his custom, kept the king a long time waiting with nothing better than words. Finally, having become old, he lay sick for many months, and, finding himself near death, wrought diligently to make himself acquainted with the Catholic ritual, and with the good and holy path of the Christian religion: he then confessed with great penitence and many tears, and although he could not support himself on his feet, yet, being sustained in the arms of his servants and friends, he devoutly received the Holy Sacrament, while thus out of his bed. The king, who was accustomed frequently and affectionately to visit him, came immediately afterwards to his room, and he, causing himself out of reverence to be raised up, sat in his bed describing his malady and the different circumstances connected with it, lamenting, besides, that he had offended God and man, inasmuch as that he had not labored in art as he ought to have done. He was then seized with a violent paroxysm, the forerunner of death, when the king, rising and supporting his head to give him such assistance and do him such favor as he could, in the hope of alleviating his sufferings, the spirit of Leonardo, which was most divine, conscious that he could attain no greater honor, departed in the arms of the monarch, being at that time in the seventy-fifth year of his age.

The death of Leonardo caused great sorrow to all who had known him, nor was there ever an artist who did more honor to the art of painting. The radiance of his countenance, which was splendidly beautiful, brought cheerfulness to the heart of the most melancholy, and the power of his word could move the most obstinate to say, "No," or "Yes," as he desired; he possessed so great a degree of physical strength, that he was capable of restraining the most impetuous violence, and was able to bend one of the iron rings used for the knockers of doors, or a horse-shoe, as if it were lead: with the generous liberality of his nature, he extended shelter and hospitality to every friend, rich or poor, provided only that he were distinguished by talent or excellence; the poorest and most significant abode was rendered beautiful and honorable by his works; and as the city of Florence received a great gift in the birth of Leonardo, so did it suffer a more than grievous loss at his death. To the art of painting in oil this master contributed the discovery of a certain mode of deepening shadows, whereby the later artists have been enabled to give great force and relief to their figures. His abilities in statuary were proved by three figures in bronze, which are over the north door of San Giovanni; they were cast by Gio Francesco Rustici, but conducted under the advice of Leonardo, and are, without doubt, the most beautiful castings that have been seen in these later days, whether for design or finish.

We are indebted to Leonardo for a work on the anatomy of the horse, and for another much more valuable, on that of man; wherefore, for the many admirable qualities with which he was so richly endowed, although he labored much more by his word than in fact and by deed, his name and fame can never be extinguished. . . .

This is the complete text of the letter that Leonardo da Vinci sent to
Duke Ludovico il Moro of Milan, referred to in the first essay of this chapter.
How was Leonardo caught up with the myth, the canon, and the hangup?

A Genius Applies for a Job

Leonardo da Vinci

Having now sufficiently seen and considered the proofs of all those
who count themselves masters and inventors of instruments of war,
and finding that their invention and use of the said instruments does
not differ in any respect from those in common practice, I am em-
boldened without prejudice to anyone else to put myself in communication with Your Excellency, in order to acquaint you with my secrets,
thereafter offering myself at your pleasure effectually to demonstrate
at any convenient time all those matters which are in part briefly
recorded below.

1. I have plans for bridges, very light and strong and suitable for
carrying very easily, with which to pursue and at times defeat the
enemy; and others solid and indestructible by fire or assault, easy and
convenient to carry away and place in position. And plans for burning and destroying those of the enemy.

2. When a place is besieged I know how to cut off water from the
trenches, and how to construct an infinite number of bridges, mantlets, scaling ladders, and other instruments which have to do with
the same enterprise.

3. Also if a place cannot be reduced by the method of bombard-
ment, either through the height of its glacis or the strength of its
position, I have plans for destroying every fortress or other strong-
hold unless it has been founded upon rock.

4. I have also plans for making cannon, very convenient and easy
of transport, with which to hurl small stones in the manner almost of
hail, causing great terror to the enemy from their smoke, and great
loss and confusion.

5. Also I have ways of arriving at a certain fixed spot by caverns
and secret winding passages, made without any noise, even though
it may be necessary to pass underneath trenches or a river.

6. Also I can make armored cars, safe and unassailable, which will
enter the serried ranks of the enemy with their artillery, and there is

From *The Literary Works of Leonardo da Vinci* by Jean Paul Richter, edited,
enlarged, and revised by Jean Paul Richter and Irma A. Richter (New York:
Oxford University Press, 1939), pp. 92–93.

no company of men at arms so great that they will not break it. And behind these the infantry will be able to follow quite unharmed and without any opposition.

7. Also, if need shall arise, I can make cannon, mortars, and light ordnance, of very beautiful and useful shapes, quite different from those in common use.

8. Where it is not possible to employ cannon, I can supply catapults, mangonels, *trabocchi* [old war engines: trébuchets], and other engines of wonderful efficacy not in general use. In short, as the variety of circumstances shall necessitate, I can supply an infinite number of different engines of attack and defense.

9. And if it should happen that the engagement is at sea, I have plans for constructing many engines most suitable either for attack or defense, and ships which can resist the fire of all the heaviest cannon, and powder and smoke.

10. In time of peace I believe that I can give you as complete satisfaction as anyone else in architecture in the construction of buildings both public and private, and in conducting water from one place to another.

Also I can execute sculpture in marble, bronze, or clay, and also painting, in which my work will stand comparison with that of anyone else, whoever he may be.

Moreover, I would undertake the work of the bronze horse, which shall perpetuate with immortal glory and eternal honor the auspicious memory of the Prince your father and of the illustrious house of Sforza.

And if any of the aforesaid things should seem impossible or impracticable to anyone, I offer myself as ready to make trial of them in your park or in whatever place shall please Your Excellency, to whom I commend myself with all possible humility.

Questions

1 Do you think there is any connection between Muhammad Ali's (Cassius Clay's) boasting and the new black consciousness that accompanies the black power movement?

2 Is it not less hypocritical to honestly boast about one's achievements than to feign modesty?

3 Do you see any contradiction in the fierce competitive nature of American society and its taboo on braggadocio?

4   If you were to achieve some great honor, how many people would you want to know about it? How would you go about arranging for them to find out? Whom are you trying to impress? Parents? Friends? Potential employers? Enemies?

5   What percentage of the Renaissance population actually had good opportunities for individual self-fulfillment?

6   Is history the study of a minority elite?

7   What are the difficulties in becoming a "Renaissance Man" in an age of specialization?

8   Who can compare with Leonardo?

9   Muhammad Ali eventually became a Black Muslim minister and refused to serve in the army, claiming conscientious objection. As a result, he was fined, sentenced to prison, and stripped of his title, though no one had defeated him in the ring. Does this description of his activities and sacrifices jibe with the picture of Ali as a braggadocio-practitioner?

10   Who are some of the multitalented people today who come close to the ideal of the "uomo universale" of the Renaissance, as exemplified by Leonardo?

11   Why do you suppose you are having such a difficult time answering question 10?

12   Which age provided the most opportunities for individualism—the Hellenic years, the Renaissance, or the present?

13   From the standpoint of emotional health, would a psychologist recommend to his patients the posture of the braggadocio of the Renaissance or the humility of the Middle Ages?

10 The Impact of the Scientific Revolution

We avoid describing the dramatic unfolding of the Scientific Revolution of the sixteenth and seventeenth centuries because we assume that students will have at least a textbook familiarity with the collapse of the geocentric world, a collapse that resulted from attacks upon the Ptolemaic system by such figures as Copernicus, Brahe, Bruno, Galileo, Kepler, and Newton. What we do deal with, however, are the relationships between the attitudes generated by the Scientific Revolution and the broader cultural canons developed during the eighteenth century. The theme is the impact of the Scientific Revolution upon the centuries that followed.

Science, Sex, and Society

Melvin Steinfield

The teenaged couple passionately petting in their automobile at the local drive-in movie personifies a reality of the twentieth century that both Sigmund Freud and Henry Ford helped create: the portable bed in the public boudoir of the permissive society. Without mass production of steel cars from Detroit and sexy films from Hollywood, a popular form of recreation that frequently leads to procreation would not exist as we know it today. Indirectly, then, both Freud and Ford can be blamed for soaring college enrollments and crowded college classrooms.

In an effort to prevent unwanted pregnancies at drive-in movies and elsewhere, medical researchers have produced a pill. The development of the birth-control pill has not only helped reduce the undesired aftereffects of sexual enlightenment but also opened up a Pandora's box of controversial questions. Pompous politicians are proposing, "Can the government require use of The Pill by unmarried mothers who are receiving welfare aid for dependent children?" Pontificating priests are promulgating, "The Pill is evil. Beware!" Paternalistic parents are probing, "Should we buy a year's supply for our daughter?"

The point is that science can make an impact upon man's culture in areas that go far beyond the specialized boundaries of science itself. In the twentieth century there are numerous examples of the far-reaching implications of science for religious values, political decisions, and social customs. For instance, consider the ethical dilemmas and controversial questions that are posed by twentieth-century medical advances. Some of the questions raised by human-heart transplant operations have shaken the roots of medical ethics and challenged ancient canons. They have also had an influence upon general moral concerns. Thus laymen as well as medical men are asking: Do we need to revise our definition of death? At what point does a physician have a right to remove a vital organ from the body of a dying patient for the purpose of transplanting it into the body of another patient? Should the doctor play God with the donor's life?

Just as the startling achievements of modern science in birth-control, heart-transplants, and even moon-landings have opened up panoramic vistas of potential controversy, the achievements of the Scientific Revolution caused man to re-evaluate his basic religious, social, and political institutions. In many cases, then as now, his conclusions contained revolutionary implications.

And then, as now, it was a practical medical decision that focused attention on the broader issues of the scientific achievement. In the 1720's the inoculation and then in the 1790's the vaccination, perfected by Sir Edward Jenner, provided an opportunity to be immunized against the dreaded smallpox germs. But this raised questions about the right of man to tamper with the will of God. Did not the Scriptures state that God visited plagues and diseases upon man as punishment for his sins? Wouldn't it amount to defiance of God's will and wouldn't it be expressly contrary to Scriptures for man to thwart the natural progress of disease? The debate raged.

Is it not written that Woman must suffer pain in childbirth as punishment for having given Adam the forbidden fruit? Is not the administration of anesthesia during childbirth therefore open violation of God's word? These kinds of questions were just as lively and important to men and women of the seventeenth and eighteenth centuries as is the question today of blood transfusions for Jehovah's Witnesses or surgery for Christian Scientists.

The medical decision depends upon an entire attitude toward human nature. If man is evil by nature, then he deserves to suffer and has no right to seek to alleviate his suffering. In the seventeenth century the religious tradition in Europe tended to uphold this view. But the view of the eighteenth century rationalists was founded upon the assumption that man is basically good. They believed that through use of his reason he could discover the beautiful and harmonious laws of nature and apply his discoveries to an increased measure of happiness upon this earth.

What was at stake, then, in the debate on the propriety of the smallpox vaccination, was a complete system of values founded upon an assumption about the nature of man. The traditional religious assumption that man is evil, and the value system that this belief supported, were being challenged by a new system based upon a different assumption about the nature of man. Thus the narrow medical question served as a lead-in to broader questions about man's nature and religion's pronouncements about man's nature.

Not just the question of health, but also the question of government, was affected by the long-range impact of the Scientific Revolution. People reasoned that if there was a universal system of laws governing the physical universe, there must be a similar rational system in the human arena. A surge of faith arose in man's ability to strip away the mysteries of ideal human organization; man came to believe that if he persisted patiently in applying reason to the affairs of government, he would soon discover the most simple and most natural forms of government.

"That government is best which governs least," concluded Thomas Jefferson. He clearly spoke for the Enlightenment generation, which stood for the simplest and most natural form of government. To many, absolute monarchy was not necessarily the simplest or most logical form. Nor did the "divine right of kings" seem to conform to any natural and universal laws. It was not by accident, then, that the men who were seeking to apply the methods and principles of Newtonian science to human affairs soon discovered that some of the most sacred myths of their society were not founded upon a rational base.

These revolutionary implications of eighteenth-century political theory had their roots in John Locke's ideas of the seventeenth century and their fruits in the French and American Revolutions. The connection is a solid one and can be traced directly by comparing Locke's Essay on Civil Government, which was written in 1690, with Jefferson's Declaration of Independence, which was written in 1776.

The search for order in government was stimulated by the orderly searches of science a century earlier. Besides weakening the basis for absolute monarchy, the Enlightenment quest for natural law led to a serious questioning of the authority of Scriptures as well. The strongest blows came from the heavens, or, more precisely, from the speculations about them. Astronomy challenged the Bible as soon as the heliocentric theory of Copernicus was proposed, for is it not written in the Book of Joshua that, contrary to its usual procedure, the sun was made to stand still? If it says in an unimpeachably authoritative source that the sun normally did the moving, how, then, can the earth move? This was a war between two views of the world, and Copernicus knew it. He postponed the publication of his book for twenty years, not for the fun of it, but for his health, which was clearly at stake. Only when he was on his death bed did he permit his heretical views to come forth in print.

Because the Church was so heavily committed to the geocentric theory, it became the most vigorous opponent of the new ideas of the Scientific Revolution. An enduring example of the Church's opposition to the heliocentric theory is the treatment accorded Galileo and Bruno. At the age of 70, Galileo was threatened with torture and forced to recant his view that the sun is the center of the solar system and that the earth revolves around it. His book in support of Copernicus' theory was placed on the Index of Prohibited Books, as were those by Kepler and Copernicus. Not until 1835 were these books removed from the Index. Giordano Bruno also supported the heliocentric theory and was therefore also considered to be a heretic who was threatening the authority of the Church. The heated controversy about the nature of the physical universe spread until it destroyed the possibility that a literal interpretation of Scriptures could remain supported by a majority of Christians much longer.

The two most severely challenged institutions were the Church and the Monarchy, but they certainly were not the only ones. The eighteenth-century application of the principles of reason, order, harmony, and other elements of the Scientific Revolution reached into many corners of human activity. For example, religious tolerance grew into a reality in the eighteenth century. This was a practical necessity because Europe was tearing itself apart with religious wars. But there was another factor that contributed to the spread of tolerance. The *philosophes* of the eighteenth century began to ask: "Is there a truth certain enough to justify persecution?" "Since Scriptures have been proven wrong in astronomy, can they not also be wrong in other areas?"

Freedom of speech also received a powerful thrust from the new attitude, which encouraged expression of all points of view in an atmosphere of free inquiry. Rational men were capable of sorting out the wheat from the chaff, it was believed, without being any worse for the effort—that is, if one believed that man could be exposed to incorrect doctrines without being poisoned or contaminated by them. The Church, of course, still did not share in the positive view of human nature that was held by the eighteenth-century *philosophes*. Rooted in a belief in the fundamental evil of man's nature, the Church would naturally come to rely upon censorship as a protection from harmful doctrines. But the Index ultimately lost out to the first amendment to the American Constitution. One might well wonder, will the opposition to the Pill lose out to the world population explosion? And, if so, what will the effect be on the authority of the Church?

Despite the dampening effect of medieval otherworldliness upon secular happiness in this life, first the Renaissance and then the Scientific Revolution successfully established the legitimacy of concern about the physical universe and man's pleasure. Out of the solemnity of medieval spirituality came a disparagement of learning about the world for its own sake. But the secular spirit of the Renaissance inspired inquiries into the nature of the universe and the physical objects in it. After the Renaissance, a new era of optimism was created by the effects of the Scientific Revolution. This is illustrated by the following statement by d'Alembert, a famous eighteenth-century French philosopher, who could hardly contain his enthusiasm:

Natural science from day to day accumulates new riches. Geometry, by extending its limits, has borne its torch into the regions of physical science which lay nearest at hand. The true system of the world has been recognized. . . . In short, from the earth to Saturn, from the history of the heavens to that of insects, natural philosophy has been revolutionized; and nearly all other fields of knowledge have assumed new forms . . . the discovery and application of a new method of philosophizing, the kind of enthusiasm which accompanies discoveries, a certain exaltation of ideas which the spectacle of the universe produces in us; all these causes have brought about a lively fermentation of minds. Spreading throughout nature in all directions, this fermentation has swept with a sort of violence everything before it which stood in its way, like a river which has burst its dams. . . . Thus, from the principles of the secular sciences to the foundations of religious revelation, from metaphysics to matters of taste, from music to morals, from the scholastic disputes of theologians to matters of commerce, from natural law to the arbitrary laws of nations . . . everything has been discussed, analyzed, or at least mentioned.[1]

D'Alembert speaks of a general "effervescence of minds," and that is a good way to describe the general tendency of the eighteenth century. Monarchy was liberated from tradition, science was liberated from theology, and culture in general was liberated from a stultifying inheritance.

During the eighteenth century virtually every major institution was closely examined under the bright light of rational inquiry. Some well-known examples of this trend are: references to "natural law" in politics and religion; new conceptions of "God," such as pantheism and Deism; the concept of progress, especially as elucidated in Condorcet's *Sketch for the Historical Picture of the Progress of the*

Human Mind; the growth of humanitarian reforms in prisons and insane asylums on the grounds that men are naturally good and no one voluntarily chooses to become a criminal or misfit; deliberate attempts to subdue passions, as evidenced in the refined rococo mannerisms of the wig-wearing, snuff-inhaling, minuet-dancing Enlightenment tough-guys like George Washington; a more cosmopolitan outlook toward the nations of mankind and toward the abilities of individual men; and the belief that became the root of "liberal" theory today, namely, that evil can be corrected by improving the environment, changing the society, spreading education, and in general, bringing human affairs to a rational, orderly, natural state.

In order to achieve these reforms, however, it was first necessary to destroy prevailing institutions, and also those attitudes that supported the institutions. The next three centuries after the Scientific Revolution witnessed the continued wearing-away of faith in inherited absolute values. Today's bewildering pace is largely the result of the long-range effects of the Scientific Revolution, both in its practical technological applications and its broad theoretical revelations.

Despite the shattering of the medieval world-view and its replacement by new concepts generated first by the Renaissance and then by the Scientific Revolution, some things remain as they were long ago. Men still ask: What is the best form of government? Is human nature good or evil? What types of cooperative behavior can the humanities and science develop? What is Man capable of achieving? And the circle is complete. We are still obsessed by problems of love and hate on Planet III, as we stand, with our hangups from way back, poised on the threshold of unprecedented scientific successes.

Or unprecedented social failures.

Note

1 Ernest Cassirer, *The Philosophy of the Enlightenment* (Boston: Beacon Press, 1955) pp. 46–47. From d'Alembert, *Elements de Philosophie,* 1759.

Descartes and Newton formulated new methods of inquiring after truth. In the two brief selections below, they each explain the simple rules they tried to observe in their own work.

The New Rules of the Game

René Descartes and Isaac Newton

Descartes

The *first* was to accept nothing as true which I did not evidently know to be such, that is to say, scrupulously to avoid precipitance and prejudice, and in the judgments I passed to include nothing additional to what had presented itself to my mind so clearly and so distinctly that I could have no occasion for doubting it.

The *second,* to divide each of the difficulties I examined into as many parts as may be required for its adequate solution.

The *third,* to arrange my thoughts in order, beginning with things the simplest and easiest to know, so that I may then ascend little by little, as it were step by step, to the knowledge of the more complex, and, in doing so, to assign an order of thought even to those objects which are not of themselves in any such order of precedence.

And the *last,* in all cases to make enumerations so complete, and reviews so general, that I should be assured of omitting nothing.

Newton

> *Rule I. We are to admit no more causes of natural things than such as are both true and sufficient to explain their appearances.*

To this purpose the philosophers say that Nature does nothing in vain, and more is in vain when less will serve; for Nature is pleased with simplicity, and affects not the pomp of superfluous causes.

> *Rule II. Therefore to the same natural effects we must, as far as possible, assign the same causes.*

As to respiration in a man and in a beast; the descent of stones in

From *Problems in Western Civilization,* Ludwig Schaefer, David Fowler, and Jacob Cooke, eds. (New York: Charles Scribner's Sons, 1968), Vol. I, pp. 373–374. From *Newton's Mathematical Principles of Natural Philosophy and His System of the World,* Sir Isaac Newton (Berkeley, Calif.: University of California Press, 1947), pp. 398–400, Andrew Motte, trans. (1729); translation revised by Florian Cajori. Reprinted by permission of The Regents of the University of California.

Europe and in *America*; the light of our culinary fire and of the sun; the reflection of light in the earth, and in the planets.

>*Rule III. The qualities of bodies, which admit neither intensi-fication nor remission of degrees, and which are found to belong to all bodies within the reach of our experiments, are to be esteemed the universal qualities of all bodies whatsoever.*

For since the qualities of bodies are only known to us by experiments, we are to hold for universal all such as universally agree with experiments; and such as are not liable to diminution can never be quite taken away. We are certainly not to relinquish the evidence of experiments for the sake of dreams and vain fictions of our own devising; nor are we to recede from the analogy of Nature, which is wont to be simple, and always consonant to itself. We no other way know the extension of bodies than by our senses, nor do these reach it in all bodies; but because we perceive extension in all that are sensible, therefore we ascribe it universally to all others also. That abundance of bodies are hard, we learn by experience; and because the hardness of the whole arises from the hardness of the parts, we therefore justly infer the hardness of the undivided particles not only of the bodies we feel but of all others. That all bodies are impenetrable, we gather not from reason, but from sensation. The bodies which we handle we find impenetrable, and thence conclude impenetrability to be an universal property of all bodies whatsoever. That all bodies are movable, and endowed with certain powers (which we call the inertia) of persevering in their motion, or in their rest, we only infer from the like properties observed in the bodies which we have seen. The extension, hardness, impenetrability, mobility, and inertia of the whole, result from the extension, hardness, impenetrability, mobility, and inertia of the parts; and hence we conclude the least particles of all bodies to be also all extended, and hard and impenetrable, and movable, and endowed with their proper inertia. And this is the foundation of all philosophy. Moreover, that the divided but contiguous particles of bodies may be separated from one another, is matter of observation; and, in the particles that remain undivided, our minds are able to distinguish yet lesser parts, as is mathematically demonstrated. But whether the parts so distinguished, and not yet divided, may, by the powers of Nature, be actually divided and separated from one another, we cannot certainly determine. Yet, had we the proof of but one experiment that any undivided particle, in breaking a hard and solid body, suffered a division, we might by virtue of this rule conclude that the undivided as well as the divided particles may be divided and actually separated to infinity.

Lastly, if it universally appears, by experiments and astronomical observations, that all bodies about the earth gravitate towards the earth, and that in proportion to the quantity of matter which they severally contain; that the moon likewise, according to the quantity of its matter, gravitates towards the earth; that, on the other hand, our sea gravitates towards the moon; and all the planets one towards another; and the comets in like manner towards the sun; we must, in consequence of this rule, universally allow that all bodies whatsoever are endowed with a principle of mutual gravitation. For the argument from the appearances concludes with more force for the universal gravitation of all bodies than for their impenetrability; of which, among those in the celestial regions, we have no experiments, nor any manner of observation. Not that I affirm gravity to be essential to bodies: by their *vis insita* I mean nothing but their inertia. This is immutable. Their gravity is diminished as they recede from the earth.

Rule IV. *In experimental philosophy we are to look upon propositions collected by general induction from phenomena as accurately or very nearly true, notwithstanding any contrary hypotheses that may be imagined, till such time as other phenomena occur, by which they may either be made more accurate, or liable to exceptions.*

This rule must follow, that the argument of induction may not be evaded by hypotheses.

The influence of the Newtonian World Machine upon the eighteenth century is discussed in detail in the selection below.

The Newtonian World Machine

J. H. Randall

In the front of an old edition of the works of Rousseau there is an engraving which beautifully illustrates the intellectual spirit of the eighteenth century. Rousseau is seated at his writing-table, facing a pleasant pastoral landscape of green fields, sheep, and graceful willows—that rationally ordered Nature which he and his contemporaries accorded so respectful an admiration. On his desk are two volumes, which, in the absence of any other books, seem designed to sum up the learning of the age—the *Principia Mathematica* of Isaac Newton, and the *Essay Concerning Human Understanding* of John Locke.

In truth Newton and Locke were the two luminaries of that brilliant Augustan age in which, under William III and Queen Anne, England assumed for a period of some forty years, from 1680 to 1720, the undisputed intellectual leadership of the world, only to lose it again or at least to share it with first France and then Germany. Theirs are beyond doubt the outstanding names in that epoch which, succeeding to the discoveries and the liberations of the Renaissance and the Reformation, and preceding the rapid change and varied currents of the nineteenth century, made so heroic an attempt to order the world on the basis of the new "Physico-Mathematicall Experimental Learning." The significance of these two men, in spite of their own outstanding achievements, lies not so much in what they themselves did, as in what they stood for to that age, and in the very fact that they became to an increasing multitude the symbols for certain great ideas. Under their standards the new science for the first time actually entered into every field of human interest, and captured the mind of every educated man. Under such banners was actually effected that outstanding revolution in beliefs and habits of thought which we sometimes mistakenly associate with the Renaissance— that complete break with the spirit of the Middle Ages that prepared the way for the further growth of the next century. The age that hailed them as acknowledged masters, that introduced the spirit of the

From *The Making of the Modern Mind* by J. H. Randall (Boston: Houghton Mifflin, 1940), pp. 253–261.

Renaissance into religion, that placed man squarely in the midst of the new ordered world, that erected a science of man and of social relations, that formulated a complete and rounded philosophical view admirably framed for the middle class which the Industrial and the French Revolutions were so soon to bring into direct control, and which disseminated these ideas among the whole membership of this class—such an age is fittingly styled the "Age of Enlightenment and Reason." It laid the foundations for our present-day beliefs in every field, and it led on naturally to the two great ideas which the nineteenth century has added to the achievements of its predecessor, evolution and relativity.

In one sense both Newton and Locke were the systematizers of the ideas we have already traced in their formative stage. Newton stands at the end of that row of scientific geniuses who effected the Copernican and the Cartesian revolutions: he finally drew up in complete mathematical form the mechanical view of nature, that first great physical synthesis on which succeeding science has rested, and which has endured unchanged until a present-day revolution bids fair to modify it. Locke stands as apologist and heir of the great seventeenth-century struggles for constitutional liberties and rights and toleration. It is to this expression in systematic form of ideas which had become common property by 1700 that the two owed their immense popularity in the new century. But in another sense both Locke and Newton stand at the threshold of a new era, Newton as the prophet of the science of nature, and Locke as the prophet of the science of human nature. From their inspiration flow the great achievements of the Age of Enlightenment; in their light men went on to transform their beliefs and their society into what we know today.

Possessed of a successful scientific method, a combination of mathematics and experiment, and of a guarantee of truth, that "reason" which was both an individual and a universal authority, men set about the task of discovering a natural order that should be both simple and all-embracing. In the words of Fontenelle, the popularizer of Cartesianism, "The geometric spirit is not so bound up with geometry that it cannot be disentagled and carried into other fields. A work of morals, of politics, of criticism, perhaps even of eloquence, will be the finer, other things being equal, if it is written by the hand of a geometer." Isaac Newton effected so successful a synthesis of the mathematical principles of nature that he stamped the mathematical ideal of science, and the identification of the natural with the rational, upon the entire field of thought. Under the inspiration of Locke, the attempt was made to discover and formulate a science of human nature and human society, and to criticize existing religious and social traditions in the light of what seemed rational and reasonable. The two leading ideas of the eighteenth century, Nature and Reason, as outstanding then as Evolution in the last generation, derived their meaning from the natural sciences, and, carried over to man, led to the attempt to discover a social physics. Man and his institutions were included in the order of nature and the scope of the recognized scientific method, and in all things the newly invented social sciences were assimilated to the physical sciences. There grew up the idea of a simple and all-embracing social order in which free play should be left to the activities of every man. It is this great eighteenth-century synthesis in its most important ramifications that we shall now examine, starting with the rational order of the world, as expressed in the Newtonian system of nature, scientific method, and scientific ideals, and proceeding to trace its applications in religion, and in the comprehensive science of human nature that embraced a rational science of the mind, of society, of business, of government, of ethics, and of international relations.

The Success of the Mathematical Interpretation of Nature

The outstanding fact that colors every other belief in this age of the Newtonian world is the overwhelming success of the mathematical interpretation of nature. We have seen how Galileo found that he could explain and predict motion by applying the language of mathematics to the book of Nature, and how Descartes generalized from his method and its success a universal principle of scientific investigation and a sweeping picture of the universe as a great machine; how both thinkers arrived at the conception of uniform natural laws that are essentially mechanical in nature. But Descartes' cosmic picture was a sketch which neither the progress of mathematics nor of physical observation enabled him to fill in by the time of his early death. To his disciples he left a system of the world worked out as a provisional hypothesis, which he had not had time to verify by those careful experiments that he increasingly recognized as necessary to determine just what actual phenomena, of the many possible ones that could be deduced from the mechanical principle, really took place. Not to the strict Cartesians, who accepted as final this sketch and did not bother to verify it by the master's method, but to the more original minds who shared Galileo's emphasis on experiment and refrained for a generation from attempting a general hypothesis, were due the discoveries that made Newton's work possible. Especially successful were the triumphs of mathematics in the fields of fluids and gases. Torricelli, Galileo's pupil, in 1643 invented the barometer and weighed the atmosphere, and Pascal confirmed his measurements four years later by his famous experiment of carrying a barometer up a mountain and observing the diminishing atmopsheric pressure. To Pascal, too, is due the formulation of the laws of pressure in liquids, while Robert Boyle, who had studied under Galileo, discovered the law of pressure in gases. It is significant that within twenty years these facts had been used in machines for raising water, and that by the end of the century Newcomen's steam engine had begun the application of steam power to industry. To light, too, mathematics was astoundingly applied, and the science of optics, originated by Kepler and Descartes, was systematically developed by the Dutch Huygens and by Newton, who gave it its classic formulation; in 1695, Roemer actually measured the speed of light.

In all this work, mathematics and experimentation were successful allies. The spirit of the new science is exemplified in the foundation of the Royal Society in London in 1662 "for the promoting of Physico-Mathematicall Experimental Learning." This institution for that scientific cooperation so urgently demanded by Descartes, was largely inspired by Bacon's vision of a great scientific establishment; but it wisely followed the mathematical methods of Galileo rather than the purely experimental searching of the Elizabethan. Science rested on experiment, but its main object, for another century at least, was to connect the observed processes of nature with mathematical law. The leading member of the Royal Society, Robert Boyle, shares with Huygens the distinction of being the greatest investigator between Galileo and Newton; he managed to draw together the threads of alchemy and mathematical physics, and his generalization of Galileo's method of mathematical experimentation strongly influenced Newton. Mayow, another member, in 1674 discovered oxygen, although it was a century before Priestley and Lavoisier were able to fit it into a chemical science.

The Mathematical Synthesis of Newton

All this experimental work, together with much advance in mathematical theory, took place in the single generation after Descartes' death. But the great formulator of seventeenth-century science, the man who realized Descartes' dream, was born in 1642, the very year of Galileo's death. Though he did not publish his immortal work, the *Philosophia Naturalis Principia Mathematica,* till 1687, Newton made his chief discoveries when he was but twenty-three years of age. At that time, he tells us, he discovered:

> . . . first the binomial theorem, then the method of fluxions [the calculus], and began to think of gravity extending to the orb of the moon, and having found out how to estimate the force with which a globe, revolving within a sphere, presses the surface of the sphere, from Kepler's rule I deduced that the forces which keep the planets in their orb must be reciprocally as the squares of their distances from their centres: and thereby compared the force requisite to keep the moon in her orb with the force of gravity at the surface of the earth, and found them to answer pretty nearly. All this was in the two plague years of 1665 and 1666, for in those days I was in the prime of my age for invention and minded Mathematicks and Philosophy more than at any time since.

The thirty years that had passed since Galileo published his *Dialogue on the Two Systems* had seen an enormous intellectual change. Where Galileo was still arguing with the past, Newton ignores old discussions, and, looking wholly to the future, calmly enunciates definitions, principles, and proofs that have ever since formed the basis of natural science. Galileo represents the assault; after a single generation comes the victory. Newton himself made two outstanding discoveries: he found the mathematical method that would describe mechanical motion, and he applied it universally. At last what Descartes had dreamed was true: men had arrived at a complete mechanical interpretation of the world in exact, mathematical, deductive terms. In thus placing the keystone in the arch of seventeenth-century science, Newton properly stamped his name upon the picture of the universe that was to last unchanged in its outlines till Darwin; he had completed the sketch of the Newtonian world that was to remain through the eighteenth century as the fundamental scientific verity.

That Newton invented the calculus is perhaps an accident; Leibniz, building on Descartes' analytic geometry, arrived at it independently, while several other mathematicians, like Pascal, seemed almost on the verge of it. Be that as it may, it was inevitable that after the Frenchman had brought algebra and geometry together, men should advance and apply algebra also to motion. Descartes had shown how to find the equation that would represent any curve, and thus conveniently and accurately measure it and enable calculated prediction to be applied to all figures; but the science of mechanics, and with it any measurement of the processes of change in the world, demands a formula for the law of the growth or falling-off of a curve, that is, the direction of its movement at any point. Such a method of measuring movement and continuous growth Newton discovered; he had arrived at the most potent instrument yet found for bringing the world into subjection to man. Since any regular motion, be it of a falling body, an electric current, or the cooling of a molten mass, can be represented by a curve, he had forged the tool by which to attack, not only the figures, but the processes of nature—the last link in the mathematical interpretation of the world. By its means a Lagrange in the eighteenth or a Clerk-Maxwell in the nineteenth century could bring all measurable phenomena into the unified world of mathematics, and calculate, predict, and control light, heat, magnetism, and electricity.

Newton himself used it to formulate the general laws governing every body in the solar system. Kepler had arrived at the law of planetary motion by induction from observed facts, Galileo had similarly discovered the laws of falling bodies upon the earth. Newton united both in one comprehensive set of principles, by calculating that the deflection of the moon from a straight path, that is, her fall towards the earth, exactly corresponded with the observed force of terrestrial gravitation; and he further showed that on his hypothesis Kepler's law of planetary motion followed mathematically from the law of gravitation. The significance of this lay in the proof that the physical laws which hold good on the surface of the earth are valid throughout the solar system. What Galileo divined, what Descartes believed but could not prove, was both confirmed and made more comprehensive. This meant, on the one hand, that the secrets of the whole world could be investigated by man's experiments on this planet; and on the other, that the world was one huge, related, and uniform machine, the fundamental principles of whose action were known. One law could describe the whirling planet and the falling grass blade; one law could explain the action of every body in the universe. Newton expressed this fundamental principle in a famous rule:

> We are to admit no more causes of natural things than such as are both true and sufficient to explain their appearances. Therefore, to the same natural effects we must, as far as possible, assign the same causes. The qualities of bodies that cannot be diminished or increased, and are found to belong to all bodies within the reach of our experiments, are to be esteemed the universal qualities of all bodies whatsoever. For since the qualities of bodies are only known to us by experiments, we are to hold for universal all such as universally agree with experiments. . . .

We are certainly not to relinquish the evidence of experiments for the sake of dreams and vain fictions of our own; nor are we to recede from the analogy of Nature, which uses to be simple, and always consonant with itself. . . . We must, in consequence of this rule, universally allow, that all bodies whatsoever are endowed with a principle of mutual gravitation.

Using this principle and his new mathematical tool, Newton proceeded "to subject the phenomena of nature to the laws of mathematics." "I am induced by many reasons to suspect," he says, "that all the phenomena of nature may depend upon certain forces by which the particles of bodies, by some causes hitherto unknown, are either mutually impelled towards each other, and cohere in regular figures, or are repelled and recede from each other." Every event in nature is to be explained by the same kind of reasoning from mechanical principles: the whole program of science is "from the phenomena of motions to investigate the forces of nature, and then from these forces to demonstrate the other phenomena." The world is a vast perpetual motion machine, and every event in it can be deduced mathematically from the fundamental principles of its mechanical action; the discovery of these mathematical relations is the goal of science. The universe is one great harmonious order not, as for Thomas and the Middle Ages, on ascending hierarchy of purposes, but a uniform mathematical system.

The universal order, symbolized henceforth by the law of gravitation, takes on a clear and positive meaning. This order is accessible to the mind, it is not preestablished mysteriously, it is the most evident of all facts. From this it follows that the sole reality that can be accessible to our means of knowledge, matter, nature, appears to us as a tissue of properties, precisely ordered, and of which the connection can be expressed in terms of mathematics.

Newton's great mathematical system of the world struck the imagination of the educated class of his time, and spread with amazing swiftness, completing what Descartes had begun. Prior to 1789 some eighteen editions of the difficult and technical *Principia* were called for; British universities were teaching it by the end of the seventeenth century, and Newton was accorded a royal funeral when he died in 1727. In 1734, Bernoulli won the prize of the French Academy of Sciences with a Newtonian memoir; in 1740 the last prize was granted to an upholder of Descartes' physics. Voltaire was struck by Newtonianism during his visit to England in 1726–1728, and popularized him in France in his *English Letters,* in 1734, and his *Elements of the Newtonian Philosophy* in 1738; thenceforth Newton reigned in France as in England. From the presses there poured forth an immense stream of popular accounts for those unable or unwilling to peruse the classic work. His conclusions and his picture of the world were accepted on authority. By 1789 there had appeared about the *Principia* forty books in English, seventeen in French, three in German, eleven in Latin, one in Portuguese, and one in Italian, many of them, like those of Desaguliers, Benjamin Martin, Ferguson's *Lectures for Ladies and Gentlemen,* and Count Alogrotti's *Le Newtonianisme pour les Dames,* running through edition after edition. Newton's name became a symbol which called up the picture of the scientific machine-universe, the last word in science, one of those uncriticized preconceptions which largely determined the social and political and religious as well as the strictly scientific thinking of the age. Newton *was* science, and science was the eighteenth-century ideal.

The Method of Newtonian Science

Hence the method of the new physical science became all important, for men proceeded to apply it in every field of investigation. Just as the success of biology under Darwin led to the importation of the biological method into all the social sciences, and the more recent success of psychology has led to the wider application of its methods, so the social sciences, which, in the absence of any sure method of their own, always borrow from the striking science of the day, were in the Age of Enlightenment almost completely under the domination of the physico-mathematical method.

Science and Religion

Peter Gay

The philosophical and the scientific revolutions of the seventeenth century were one and the same, and it was essentially this great revolution, though not led by deists, that gave rise to modern deism. It began with Bacon, Galileo, and Descartes early in the century: it produced such mavericks as Hobbes and Spinoza; and it culminated in the writings of Newton and Locke at the end of the century.

Bacon, Galileo, Descartes

It is fashionable to pit Bacon, the prophet of empiricism, against Descartes, the pioneer of modern rationalism—and both Bacon and Descartes, the philosophers, against Galileo, the superb practitioner. Differences in emphasis, mood, and even philosophy certainly existed among these three men, but from a larger perspective it is clear that they were allies. All, each in his own way, were the philosophical prophets of the new science. All agreed with Bacon's ambitious formulation: mankind must do nothing less than undertake "a total reconstruction of sciences, arts, and all human knowledge, raised upon proper foundations." And it was the business of these thinkers to discover those proper foundations, for one thing was clear—these foundations had not been laid by the Scholastics or the philosophers of the Renaissance.

> The knowledge whereof the world is now possessed [Bacon insisted] especially that of nature, extendeth not to magnitude and certainty of works. The Physician pronounceth many diseases incurable, and faileth oft in the rest. The Alchemists wax old and die in hopes. The Magicians perform nothing that is permanent and profitable. The mechanics take small light from natural philosophy, and do but spin on their own little threads.

What was needed, therefore, was not a new discovery, or even a host of new discoveries, but a new method. And that method, Bacon said, and Galileo and Descartes said with him, was the method of the sciences: the mixture of mathematical intuition and laborious empirical enquiry, the fashioning of mechanical and intellectual instruments that would enable the researcher to probe more deeply into the mysteries of nature than had been possible before and (which was more significant) to develop a systematic intellectual procedure that would enable successive generations of scientists to confirm and correct the findings of their predecessors. Bacon, Galileo, and Descartes sought to make science cumulative and self-correcting.

This was essential work for the deists, for, despite their own intentions, the scientific revolutionaries threw doubt on most of the accepted stories of Christianity. They did so neither directly nor deliberately. But they were developing a method that would construct a body of knowledge on which all men could agree—and if there was anything certain in the world, it was that theologians did not agree, and could not agree, and would never agree.

Hobbes and Spinoza

In the midst of this revolution, a number of intellectuals turned quite directly to the claims of the theologians and pronounced them all unproved, unprovable, and probably false. Some of these radicals were modern Epicureans, citing their favorite text, Lucretius' *De rerum natura*. These had little influence. But there were also two thinkers of stature, Hobbes and Spinoza, despised and rejected—and read.

Thomas Hobbes (1588–1679) is a complicated and in some respects a shadowy figure: the precise nature of his own religious beliefs remains a matter of some dispute. But it is clear that his influence was on the side of disbelief, and it is certain that the deists learned much from him. "The philosopher of Malmesbury," Bishop Warburton wrote in the eighteenth century, "was the terror of the last age, as Tindal and Collins are of this." He might have added that the terrors of his own day were much indebted to their illustrious predecessor.

Hobbes himself argued steadfastly that he believed in a God, and that reason would discover him to any man ready to trust his reason. There are even occasional—very occasional—passages in which he speaks of the truths of revelation and the "blessed Savior Jesus Christ." But for the most part, his God is a remote and philosophical figure, and, while his writings against the Roman Catholic Church—"the Kingdom of Darkness"—are cast in the approved style of Protestant polemics against Papists, his specific teachings on the credibility (or rather incredibility) of tales of revelation gave good Protestants little comfort and earned him the reputation of an atheist. It was not so much that Hobbes openly denied the possibility of revelation; it was, rather, that in his persuasive epistemological writings he managed to throw doubt on nearly all the methods that Christians had used to proclaim that a revelation had taken place. If a man claims, for instance, that God has revealed something to him, there is no way for him to prove that the revelation is genuine; if he claims that the revelation came to him in a dream, this means no more than that a man dreamed that God had spoken to him. "So that though God Almighty can speak to a man by dreams, visions, voice, and inspiration; yet he obliges no man to believe he hath done so to him that pretends it; who, being a man, may err, and, which is more, may lie." Here was a prescription for skepticism that the deists would take up, at interminable length, in the decades after Hobbes's death.

Beyond this, Hobbes raised some difficult questions both as to the authorship and the authenticity of the Scriptures. Clearly—and here too the deists would read him with great profit—the church that had long been dominant in Europe had been corrupt, mendacious, power-hungry, and Reformers had effectively demolished many of their in-incredible tales of miracle-working saints and divinely blessed relics. How much more, Hobbes asked, might not a reasonable man do with, or to, the miracles that remained? It was an uncomfortable question.

Hobbes raised other questions, equally uncomfortable. In some remarkable pages of his *Leviathan,* he offered a natural history of the religious sentiment, and concluded that the "natural seed of religion" consisted of "opinion of Ghosts, ignorance of second causes, devotion toward what men fear, and taking of things casual for prognostics." In essence, this was an ancient procedure: the Greeks had already speculated on the reason why men were religious. But Hobbes went beyond them to offer a brilliant, if incomplete, psychological account of the religious impulse; nothing among the many subversive things he did was more subversive than this.

Hobbes was a master of the English language, and constantly enmeshed in controversy. Spinoza wrote as a rigorous mathematical logician, chiefly in Latin, and his influence was therefore less marked than Hobbes's. Yet he too became notorious as an atheist, and his writings were required reading for radicals in his time—most of whom did not read him well. But while the pantheism of his *Ethics* (1677) had to await the late eighteenth century before it was clearly seen and fully appreciated, the theological position of his *Theological-Political Treatise* (1670) was perfectly transparent from the beginning. The *Treatise* is a prescient masterpiece of the higher criticism, written long before scholars had, as it were, invented this discipline. Spinoza points out that once the Bible is confronted as any other book is confronted—as a book written by human authors and subject to the ordinary canons of consistency—it becomes evident that it is not the work of a single, but the work of many hands, and that many tales, especially the tales of miracles, are interpolations into earlier stories. In the *Ethics,* Spinoza had indicated his conviction that there could be no miracles, because God (who is nature) does not violate the laws of which He is Himself an embodiment; in the *Treatise,* Spinoza indicates just how the reports of miracles were written and inserted into the holy text. It was a fruitful hypothesis, and the deists made the best of it.

Newton and Locke

Neither Isaac Newton (1642–1727) nor John Locke (1632–1704) was a deist, yet both were indispensable to the deist cause. Newton gathered the scattered laws of physics and astronomy into a single imposing system, and while there was room in that system for divine intervention—God, Newton thought, set the universe right once in a while when it threatened to run down—the Newtonians could safely disregard this kind of theology as a personal idiosyncrasy. What mattered was that the regularity of the universe had been reduced to system and, in a modest way, explained. What mattered, also, was that Newton did not merely embody the empirical method of the sciences, he also wrote about it with conviction, and convincingly. "I do not feign hypotheses" (*Hypotheses non fingo*), he wrote in a much-quoted pronouncement. He refused to go beyond the evidence; he rejected systems that must be spun out of the head of the ambitious philosopher; he relied upon experiment, observation, and mathematical generalization alone. This was, as I have said, not a deist tenet, but it encouraged men to move in the direction of deism: Newton's prestige as a sage—the world's greatest man, as Voltaire admiringly called him—lent weight to speculations in which miracles, supernatural interventions, and priestcraft, had no place.

It was, finally, in the work of Locke that the groundwork of deism was completed. Locke was above all an empiricist: man acquires knowledge by his sensations upon which his reflection plays. He achieves authentic certainty only in the way of the "natural philosopher," which is to say, the scientist. In his great *Essay Concerning Human Understanding* (1690), Locke drew the consequences of this position: revelation is but reason extended; if it is anything else, if it subverts or contradicts reason, it is not authentic revelation, but a deception.

Yet Locke in his own way was a Christian, though he was sharply criticized for being something less, and something worse, in his own time. *"The Reasonableness of Christianity"* (a book Locke had published in 1695), and *"Christianity not Mysterious,"* (the deist book Toland published in the following year), "these two Titles," a critic wrote in 1706, "are different in Sound, but agree in Sense."

There we are back at the beginning. That critic was both right and wrong. Locke, in the *Reasonableness of Christianity,* had driven the call for a simple, an optimistic, a philosophical, and a reasonable piety, to as great lengths as it would go: he indicated that all a Christian need believe—but this he must believe—is that Christ is the Messiah. This was not much; it was too little for most Christians. But it was not yet deism. In this sense, the critic was wrong. But in the sense that it was indeed too little for most Christians, and that while the step from Locke to Toland was across an abyss it was still only a single, and not very surprising step, the critic was right. Liberal Protestantism was not deism, but it helped to make deism inevitable.

This selection shows the personal side of a famous contributor to the
Scientific Revolution. Here we see the intellectual conflict within the
participant himself as well as the dramatic confrontation between old
and new. How does the dilemma of Galileo compare with that of the
doctor who perfected the birth-control pill?

Dilemma of a Heretic

Angus Armitage

All his life Galileo was a devout Catholic. It distressed him to
find that the opinions to which he was irresistibly led as a scientist
were condemned by the Church of which he considered himself a
loyal son. Accordingly, he was forced to think out for himself the
relations between science and scripture. His position was one in which
Christians have been placed from time to time. For example, in the
middle of the nineteenth century, difficulties were felt in reconciling
Darwin's theory of evolution with the Biblical account of the creation
of living things. It seemed then as if man were to be deprived of his
unique central position in the world of life, just as in the sixteenth
century man's home, the Earth, had been deprived of its unique, central position in the Universe.

One way of getting over the difficulty is to say that the Bible is not
a textbook of astronomy (or of biology), intended to teach us things
that we can discover for ourselves. It reveals spiritual truths which
we could not have found out for ourselves. But it expresses these
truths in ways natural to the people to whom, and through whom,
they were originally revealed. That was roughly Galileo's position. It
did not upset him to find that the Bible pictured the world in ways
natural to the early Hebrews.

Soon after Galileo had explained his views on this matter, his
enemies seized upon a little book he had written on sunspots. They
extracted from it a statement of the principles of the Copernican
theory, and they submitted them to a committee of the Inquisition for
an opinion. This committee reported that, to make the Sun the fixed
center of the world was absurd and heretical; while to say that the
Earth was not the center and was in motion was absurd and, if not
heresy, at least a wrong belief. This report did not, in itself, make
the Copernican theory a heresy, for it was never proclaimed so by

the Pope. But it provided grounds on which Galileo, in 1616, was warned not to defend the theory. At the same time Copernicus's *Revolutions* was placed on the *Index*—the list of books that Catholics were not allowed to read without special permission—until it was "corrected." The corrections would have had the effect of reducing the theory to a mere device for calculating tables, as Osiander long since had claimed it to be.

However, some years later, when the storm had died down, Galileo wrote a great book which was really meant to be a defense of the Copernican theory. In order to keep to the letter of the command laid upon him in 1616, Galileo threw his book into the form of a debate between the supporters of the Ptolemaic and of the Copernican theories respectively.

The book is entitled *Dialogue Concerning the Two Chief Systems of the World;* and it relates how three friends meet on four successive days to discuss the two rival theories of the Universe, ignoring that of Tycho Brahe. They range over all the arguments on both sides. One of the characters acts as the spokesman of Galileo himself. He puts forward the fresh evidence based upon the telescopic discoveries. The book is written with great literary skill; and it is in Italian, so that other people besides scholars could read it.

On the first day the three friends debate whether heavy bodies fall in order to reach the fixed center of the *Universe* or (as Galileo supposed) in order to reach the center of the moving *Earth*. On the second day they discuss the Earth's daily turning on its axis. The point is made that the Earth could hardly remain at rest if everything outside were being carried round in a vast daily whirl, whereas, on the Copernican view, the Earth is so small in comparison with the rest of the Universe that it could easily rotate without affecting anything outside itself. On the third day they argue for and against the view that the Earth revolves round the Sun, just as the little moons revolve round Jupiter; and for the last day Galileo provides an explanation of the tides which later proved to be mistaken.

Although the weight of evidence goes in favor of Copernicus, Galileo did not dare to press the debate to a decision. He thus managed to get the book past the Censor. But immediately it was published in 1632, Galileo was attacked by the Jesuits on the ground that he had been commanded, in 1616, not to *teach* the Copernican theory, and that he had concealed this fact from the Censor. Thus, it was argued, he had obtained permission to publish his book on false pretenses. The Pope set up a Commission which considered the book in secret and produced a record of the command not to teach. Galileo could remember only being told not to *hold* or *defend* the theory; and he had done neither of these in his book. Whether his memory was at fault, or whether the record was a mistake, or a forgery, may never be cleared up. On the strength of the Commission's report, Galileo, now an invalid of close on seventy, was summoned to Rome to face the Inquisition in the winter of 1633. He was kept in close confinement until the summer, being questioned from time to time, but apparently not physically ill treated as things went in those days. However, he was allowed none of the facilities for legal self-defense normally granted to any criminal by the courts of a civilized state. He was tried in his absence, and brought up for sentence on June 22, 1633. But by that time his age and ill health, the depression born of confinement, the prolonged mental bullying to which he had been subjected, and the confusion of ideas between the spiritual authority of the Church and the testimony of experience—all these had done their work and had reduced Galileo to the condition in which he was prepared, on his knees, to renounce the Copernican theory. The sentence of the Inquisition upon him was one of perpetual imprisonment; but this was relaxed in time to a kind of "house arrest" in which he was able to continue his scientific work, in some measure, until his death.

Galileo is remembered today, however, not because he went down at the last before the forces of darkness, but because he fought so long and so successfully against them. There is even a legend that, as he rose to his feet after his forced submission to the Inquisition, and his denial of the Earth's motion, Galileo muttered something to the effect that the Earth *does* move all the same! Whatever the truth of the story, the words have become a sort of proverb implying that "the truth is great and shall prevail," despite all foolish attempts to suppress it in the interests of this or that school of thought. So it was with the truth of the Copernican theory. By his reformation of mechanics, by his telescopic discoveries, and by his battle against the ignorance of the learned men of his day, Galileo had brought the Copernican theory nearer to its final triumph than he could have dreamed in the moment of his downfall. For the year 1642, which saw the death of Galileo in captivity, saw also the birth of Isaac Newton.

Questions

1   More years have now elapsed since the close of World War II than passed between the end of World War I and the outbreak of World War II. While we do not live in peaceful times, at least the great powers have

shrunk back from the chasm of World War III. How much, if any, have scientific discoveries and their implications been responsible for this happy circumstance?

2   From the vantage point of the present, did the Scientific Revolution and its resultant change in man's thinking and behavior cause as many problems as it solved?

3   Can science and education solve all or almost all of mankind's ills?

4   This essay mentions The Pill and heart transplants as scientific advances that changed behavior and caused controversy. Name several other such advances (not just in medicine) that have been made in the last twenty years or that may be perfected in the next twenty years that will similarly change accepted or traditional values and cause controversy.

5   How many of our canons are based upon myths?

6   What are the main scientific hangups of Western civilization?

71 72 73 7 6